Advances in Information Security

Volume 63

Series editor

Sushil Jajodia, George Mason University, Fairfax, VA, USA

More information about this series at http://www.springer.com/series/5576

Misty Blowers
Editor

Evolution of Cyber Technologies and Operations to 2035

 Springer

Editor
Misty Blowers
Information Directorate
Air Force Research Laboratory
Rome, NY, USA

Advances in Information Security
ISBN 978-3-319-79505-8   ISBN 978-3-319-23585-1   (eBook)
DOI 10.1007/978-3-319-23585-1

Springer Cham Heidelberg New York Dordrecht London

Printed on acid-free paper

Springer International Publishing AG Switzerland is part of Springer Science+Business Media (www.springer.com)

Preface

Evolution of Cyber Technologies and Operations to 2035 explores the future of cyber technologies and cyber operations which will influence advances in social media, cyber security, cyber physical systems, ethics, law, media, economics, infrastructure, military operations, and other elements of societal interaction in the upcoming decades. It provides a review of future disruptive technologies and innovations in cyber security. It informs military strategists about the future of cyber warfare and serves as an excellent reference for professionals and researchers working in the field of security, economics, law, and more. Students will also find this book useful as a reference guide or secondary textbook.

Written by leading experts in the field, authors explore specific examples of how future technical innovations vastly increase the interconnectivity of our physical and social systems and the growing need for resiliency in this vast and dynamic cyber infrastructure. In-depth coverage is provided on the future of social media, autonomy, stateless finance, quantum information systems, the Internet of Things, the dark web, space satellite operations, and global network connectivity along with the transformation of the legal and ethical considerations of these technologies in future military operations. The international nuances of cyber alliances, capabilities, and interoperability are confronted with a growing need for new laws, international oversight, and regulation.

Chapter 1 addresses the increasing need for resiliency of future cyber systems and technologies. It discusses how cyberspace defenders can maximize the flexibility of their systems by deliberately building in "inefficient" excess capacity, planning for and expecting failure, and creating personnel flexibility through training and exercises. The author also argues that defenders should reduce their attack surface by eliminating unnecessary capability in both hardware and software, resist users' desire for continual rapid improvements in capability without adequate security testing, and segment their networks and systems into separate defended enclaves. Finally, the need for cyber defenders to position themselves to dynamically respond to attacks through improved situational awareness, effective cyberspace command

and control, and active defenses. This chapter shows how combining these approaches will enable the defenders of cyberspace systems to weather cyberspace attacks and spring upright after the passage of the storm.

Chapter 2 shows us how the "Internet of Things" (IoT) is poised to potentially change the way that human beings live their lives. This change will come about through the integration of billions of embedded devices and trillions of sensors into the world around us. These sensors will perceive the conditions around them and provide information to support an almost endless array of decision-supporting and decision-making capabilities. The effect of this capability will allow human beings to realize efficiencies in operation and slash costs in ways that would otherwise be impossible. IoT will be used to revolutionize our supply chains, manufacturing, infrastructure, transportation, clothing, homes, agriculture, and even our bodies. We will be able to instrument the world around us to the degree that we will increasingly rely on machines to augment and make decisions for us.

Chapter 3 discusses the convergence of cyber and electronic warfare. As nations embrace new and evolving communications networks, the reliance on these systems brings with it an implied vulnerability – the network itself. Understanding the current paradigm and accurately forecasting the future of communications will provide militaries with clear advantage in this facet of warfare. In this chapter we will examine the networks currently employed, their development, how they might look in the future, and finally how they relate to the overall electronic battlefield of the next several decades. Having an idea of how communication and operations will look in the future will help us craft the next generation of disruptive technologies for use during wartime.

Chapter 4 describes the relationships between the realm of cyber and space operations as they have been historically, are now, and as they will develop over the next 20 years. Space operations have long been critical for national security, providing intelligence, surveillance, and reconnaissance (ISR) capabilities from on high since the late 1950s. Predictably, American and international space assets have evolved exponentially since those early days, by now offering nations with navigation, timing, communications, weather, targeting, strategic warning, and defense abilities, among the more classical ISR roles. Both military and civilian affairs have been so enhanced by access to space that the realm has become indispensable to our day-to-day lives. However, the critical role of cyber relative to space operations is still somewhat hazy during normal space operations. Even with the dictum "You can't have Space without Cyber" well known to space operators, understanding just how true that is and space systems' vulnerabilities to cyber-attacks still needs to be fleshed out. To explore the aspects of cyber in space and cyber relative to space, this chapter will outline some of the current-generation systems, capabilities, and vulnerabilities and project what may be seen over the next 20 years from the view of space and cyber operators.

Chapter 5 discusses future trends in large data handling. From identifying prey in a distant landscape to today's Big Data analytics, the task of information processing has been at the forefront of progress and will continue to be in future innovations. In the past, quantity of collected data was limited by our capability to transform it into useful information. Factors such as low computing resources, minimal information storage, and small numbers of experienced analysts all constrained data collection by requiring careful feature and target selection. With the progression of Moore's law, rapid advance of storage technologies, cloud computing resources for hire, and distributed computing software, these constraints are relaxed. The result is an explosion in the amount of collected data from every imaginable sector of our lives. We discuss in this chapter the myriad fields in which large data analytics are being used, current and future challenges of this continued upward trend toward larger data collections, and future technology enablers in this field.

Chapter 6 presents an example of a specific visualization tool that may be used for a variety of big data problems. A specific problem is presented in which a cyber-analyst is inundated with vast amounts of data and tasked with identifying malicious network behavior. With a virtual reality (VR) head-mounted display, the display space for visualizing different information and data pertaining to cyber events becomes almost limitless. The head mounted VR display opens the door to new and innovative visualization techniques which enables a degree of spatial awareness that can be associated with information. The use of higher resolution and large panels enables analysts of the future to utilize more intuitive methods of sense-making in order to identify patterns of behavior within data making their jobs faster and easier and their information more reliable.

Chapter 7 provides an operational picture for the future use of quantum technologies. The author presents an alternative view of the future based on working quantum technologies and provides some past examples of disruptive technologies employed during WWII and technologies that rapidly developed during the 1980s. These examples highlight how the use of immature technologies can affect the strategic outcomes for war. The three phases of quantum technology development are discussed on a high level. The chapter closes on a fictional narrative to convey the perspective of an individual living in the 2025–2045 timeframe to illustrate how these quantum technologies may impact the world in that timeframe.

Chapter 8 explores the DarkNet and the future of underground networks. The future of the DarkNet is full of awe inspiring technological feats and dangers at the same time. We have been continuously plagued with technology that, from a security perspective, was not ready to be released to the general public. Knowledge of the DarkNet seems to be limited to IT professionals, hackers, and computer savvy criminals in modern times. However, more and more people are turning to this underground network as future generations become more connected and anonymity becomes an increasing concern. This is where the never-seen-before computer malware lives and thrives. You can find anything and everything known to man here, both legal and illegal (illegal drugs, weapons); even hitmen advertise in this part of the web. All of it can be conveniently delivered to your front door via UPS and FedEx. This chapter projects the dangers of the DarkNet and how underground networks may leverage it.

Chapter 9 takes an in-depth look into cryptocurrencies. Although most cryptocurrencies were created as a product of innovation in line with technological advances and with good intentions in mind, the use of such technologies by malicious users is not a nuance concept. The author focuses her attention on the most common and popular of the cryptocurrencies, the Bitcoin. The Bitcoin has created a currency that can surpass institutions and eliminate transparency, providing a perfect agency. As governments grow concerned about taxation and their lack of control over the currency, Bitcoin also poses serious means of funding illicit activities and terrorist organizations. To what extent can Bitcoin develop and morph into a serious currency utilized to finance terrorism? This chapter explores how Bitcoin can manifest a credible security threat by directly changing systems of financial support. The first part of this chapter will describe how Bitcoin operates, including what features make it appealing to illicit networks and areas of vulnerabilities. The second part of this chapter will look at how Bitcoin is shaping terrorist financing, what the government response has been, and to what degree it has been effective. Finally the author will present a projection of the role of Bitcoins in the coming future.

Chapter 10 explores the current role of social media and its projected evolution. The rise in popularity of social media in protests and revolution in the present age presents a host of possibilities in the coming decades. The exploding use of social media is staggering, and the ability for populations and governments to stay connected is unprecedented. It is the author's position that basic human psychology and habit patterns observed today will greatly inform our understanding of how social media will be used in the future. The author explores two recent protests where social media played a significant role in the way the protests unfolded and concluded. It is to the reader to determine social media's ultimate effect on social protests, but consider the effect of social media to foment peace or violent and organize the demonstration and the ability of government to coordinate a response. These examples lead the author to make loose projections on the future of social media and its global impact on society.

Chapter 11 discusses the rules for autonomous cyber capabilities. It discusses how our capability to unleash autonomous systems into the wild on our behalf outpaces the degree to which we have pondered and resolved the myriad legal questions that arise. For instance, who is responsible if something goes wrong? Can responsibility even be determined? What rules should apply? What laws govern? Should autonomous cyber responses be allowed at all? This chapter outlines some of the key questions in this regard and seeks to explore these questions in light of the developing law for other autonomous systems. It will discuss the aspects that make cyber unique and propose rules that address such distinctions.

Chapter 12 is about ethical considerations in the cyber domain in future years. Defining proper ethical behavior in the cyber domain and making sure all societies and governments agree on cyber ethics will be an increasingly difficult challenge. Under current circumstances, democratic nations could be willing to reach bilateral agreements, but other nations might not be so cooperative. Cyber society is defined in this chapter as a combination of legislative actions, state and non-state actors, the military, and public-private partnerships. The difficulties in establishing a set of standards from geographically separate and ideologically diverse worldviews are presented, as well as discussions on critical infrastructure protections in both the public and private sectors. Finally, the chapter presents ethical considerations for state and non-state actors.

Chapter 13 is about the ethical challenges of state-sponsored hacktivism and the advent of "soft" war in which warfare tactics rely on measures other than kinetic force or conventional armed conflict to achieve the political goals and national interests. The author presents a brief history of cyber conflict and malevolent activities in the cyber domain. He then discusses the rise of state-sponsored hacktivism and the subsequent advent of state-sponsored internet activism. The soft war leads to "soft" law which calls moral guidelines and ethics into consideration in which the legal framework may not suffice to provide reliable guidance. Alternatively, best practices emerge from the shared practices of the interested parties and reflect their shared experience and shared objectives.

Chapter 14 is a collection of short essays written from the perspective of a younger generation – current high school students. The graduating classes of 2015–2016 have grown up fully immersed in this technological world and have a unique perspective on how we as humans will have to continue to adapt to it. The students' task was to talk about "disruptive technologies" and how they see technology affecting our world in the year 2035. Various topics were selected such as cyber warfare, commercial and personal space travel, quantum computing, holographic enabling technologies, solar roads, and flying cars.

This book was designed to bring some of the most inquisitive, enlightened, and educated minds together to help us all understand the landscape of future cyber operations and societal concerns. We hope that the reader finds inspiration from reading this book to address some of the ethical concerns presented, to innovate new solutions to help shape a new world of interconnected devices and people, and to educate the next generation of scientist and engineers who will design technologies we could not even conceive of when writing this book.

This book could not have been made possible without the generous time commitment and passion of the authors whose ideas and insights are contained within to share with the world. In addition, I would like to express my most sincere gratitude both to the publisher and to a team of contributing technical reviewers who gave their time to ensure accuracy of technical content. Members of this team included the following:

1st Lieutenant Daniel Stambovsky, US Air Force
Captain Jon Williams, US Air Force
Mr. Jason Moore, US Air Force
Mr. Phil Zaleski, Exelis Inc.
Mr. Anthony Wong, Invincea Inc.

Thank you to all!

New York, NY   Misty Blowers

Contents

Cyberspace Resiliency: Springing Back with the Bamboo

William Bryant

> *The winds may fell the massive oak, but bamboo, bent even to the ground, will spring upright after the passage of the storm*
>
> – Japanese Proverb

Introduction

According to the ancient Japanese proverb, after the storm passes, the stronger oak lies on the ground while the weaker bamboo stands upright. The moral that resiliency is more important to success than strength applies to conflict in the cyberspace domain as well. It is important to clarify that the resilience under discussion here is in response to cyberspace attacks, not cyberspace espionage. Cyberspace attacks change friendly systems through manipulating data, causing hardware failures, or physical destruction of objects controlled from cyberspace. If pure cyberspace espionage is done well, the defenders will have no idea anyone was ever in their systems, everything will still function. Resilience is not as useful in examining cyberspace espionage as cyberspace attack.

The Department of Homeland Security Risk Steering Committee has defined resiliency as, "The ability to adapt to changing conditions and prepare for, withstand, and rapidly recover from disruption."[1] As organization after organization and system after system is successfully attacked, there is a growing realization that a perfect perimeter defense is not possible, and even if it were, attackers are often within the walls as insider threats. In addition, while shifting to multiple layers of "defense in depth" improves security, each layer will still have flaws and vulnerabilities that a determined attacker can circumvent. Accordingly, cyberspace operators have increasingly looked to resilience as a promising way to improve overall security.[2]

---

[1] Risk Steering Committee [1].

[2] Singer and Friedman have recently suggested that the classic information security "CIA Triad" of Confidentiality, Integrity, and Availability should be extended to include resilience [2], Kindle Location 720.

W. Bryant (✉)
Task Force Cyber Secure, Office of Information Dominance and Secretary of the Air Force, Pentagon, Arlington, VA, USA
e-mail: bryantcyber@outlook.com

© Springer International Publishing Switzerland 2015
M. Blowers (ed.), *Evolution of Cyber Technologies and Operations to 2035*,
Advances in Information Security 63, DOI 10.1007/978-3-319-23585-1_1

While resilience is key to success for cyberspace defenders, it is important that they do not neglect their basic defenses either. In the United States military, there has been a tendency to focus too much on offense much like was done with early bombers in the air domain before World War II.[3] This is a mistake and as noted by Martin Libicki, "in this medium, the best defense is not necessarily a good offense; it is usually a good defense."[4] Offense is widely seen as overwhelmingly powerful over defense, but that assumption ignores the historical record of cyberspace attacks thus far. Unsophisticated attacks are easily defeated by modest defenses, and even nation-state level attacks have had mixed success. Of the eight cases of nation-state on nation-state cyberspace attacks with a reasonable amount of open source data, only half of them can be qualified as a success.[5] If the offense were truly so over-whelming, it should be able to achieve greater than a 50 % success rate. When the high level attacks are analyzed, it is apparent that in most cases, the offenders did get past the defenses, but the defenders were able to react and negate the attacks in a week or two; resilience is the key to that ability to flexibly respond.[6]

Before developing the tenants of cyberspace resiliency, it is important to clarify what cyberspace is as there is great confusion on this point. The United States Joint Staff has defined cyberspace as, "a global domain within the information environment consisting of the interdependent network of information technology infrastructures and resident data, including the Internet, telecommunications networks, computer systems, and embedded processors and controllers."[7]

A very important point that comes from the definition is that while the Internet is part of cyberspace, it is not all of cyberspace. Any computer system capable of communicating to other computer systems in some way is part of cyberspace. A desktop computer, an avionics computer on an aircraft, an iPhone, an industrial controller, and the central processor on a modern car are all part of cyberspace, although only some of them are routinely connected to the Internet. Most modern military equipment more complex than an M-4 carbine has some form of processor from a humble truck to an aircraft carrier, and is thus part of cyberspace. Now that the definition of cyberspace is clear, what is required to be resilient within cyberspace?

---

[3] Analysts were convinced that the offense was overwhelmingly powerful in the air domain based on several factors. One was that pursuit aircraft only had a slight speed advantage over bomber aircraft and took so long to get to altitude that the bombers would be gone before pursuit aircraft could engage them. A second was that bomber aircraft would be able to defend themselves with their own defensive firepower. Both ideas turned out to be wrong. Fighter aircraft developed a significant speed advantage over contemporary bomber aircraft, and radar as well as better command and control greatly enhanced their capability to intercept bombers and get to altitude before the bombers arrived. Additionally, the bombers were much less able to defend themselves than expected because defensive gunners turned out to be less effective than analysts had predicted.

[4] Libicki [3].

[5] Bryant [4], 171.

[6] Bryant [4], 172.

[7] Joint Chiefs of Staff [5].

There are three elements to the bamboo's success in the storm that have application to resiliency in the cyberspace domain; flexibility, a reduced attack surface, and the ability to respond dynamically to attacks. First, the bamboo can accept deformation without failure. As noted by the proverb, the bamboo can be bent and spring back upright, while the oak can accept little deformation before failing catastrophically. Second, the bamboo presents far less attack surface to the attacking wind as it has a streamlined shape with relatively few exposed leaves compared to the oak tree which has a far larger and more complex structure. Finally, the bamboo adjusts to the wind, as it bends it reacts in a way that minimizes the effect of future wind gusts. Each of these three elements of the bamboo's success can be applied to the cyberspace domain as a way of understanding how practical cyberspace resilience can be built.

Flexibility

What does flexibility look like in cyberspace? Is flexibility even a meaningful concept when every device in cyberspace is actually running a complex rule-set that predetermines its actions in response to a given set of inputs? While the computers that make up cyberspace simply do what they are told, the flexibility in cyberspace comes from the people telling the machines what to do. People can also build in more capacity for flexibility by constructing their systems to operate in cyberspace with excess capability.

The typical business mindset focuses on efficiency to generate as much profit as possible, while the military mindset loves efficiency, order and hierarchy, but these concepts are opposed to flexibility in cyberspace. Efficiency means using 100 % of available resources with no excess capability. Yet, if you are 100 % efficient, the smallest perturbation can lead to catastrophic failure. The heart of resiliency is the ability to absorb perturbations and failures, whether natural or manmade, and continue functioning. Thus, a system built for resiliency will look very different than one built for efficiency.

Too much efficiency will hamper resiliency and cyberspace defenders would do well to build less-efficient redundant systems if they want to achieve resiliency under attack. There are several efficiency trends that cyberspace operators who want to build a resilient system will need to oppose. In the perfectly efficient network every device on the network will run the same operating system, utilize the same applications for specific tasks, have a minimum of sub-networks or enclaves all structured the same way, and even utilize the same hardware throughout for the same functions. While each of these concepts are efficient, they hurt resiliency.

An entire network that runs a single operating system is efficient and easy to administer; and also just as easy to take down via a single vulnerability. A heterogeneous network made up of Windows 7, Windows 8, and Linux with a few Apple machines thrown in for good measure cannot be completely taken down by a single vulnerability. Edward Luttwak noted that in the strategic realm with a thinking enemy, "homogeneity can easily become a potential vulnerability."[8] Of course, there must be a balance between efficiency and resiliency, a system where every single device runs a unique operating system would be resilient in a sense, but would be so difficult to administer that it would likely be full of unpatched machines and unknown vulnerabilities. Aristotle taught that virtue always lies on a continuum between two vices.[9] The virtue of cyberspace resilience lies between rigid conformity to a single system that can be taken down with a single attack on one side, and complete chaos within an unworkable mess of a network on the other. A reasonable middle ground is for cyberspace operators to select a handful of different well-designed operating systems and then implement them throughout their networks. Thus if three operating systems are used, two thirds of the network should be available following an attack against any particular operating system. Cyberspace operators should also find the right balance between too many and two few different types when it comes to applications and hardware for very much the same reasons as discussed above for operating systems. Heterogeneous systems are a start, but the defender can also break those systems into separate enclaves to further increase resiliency.

Network segmentation into separate sub-networks that can function even if other networks around them fail is a key component of cyberspace resiliency. Consider the changes that the network on a typical U.S. Air Force base has gone through. At first, every base was unique, IT equipment was purchased locally and every network ran different software and applications depending on what the local communications squadron had purchased. This structure was extremely inefficient and the level of security achieved was highly variable and often quite low partially because the different networks still had to be connected to each other, often in not very secure ways. The next step was to bring control of the networks up to a regional level which took control of base networks largely out of the hands of local units. While this resulted in a more efficient network, it also meant that a successful attack against the regional hub could bring down multiple bases at the same time, whereas before, each base would have to have been reconnoitered and attacked separately. Now, the Department of Defense (DoD) has mandated that the military services all utilize the same structure under the Joint Information Enterprise (JIE) and the same gateways in the form of Joint Regional Security Stacks (JRSS). If every service is using the same equipment running the same software, one successful attack against a single vulnerability could conceivably take down the entire DoD network.

Returning to the "Wild Wild West" mindset where every local unit does whatever it wants will not improve operational effectiveness. Instead, resiliency and a reasonable level of efficiency can be achieved by a planned and deliberate diversification of networked systems. Homogeneity is good for ensuring patches and protocols are followed against known threats, and heterogeneity helps protect a

---

[8] Luttwak [6].
[9] Aristotle [7].

system from unknown and unpredictable threats. System architects should buck the trend towards ever larger and homogenous networks and deliberately build in heterogeneous enclaves based on a small number of carefully selected hardware and software configurations. It is important that network architects do not build systems with a single type of system performing a function across the network. For example, a segmented network of heterogeneous enclaves that all use the exact same hardware and software as a gateway will be less resilient than one that uses different types of gateways. Resiliency is best increased by parallel lanes of different systems, if a network relies on a single type of system at any level there is still a single point of failure. Like with operating systems, finding Aristotle's "golden mean" of diverse enough to be resilient with enough efficiency to be manageable and low cost is the key.

Even if a network is heterogeneous and cannot be completely taken down by a single vulnerability, cyberspace operators still need to expect and plan for failure.[10] Planning for failure does not come naturally, especially in the military environment. Antoine Bousquet has noted that the military often attempts to achieve, "100 % relevant content, 100 % accuracy, and zero time delay" in the pursuit of a frictionless cybernetic war machine, but that goal is illusory.[11] Instead, cyberspace operators should be, "embracing uncertainty and designing a resilient and flexible military that is capable of adapting to the unforeseen and contingent."[12] Cyberspace operators need to move beyond asking "how can I best secure this system against attack?" to "how do I design my system to still work after my defenses fail?" This requires a significant mindset shift for military cyberspace operators to include focusing on response capabilities such as emergency and incident response teams and plans.[13] One of the best ways to accomplish this shift is through aggressive and thorough red teaming.

Well-resourced and extensive red teaming of cyberspace systems is a critical part of building cyberspace resiliency. A red team is the military term for a group of friendly attackers who attack systems to find their vulnerabilities and weaknesses so that defenses can be improved. In the civilian sector, the same type of work is normally called ethical hacking or penetration testing. They use the same techniques as real attackers and provide an invaluable service in not only finding vulnerabilities, but giving defenders practice in how to respond to attacks and keep their systems functioning. Historically the DoD has under-resourced red teams due to the persistent focus on offensive cyber capabilities. Red teams require the same people and resources that are needed for offensive cyberspace capabilities. However, offensive capabilities and red teams are not locked in a zero sum resource game. Since the same attack techniques are used, red teaming can be excellent training for offensive cyberspace operators and can also help overcome classification barriers.

---

[10] Rosenzweig [8], Kindle Location 3727.

[11] Bousquet [9], 222.

[12] Bousquet [9], 222.

[13] Rattray [10], Kindle Location 220.

Compartmentalization continues to me a major issue preventing defenders and attackers from learning from each other.[14] According to former Vice Chairman of the Joint Chiefs of Staff, General Cartwright, "We make sure the recce teams don't tell the defenders what they found, or the attacker, and the attackers go out and attack and don't tell anybody they did. It's a complete secret to everybody in the loop and it's dysfunctional."[15] Compartmentalization and security is essential in cyberspace weapons, but it is foolish for attackers to assume that the clever techniques they develop will not be discovered and utilized by their enemies. Attackers need to inform defenders of their attack methods in appropriate ways that allow defenders to defend their systems while not giving away the attack methods to adversaries. Once again, there is a balance required between disclosure and security, sometimes a particular offensive technique may be so critical that it must be protected at the cost of leaving friendly systems vulnerable. However, this decision needs to be made at the appropriate level by commanders who have responsibility to both the offense and defense. In the DoD it appears that the need is for more disclosure to defenders and not less. Red teaming and improved disclosure helps to develop resiliency in the people operating in cyberspace, but there are a number of other ways to build resiliency into cyberspace operators.

The highest payoff in building cyberspace resiliency lies in building resilient people. People are the ones who react, not machines. The machines will simply do what their instructions tell them to do, even if those instructions are complex and allow for some ability to respond to stimuli. It is not only cyberspace operators who need to be resilient, improved resiliency and security needs to be built into regular users as well.

Users can be "hardened" via training as they are currently the weakest spot in the armor of most cyberspace systems. Users are the bane of system administrators the world over and many attacks rely on finding a user who can be tricked into doing something they should not do. Most users have only a rudimentary knowledge of computer security, so spending time and money training them can produce a significant payoff. Mandatory training programs are a start, but not all users will pay attention to training or be convinced that it is important to them. Organizational leaders need to convince users that there is significant benefit to following good security practices whether it is monetary rewards for best practices or reprimands for those who do not follow procedures.

Most organizations have user training programs in place, what is missing is accountability to make users take cyberspace security seriously. In a recent study, security testers left USB thumb drives on the ground in a parking lot outside of a federal office building. All federal employees receive regular training on the dangers of plugging in unknown USB devices, but 60 % of these highly trained employees plugged them in anyway. The addition of an official looking logo on the drive

---

[14] Lonsdale [11].

[15] General James E. Cartwright, USMC, comments at Air Force Association Air Warfare Symposium, February 8, 2007, reported in Kramer [12].

increased the percentage of USB drives employees plugged in to 90 %.[16] How many of these employees were fired or even mildly reprimanded for their failure to follow procedures they have been trained on multiple times? Performance ratings and rewards need to be explicitly tied to following security practices, and there should be consequences for security failures that are regularly tested via a continuing testing program.

Users should be routinely tested and probed and those who do not perform well should face escalating consequences. For example, cyberspace operators should routinely send out "phishing" style e-mails based on actual real-world attacks to users of their systems. If a user is duped into clicking on the link, instead of unleashing a virus, the user should be directed to retake the organization's computer security training. Subsequent failures should have increasingly unpleasant consequences to include eventual termination for employees who are incapable of following good security practices. A similar escalation ladder could be followed for users who continue to visit questionable sites or are caught deliberately circumventing security safeguards. Escalating consequences are for well-intentioned, but security inept employees; insider threats are a different matter and should be dealt with according to organizational and legal rules. These types of changes will normally not be received well because they involve changing organizational culture and they will require support from top executives in the organization to be successful. For the military in particular, cyberspace resilience will also include a significant amount of resilience outside of cyberspace systems.

For most Western militaries, cyberspace systems are principally important because they enable effectiveness in the physical domains of combat. Thus, cyberspace resilience includes the ability of military forces to fight effectively even if their cyberspace systems are compromised or unavailable.[17] Martin Libicki has recently identified that networked militaries need to be careful not to focus on the network for its own sake through information assurance, but need to stay focused on the mission and mission assurance.[18] This is deeply uncomfortable for a generation that has gotten used to continual connection and reliability of cyberspace systems since Western militaries have not yet fought a significant cyberspace adversary. However, there are a number of potential adversaries who have been very clear that they intend to fight hard in cyberspace in the case of a conflict, and Western militaries would be exceedingly foolish to assume that the enemy will never have a "good day" and be able to disrupt many of their critical systems.

Much like with cyberspace operators and system users, resilience in regular military forces can best be built through realistic training and exercises. Currently, if there is cyberspace play in military exercises, it is usually discounted by exercise referees so that regular forces can get "good training" and utilize all their systems. On the contrary, I maintain that the "good training" is when they don't have all their systems. Consider a single cyberspace enabled system, the Global Positioning

---

[16]Rosenzweig [8], Kindle Location 815, chap. 3.

[17]Rattray [10], Kindle Location 219.

[18]Libicki [13].

System or GPS. What would a major exercise such as Red Flag look like if none of the participants were allowed to utilize GPS? What about a land based combat exercise at the National Training Center? How many young platoon leaders would be able to maneuver their forces quickly and expertly using only a compass and a map? What if their radios stopped working as well? Would forces continue to maneuver and operate in the absence of communication from headquarters? There are some hopeful signs that some leaders in the military are taking this threat seriously, Gen Hostage's distributed control is one promising approach,[19] but these ideas must be thoroughly tested and exercised on a regular basis if military forces are going to have any ability to operate in a cyberspace denied environment. The flexibility created by these changes can be enhanced by also reducing cyberspace system's attack surface.

Reducing Attack Surfaces

The bamboo has far less surface area in its structure than the massive oak tree and thus presents a much smaller surface for the wind to push against. In cyberspace, the surface area open to be pushed against is normally referred to as the "attack surface." The attack surface is made up of all the potential access points for an attacker and cyberspace operators should actively seek to make their attack surface as small as possible to help improve cyberspace resiliency.

Every piece of software, every capability added to that software, and every communications pathway represents a potential avenue of enemy attack. Thus, the first thing cyberspace operators should do to reduce the attack surface they present to the enemy is to eliminate non-essential features as they represent added risk.[20] This is a mammoth task and not one that most cyberspace operators are well prepared to do as modern software is written to appeal to the largest number of customers with "all the bells and whistles" on by default. It can be nearly impossible, not only to determine what functionality is not needed, but then to disable it across the network to prevent it from being used as an attack vector. While swallowing the elephant all at once is not immediately achievable, there are concrete steps that can be taken in both the software and hardware arenas.

An organization's hardware attack surface can be reduced by disabling unnecessary ports and communications pathways where possible. The best method for disabling unnecessary communications pathways is via physical means. If a computer's wireless network or modem card is removed, there is complete certainty that it can't be used as a clandestine back door into the organization's network. The same can be said for unnecessary physical ports such as USB ports. It may be crude to cut the wire behind the port, or fill the port opening with hot glue, but it is certainly effective. Software methods can be used as well, but they are not

---

[19] Hostage and Broadwell [14].
[20] Owens et al. [15], 84.

as certain. Most devices can be easily disabled via the operating system, but they can be just as easily surreptitiously re-enabled. Cyberspace operators would do well to run periodic checks to ensure that the disabled ports have not been turned back on. While closing hardware based vulnerabilities is a start, the majority of an organization's attack surface lies in its software.

If an organization is serious about its cyberspace security, then there should be an increased level of scrutiny put towards every piece of software on the organization's networks. As with operating systems, there is a balance to be struck between having too many different applications to accomplish the same function and too few. Having too many applications opens up unnecessary avenues of attack, but having too few can also hamper resiliency. For example, if an organization mandates the use of only one particular build of one Internet browser, it is difficult for the organization to react quickly if a vulnerability is discovered in that browser. If the same organization had two browsers allowed on the network, all functionality could be quickly switched to the second browser while the first was patched. However, in most networks it appears that there are far too many applications, not too few. It is reasonable to have a primary and a spare application for each function, but it is not reasonable to have twelve applications that do mostly the same thing. Of course, a system administrator telling users they cannot utilize their favorite application is about as popular as the IRS auditor. Most cyberspace operators do not have the support of their executive leadership as the importance of reducing an organization's attack surface presented via too many applications is not well understood. Users will often push back against security requirements if it means they cannot get the software they want as quickly as they want to get it.

There is a natural tension between the desire of users for continual connection with constant improvements and security requirements to restrict unnecessary communications pathways and comprehensively check all new software. Once again, balance is the key and cyberspace operators must find the correct balance between competing requirements. That balance will be different for each organization and operational environment; the right balance for a small IT firm developing iPhone applications is very different than the right balance for the Central Intelligence Agency. Once an organization has done all it can to reduce its software and hardware attack surfaces, it can take one more step.

The final step in reducing the attack surface shown to a cyberspace attacker is to hide as much of it as possible behind different segments of the network. This is very similar in many respects to a defense in depth where once the attackers get over one wall, they are faced with a whole new series of walls to attack that are different than the first wall already conquered.[21] There is some overlap with the previous discussion on flexibility as segmentation can aid flexibility and also reduce an organization's apparent attack surface. True air gaps remain very difficult to maintain without some connection for maintenance or communication, but segmenting a network into different areas with strictly controlled communication links can reduce an organization's apparent attack surface. The amount of communication allowed into

---

[21] Carr [16].

or out of the segments can be adjusted to account for the level of security required. The control system for a nuclear power plant should have very little and strictly controlled access to communication flows, whereas the segmented network for an operating division inside a corporation will have much freer communication links.

The key to reducing attack surfaces appropriately is finding the right balance between connectivity and security. However, the world is full of aggressive actors in cyberspace and it is likely that an attacker will find a vulnerable attack surface eventually. Than the flexibility an organization has built will be tested as it reacts to the storm and bends like the bamboo.

Reacting to Attack

When bamboo bends during a storm it is in response to the pushing of the wind. The bamboo bends away from the wind which reduces the amount of the bamboo's surface the wind can push on and the bamboo's leaves and branches streamline, which reduces the force on the bamboo even more. If cyberspace operators are going to react to attacks in an analogous way, they will have to start by understanding the nature and characteristics of the attack they are under.

Cyberspace situational awareness is normally key for cyberspace operators to be able to defend their systems. When most cyberspace attacks are examined, their persistence is extremely low. Despite the media attention given to major worms such as Melissa or Slammer, most IT operations were back in full operation in a couple of days.[22] When serious nation-state cyberspace attacks are examined, only Stuxnet can be shown to have lasted more than a few weeks and that was because the defender did not know it was under attack.[23] This finding refers to direct attacks on systems and not cyberspace espionage, which is much harder to track and analyze for if analysts know it happened, the espionage was a failure at some level no matter how much information was collected. It is difficult to do an analysis of cyberspace espionage when the only cases that can be examined were all at least partial failures simply because you know about them.

Cyberspace situational awareness starts in the cyberspace defender's portion of cyberspace; cyberspace operators need to understand their own networks. This point at first may seem so obvious as to be hardly worth stating, but it may surprise people outside the IT business that many large organizations, to include the military services, do not have a complete picture of what their networks look like, exactly how they are connected to what, or even what applications are running on their networks. Large amounts of money are being spent to attempt to solve this problem, but an immediate solution is not apparent. Automated tools do a good job finding what they know to look for, but unique systems and applications are often missed as the automated tools do a poor job of finding and categorizing unknown software.

---

[22] Libicki [17], 37.
[23] Bryant [4], 171.

Legacy networks can be riddled with "servers" that are actually desktop computers sitting under a desk somewhere that were configured years ago to do a specific task that may, or may not, still be required. Once a picture of your own network is built, the next step is to consider what the enemy may be trying to do to it.

Intelligence on cyberspace threats is extremely difficult to collect. Cyberspace weapons are easy to build in extreme secrecy as the resources needed to create them can be easily hidden, as opposed to the resources required to build a battleship or bomber. Intelligence agencies should pursue information on cyberspace capabilities and intentions, but much of their best work will likely not be via cyberspace but via other more traditional methods since people are the ones who drive cyberspace and people may yield better intelligence than computers and networks in this area. Consider for a moment the presumed difficulty a nation-state would have hacking into the NSA compared to how easy it apparently was for Edward Snowden to walk out with an enormous amount of information. Once intelligence has been collected, via whatever means are available, cyberspace operators must overcome their own organization's security policies if it is to have any real effect.

While cyberspace weapons are very vulnerable to compromise and must be protected to be successful, the current extreme levels of secrecy hamper cyberspace resilience. Cyberspace capabilities were developed in a world steeped in high levels of classification and compartmentalization and it is true that cyberspace weapons are very frangible. Once an enemy knows about an exploit or technique, the target can normally block it very quickly.[24] However, a better balance between security and strengthening defenses needs to be struck in this area. Cyberspace attackers should not share the details of their latest weapons and techniques, but they should provide generalized threat information based on their weapons to their own cyberspace defenders. For cyberspace attackers to assume that their enemy could not possibly be smart enough to discover the same vulnerabilities and techniques would be extremely foolish. Striking the right balance in this area will have to be done by senior leaders who can balance improved defenses against possible loss of offensive capability. Sometimes the answer will be to disclose, sometimes the offensive capability will be so important that the risk to friendly networks of leaving them unpatched will be deemed acceptable. Right now, it appears that the default is that offensive forces share almost nothing with their defensive brethren. Aristotle's golden mean appears to lie in the direction of more disclosure, not less, for most organizations. The next question for cyberspace operators is how to effectively command and control cyberspace forces.

Resilient operational cyberspace organizations should be commanded and controlled more like maneuver forces in the physical domains, than managed as IT departments. Despite protestations by some that there is no maneuver in cyberspace, conflict in the cyberspace domain remains driven by humans who make decisions and react to their adversaries in ways that would still be familiar to Clausewitz and other military thinkers.[25] Attempting to reduce military conflict to

---

[24] Libicki [17], 74.

[25] Clausewitz [18], 75.

an engineering problem was a bad idea in the physical domains, why would we expect it to be a good idea in cyberspace? Accordingly, structuring cyberspace forces as maneuver units that are expected to react and maneuver to defeat a thinking and reacting adversary is a good start. Currently, cyberspace command and control is also far too complex with decision to employ too far up in the chain of command and examined by too many different teams of lawyers. Streamlining the process is important, but that will likely take time as understanding of the cyberspace domain continues to develop. In the meanwhile, maneuver and counterattack will remain important tools for resilient defenders.

According to Clausewitz, defenders should not simply wait passively, "...the defensive form of war is not a simple shield, but a shield made up of well-directed blows."[26] Owens, Dam, and Lin identified that with only a passive defense the defenders have to succeed every time, and since there are no penalties for the attacker, he can continue attacking until he is successful.[27] This difference places, "a heavy and asymmetric burden on a defensive posture that employs only passive defense."[28] A defender can be attempting to accomplish several things when utilizing hackbacks. A defender can disable the computers executing the attack. A defender can also attempt to trace an attack back to its source. Attackers will normally bounce attacks through multiple servers to attempt to hide themselves, but a persistent defender can sometimes work back through the servers to the source, or utilize more creative methods to identify the attacker. If a defender makes it all the way back to the originator of the attack, there are now a number of unpleasant things he or she could theoretically do to the attacker's networks in retaliation. Unfortunately, most of those things are currently illegal for defenders to do under U.S. law.

Since active defense normally involves breaking into a number of privately owned computers along the way, it is generally illegal under the Computer Fraud and Abuse Act (CFAA.) According to Paul Rosenzweig, any active defense that reaches outside of the defender's computer system is "almost certainly a crime in and of itself."[29] This legal issue opens cyberspace defenders up to prosecution and lawsuits whether they are military or civilian. And that is just if the attacking computers are only in the United States, which is normally not the case. Breaking into computers in foreign countries brings on an entirely new set of legal and political problems. The difficulty in attributing attacks might work in the defender's favor, as it can be hard to attribute hackbacks if the defender chooses to mask where he is coming from, but that does not actually deal with the legal and ethical issues. Hackbacks quickly devolve into a legal and political Gordian knot. Hackbacks are a key element in an effective defense, but they are clearly illegal, and just as clearly even private organizations are now using them.[30] Hopefully, policy and legal

---

[26] Clausewitz [18], 357.

[27] Owens et al. [15], 13.

[28] Owens et al. [15], 13.

[29] Rosenzweig [8], Kindle Location 2024, chap. 7.

[30] Higgins [19].

authorities will catch up in this important area. Fortunately for defenders, there are other types of active defenses that have less legal issues.

A less legally problematic technique that a resilient cyberspace defender can utilize against an attacker is a honey net. A honey net diverts attackers into a false network full of whatever the defender wants the attacker to see. If a cyberspace attacker is attempting to break into a highly classified system and the defenders know it, they can divert him into a false network. If you block the attacker, there is nothing preventing him from trying again using a different access that the defender might miss. If the defender instead diverts the attacker but provides him with false information, it can be far more effective. For the defenders to be effective in their deception, they have to understand the expectations of the attacker and provide an environment tailored to what the attacker expects to find.[31] Something similar to this may have happened in the early 1980s when a U.S. spy provided information that the Soviet Union was planning secretly to acquire gas pipeline technology. Instead of blocking the sale, the U.S. allegedly quietly altered the computer code that eventually led to, "the most monumental non-nuclear explosion and fire ever seen from space."[32] Defenders can do much the same thing in cyberspace. Once a defender captures an attacker in a honey net, the defender can keep the attacker busy with false information, examine attack patterns and techniques, embed beacons to phone home in the data that the attacker is taking, or whatever is most useful. One of the most useful techniques for a defender is instilling doubt in the mind of the attacker.

Introducing doubt into the mind of an attacker is one of the more useful things a resilient cyberspace defender can do with a honey net. A defender does not have to falsify everything; successfully falsifying one piece of information can make the attacker doubt everything else he or she got as well. One way of accomplishing this increased doubt is through a defender falsifying Battle Damage Assessment (BDA.) It is normally difficult for an attacker to understand how effective her or his attacks have been; a honey net can make it even worse. A defender can use a honey net to make it look like an attack has been successful, but then suddenly turn the system back on to ambush the attacker's forces at the most opportune time.[33] Tricking the enemy this way once, will also have the effect of making the enemy very reluctant to trust any future cyberspace BDA. If an adversary does not fall for a honey net, a resilient cyberspace defender should have multiple copies of critical data available.

Backups enable a defender to rapidly reconstitute damaged systems and data, and provide a way for defenders to minimize the effect of even a successful attack.[34] An attacker who breaks into a logistics system and erases all the data can cause significant problems for a defender. However, if the defender has a backup and can have the system restored and operating in a day, the defender can minimize the attack's long-term effects. One of the hopeful trends for cyberspace defenders is the decreasing cost of electronic data storage. This decreasing cost makes it far easier

---

[31] Gray [20], 35.

[32] O'Harrow [21].

[33] Owens et al. [15], 125.

[34] Libicki links the replicability of cyberspace with its reparability in Libicki [17], 5.

for defenders to keep one, two, or ten copies of the data needed to restore a system. Of course, defenders need to keep the copies in a manner that prevents an attacker from getting to the backups and the primary system at the same time.[35] Automatic backup systems may be convenient, but they are automatic and will copy a cyberspace weapon just as easily as valid data. Backups are part of resilience, but cyberspace defenders can also build hidden additional capability into their networks.

War Reserve Modes or WARM is a concept from electronic warfare that has great applicability in cyberspace combat. Electronic warfare equipment such as radars or radios is often built with additional functionality that is not used unless needed in a major conflict against a top tier enemy. The reason for these hidden modes is that every technique has a countermeasure and if all of a combatant's techniques are used routinely, the enemy will find out what they are and develop countermeasures. If the best techniques are hidden and not used until combat starts, it can give one side a decisive advantage.

WARM applied to cyberspace would suggest that defenders should have preplanned ways to significantly alter not just their defenses, but also their networks in ways that make an attacker's careful reconnaissance obsolete. Gregory Rattray has identified that in cyberspace, the equivalents of mountains and oceans can be moved with the "flick of a switch"[36] and defenders don't have to accept the geography of their environment, they can actively change the terrain to make it harder to attack.[37] Cyberspace attackers often have to spend enormous time and effort mapping out exactly how a network is configured and what software it is running. If a defender was to change all the software on his routers to a previously unknown version as a conflict starts, it could disrupt many of the attacker's plans. The new software does not even have to be better than the old one or have less vulnerabilities, the new vulnerabilities will still have to be discovered which can buy the defender significant time and breathing space. The same principle could be utilized for any software on the network, and even has applicability to hardware.

A well-resourced defender could have significant spare hardware on hand of different types to enable him to quickly rebuild a network. For example, if a defender has a diversified network with three types of routers and one of them is successfully attacked, a cyberspace defender could replace the vulnerable one with one of the other two types from storage. Defenders could go so far as to build entire networks using different types of hardware that are then left in a standby mode and disconnected from other systems, which makes them very difficult to attack. If the primary system is successfully attacked, the defender can switch to the backup. Defenders cannot simply set up a backup system and assume it will work when needed; they have to extensively test and evaluate it. Otherwise a backup system may be worse than useless as it provides a false sense of security but no capability when it is needed.

---

[35] Singer and Friedman [2], Kindle Location 3177.
[36] Rattray [22], 256.
[37] Libicki [13], 324.

Of course, setting up an entire backup network is extremely expensive and will likely only be worthwhile on a small scale and when the information or network is so critical that it cannot be allowed to fail. Nuclear command and control is one obvious area where the requirement for surety is so high that a complete backup network is reasonable. These techniques of improved situational awareness, effective command and control, hackbacks, honey nets, backups, WARM and backup networks will help cyberspace defenders to dynamically maneuver and bend in the right direction when the attacking wind comes.

Conclusion

There are many ways that cyberspace defenders can bend under attack before springing upright like the bamboo in the ancient Japanese proverb. The three key elements that apply to the resilience of the bamboo as well as resilience in cyberspace are flexibility, reducing attack surfaces, and reacting dynamically to attack.

Flexibility in cyberspace conflict will largely stem from creating flexible people although good network design that allows flexible cyberspace operators more options will also help. Flexibility in cyberspace systems will be expensive and efficiency will be lowered due to the necessary excess capacity that must be built into a more flexible system. A flexible cyberspace system is also one that is heterogeneous and broken into defensible enclaves, not one large and easy to administer network running the same software on every device. Flexible cyberspace personnel are best grown through extensive training and exercises to include red teaming, full scale exercises with cyberspace play allowed to affect the physical domains and accountability for users who prove unable to adopt good security practices. Many of these changes will be very hard to implement as they will be extremely uncomfortable to organizations and will require significant cultural change.

Reducing attack surfaces is the second element to creating cyberspace resiliency. The first, and extremely difficult step is to eliminate unnecessary capability across the network, both in software and in hardware. Users will be discomfited by having to use different tools than they are used to, but the payoff in security can be significant. Not every backup system should be eliminated, wherever possible a primary and backup for each key mission area should be available to allow cyberspace operators to rapidly shift from one to the other if vulnerabilities are discovered. User's desire for continual rapid improvements in communication and capability will also have to be balanced against security requirements as each new capability or communications pathway introduces a potential attack vector. Striking the correct balance between security and capability will be a difficult and continuing challenge and the correct balance will change depending on the organization and environment it operates within.

The final element to resiliency in cyberspace is the ability to react dynamically to attack. Cyberspace operators need to develop better situational awareness of their own networks and develop intelligence capabilities to understand what the enemy is planning. Attackers and defenders on the same side also need to lower the walls between them and share more information to enable cyberspace defenders to be better able to defend their networks, while protecting offensive capabilities. Effective cyberspace command and control that treats cyberspace operators as maneuvering forces to be commanded, versus an IT management problem with an engineering solution is also important. Active defenses to include hackbacks, honey nets, backups, war reserve modes, and backup hardware all contribute to cyberspace resilience.

For an organization to create enduring cyberspace resilience, some aspects of all three elements will be required and building in cyberspace resilience will not be cheap. The additional costs incurred for redundancy and training alone will overwhelm any potential savings from streamlining and reducing excess capacity. However, if an organization is serious about protecting its ability to accomplish its mission in cyberspace, resilience under attack will be the key. If cyberspace operators and their defended networks and systems adopt the characteristics of the wise bamboo, they too will be resilient enough to spring upright after the passage of the storm.

References

1. Risk Steering Committee (2010) DHS risk lexicon: 2010 edition. p 26. http://www.dhs.gov/xlibrary/assets/dhs-risk-lexicon-2010.pdf. Accessed 17 Jan 2015
2. Singer PW, Friedman A (2013) Cybersecurity and cyberwar: what everyone needs to know. Oxford University Press, Amazon, Kindle Location 720
3. Libicki MC (2009) Cyberdeterrence and cyberwar. RAND Corporation, Santa Monica, p 176
4. Bryant WD (2015) International conflict and cyberspace superiority: theory and practice. Routledge, London
5. Joint Chiefs of Staff, Joint Operations (2012) Information Operations 3–13, U.S. Government Printing Office, Washington DC, II-9
6. Luttwak EN (2003) Strategy: the logic of war and peace. Belknap Press, Cambridge, MA, pp 39–40
7. Aristotle (1993) Nicomachean ethics. In: Bennett WJ (ed) The book of virtues. Simon & Schuster, New York, p 102
8. Rosenzweig P (2013) Cyber warfare: how conflicts in cyberspace are challenging America and changing the world. Praeger, Santa Barbara
9. Bousquet A (2009) The scientific way of warfare. Columbia University Press, New York
10. Rattray GJ (2001) Strategic warfare in cyberspace. MIT Press, Amazon
11. Lonsdale DJ (2004) The nature of war in the information age. Frank Cass, London, p 154
12. Kramer FD (2009) Cyberpower and national security: policy recommendations for a strategic framework. In: Kramer FD, Starr SH, Wentz LK (eds) Cyberpower and national security. Potomac Books, Washington, DC, p 14
13. Libicki MC (2012) Cyberspace is not a warfighting domain. I/S: A Journal of Law and Policy for the Information Society 8(2):330
14. Hostage GM III, Broadwell LR Jr (2014) Resilient command and control: the need for distributed control. Joint Forces Quarterly 75:38–43
15. Owens WA, Dam KW, Lin HS (eds) (2009) Technology, policy, law, and ethics regarding U.S. acquisition and use of cyberattack capabilities. National Academies Press, Washington, DC

16. Jeffrey Carr (2011) Inside cyber warfare: mapping the cyber underworld. O'Reilly Media, Beijing, Kindle location 3674
17. Libicki MC (2007) conquest in cyberspace: national security and information warfare. Cambridge University Press, Cambridge
18. von Clausewitz C (1976) On war (ed and trans: Howard M, Paret P). Princeton University Press, Princeton, p 75
19. Higgins KJ (2013) Free 'active defense' tools emerge. Security Dark Reading, 11 July 2013. http://www.darkreading.com/intrusion-prevention/free-active-defense-tools-emerge/240158160
20. Gray CS (1999) Modern strategy. Oxford University Press, Oxford
21. O'Harrow R, Zero day. Diversion Books, New York, Kindle Location 345, part 2
22. Rattray GJ (2009) An environmental approach to understanding cyberpower. In: Kramer FD, Starr SH, Wentz LK (eds) Cyberpower and national security. Potomac Books, Washington, DC

Internet of Things

David Fletcher

Introduction

The Internet of Things (IoT) got its start in 1999 with the founding of the MIT Auto-ID Center. The goal of the Auto-ID Center was to develop a broad class of identification technologies for use in industry to support automation, reduce errors, and increase efficiency. The cornerstone of this technology was the Radio Frequency Identification (RFID) tag. The RFID tag allows one to uniquely identify any tagged object and discover details regarding the object via a centralized service. This initial work culminated in the launch of the EPC Network in 2003. This network demonstrated that computers could be used to automatically identify and track man-made objects through the production, distribution, and delivery processes. It also opened the door to realizing new efficiencies in manufacturing and distribution. Now, production objects could be tracked in mass to identify bottlenecks in production, reduce the amount of human labor required, and deter item theft [1].

After the EPC Network demonstration, the Auto-ID Center was split into Auto-ID Labs and EPCglobal. The purpose of Auto-ID Labs was to develop the hardware, software, and languages that could be integrated into the current internet in order to realize the IoT. In contrast, EPCglobal was charged with commercialization of IoT. Since this time, advancements in wireless communication and embedded computing have broadened the scope of IoT to include virtually any device that can be used to sense and communicate across the internet [1].

This broadening of scope has caused a fair amount of confusion regarding the definition of the IoT. A sampling of definitions includes:

- The capability to connect, communicate, and remotely manage a number of networked, automated devices via the Internet [2].

D. Fletcher (✉)
e-mail: david.fletcher.6@us.af.mil

© Springer International Publishing Switzerland 2015
M. Blowers (ed.), *Evolution of Cyber Technologies and Operations to 2035*,
Advances in Information Security 63, DOI 10.1007/978-3-319-23585-1_2

- The point in time when more "things or objects" are connected to the Internet than people [3].
- A world-wide network of interconnected objects uniquely addressable based on standard communication protocols [4].
- The interconnection via the internet of computing devices embedded in everyday objects, enabling them to send and receive data [5].

Each of these definitions paints a very broad picture of the internet of things and each includes the common characteristic of an objects' ability to communicate. In fact, it is this ability for objects to communicate that delivers the power of the IoT. This power is found in the form of data. Through arrays of sensors, each IoT device is predicted to generate of a waterfall of data that can be used to increase the collective knowledge and wisdom of the human race. More data captured results in a greater level and fidelity of knowledge and wisdom for mankind [3].

The size and scale of the Internet of Things is expected to be monumental. Various predictors of IoT scale have estimated that as many as 100 billion devices will be connected to the internet by the year 2020 [1, 3, 6]. This number does not account for traditional internet devices such as computers, tablets, and smart phones. In addition, the number of devices that will have indirect connections to the internet (typically sensors) will number in the trillions by that same date [7, 8]. If these predictions come to pass, then the number of machine to machine communication sessions will be 30 times that of human to human communication on the internet [1]. In addition, given a population estimate of 7.6 billion people in 2020 each person will be associated with six directly connected IoT devices, over 130 sensors, and innumerable embedded objects [8].

Gartner conservatively estimates that in 2020 there will be 25 billion IoT devices connected to the internet [6]. Analysis of the growth trend presented in the study indicates that the IoT grows by roughly 35 % year over year. Extrapolating this trend out to the year 2035 results in an IoT device count of 2.2 trillion devices. Because of the sheer number of devices and their pervasive deployment in our surrounding environment the Gartner study goes on to describe the IoT as disruptive across all industries and areas of society [6]. This sentiment has been echoed by several other sources including a National Intelligence Council study conducted in 2008 [9, 10].

Future Benefits

There is almost unimaginable potential for the sensing, processing, informing, and decision making power of the Internet of Things. This potential is so widely recognized that industries have begun creating their own terms that embody the intent of the IoT within their particular markets. Terms like Industrial Internet, Industry 4.0, Smart

Planet, Smart Grid, and Smart Home attempt to restrict the focus of IoT technology to a specific vertical industry. Examples of Internet of Things research can be found in nearly every industry.

At the consumer level, the Internet of Things is being developed in the form of home automation. Through this technology, individuals will be able to create efficiencies based on information that typical home appliances generate. For instance, a refrigerator will maintain a full inventory of its contents in addition to product expiration information to better inform the homeowner to support product ordering and waste minimization. This information could be further correlated with favorite recipes to determine available ingredients and potentially re-supply. Orders would be automatically transmitted to a grocery store with pick-up or delivery being the only remaining task. Gartner predicts that the efficiencies realized by the connected kitchen will reduce consumer cost by 15 % [6]. This example is a single instance of IoT in the home. Other offerings include connected televisions, entry control and alarm systems, light switches, light bulbs, etc. An almost endless array of products will exist to support the efficient management of the home.

In retail stores, RFID is poised to change the way that we shop dramatically. Once all of the products in a retail outlet are tagged and the facility is equipped with reader technology it becomes effortless to manage stock and operate with much lower overhead than today. These efficiencies will be realized in many different ways. First, the reliance on human labor will be reduced as instant inventory becomes possible. Second, shoppers will have reduced wait times to complete purchases as reader technology can be used to instantly inventory and tally their purchases for checkout. Finally, by observing consumption trends, better estimates of product demand can be made to eliminate overstock situations and reduce requirements for stock on hand [11].

Efficiencies in the delivery of these goods and services to retailers can be realized through IoT integration into supply chain logistics. An example of this activity can be seen in the Port of Hamburg which has deployed a system of sensors into the roads, parking spaces, and trucks. Drivers get real-time information in their vehicles to aid in navigating the port and delivering goods for transport to their final destination. These concepts have in-turn been applied to management of waterway and rail traffic [12]. Cascading retail efficiencies with supply chain efficiencies could allow stock on hand to be distributed to reach a wider population while potentially reducing overall cost. This is possible due to efficiencies gained in delivery of goods and reduction of stock on hand based on consumption trends. This surplus stock will consequently be available for distribution rather than being stored in a stock room or spoiling on the shelf.

In the facilities sector, efficiencies are already being realized with the inclusion of industrial control systems for everything from heating, ventilation, and air conditioning control to ambient light sensing and adjustment. These capabilities allow facility operating costs to be slashed by adjusting temperature and lighting based on occupancy. In addition, through data collection, trends for energy consumption can be developed and monitored to support problem diagnosis. However, this is just the beginning of the Internet of Things revolution for facilities. From a facility maintenance perspective, smart devices such as emergency lighting and smoke detectors can alert maintenance staff proactively when problems occur. Mundane tasks like monitoring soap levels in washrooms can also be automated to reduce staff levels and decrease response time [13]. Other technologies such as smart elevators promise to more efficiently manage resource use and minimize wait times for users by predicting peak usage and positioning cars strategically for response [14].

With intelligence embedded into individual facilities the next evolution becomes the realization of smart cities. The smart city is a superset of the smart facility concept and is used to more efficiently manage and instrument public resources. Public buildings are instrumented as described above to increase efficiency in utility monitoring and consumption. Offerings such as smart parking, lighting, waste management, traffic management, and environmental monitoring improve the effectiveness of urban infrastructure while decreasing the overall operating costs of municipalities [15].

In the realm of agriculture, smart sensors will be used to monitor and communicate soil composition and irrigation conditions to enable real-time adjustment. This information, coupled with weather forecasts, temperature, and humidity readings can be used to more accurately manage resources. Watering of crops can occur at a more accurate rate to limit the cost and environmental impact of irrigation while conserving this critical natural resource. Livestock will also be tagged and monitored to proactively manage health of the herd and farm implements will include sensing devices to provide fleet diagnostics to farmers [16].

The automotive industry also holds great promise for the Internet of Things. In addition to features such as entertainment and navigation, the automotive industry will integrate a vast array of sensors into new automobiles. These sensors will provide advanced diagnostic information as well as features such as collision avoidance and traffic management sensors. This array of features will not only revolutionize consumer vehicles but entire fleets of commercial vehicles in every industry. The ability to collect diagnostic information will allow proactive management of the fleet and reduce maintenance and overhead costs [16].

The IoT adds value to the medical field as well. Initiatives in smart medicine include technologies that support proactive rather than reactive medicine. Through wearable (such as our clothes) and implantable (artificial organs and sensors) technology as well as tele healthcare devices our physicians can get a more complete picture of our overall health rather than relying on a snapshot in time. This activity is already being observed as more and more people employ fitness bands to manage their personal health and behavior [17]. Medical breakthroughs such as the artificial pancreas will make management of diseases such as diabetes almost transparent to the sufferer while more effectively managing the effects of the disease. In addition, smart pills and nano-scale robotics will allow doctors to eliminate many of the most invasive procedures by fighting diseases like cancer where they manifest themselves [18].

Challenges

Despite all of the potential benefits outlined above, realization of the IoT faces several challenges. These challenges may result in slower than expected adoption of IoT technologies or may negate any or all of the identified benefits. A literature review reveals the following challenges to full scale deployment and adoption of the Internet of Things.

The Internet of Things relies on internet connectivity in order to transmit and receive data from the embedded processors and sensors. Currently, the public routable Internet Protocol version 4 address space is fully saturated. Evans predicts that IoT adoption and growth will be highly dependent upon deployment of the next generation Internet Protocol. Internet Protocol version 6 provides ample address space to handle the immense number of devices that IoT promises [3].

A large population of the IoT will require energy to operate. Many of these devices will also be deployed in locations that do not have energy readily available. Examples include wearable technology, retrofitted sensors, and technologies such as smart roads. This leaves two options for powering devices; energy harvesting and battery power. Without advanced power saving schemes and overall reduced consumption it may be economically unfavorable to adopt IoT technologies as the cost to operate devices may outweigh any efficiencies gained [3, 19, 20].

The Internet of Things will rely heavily on wireless communication. Another shortfall in physical capacity is the availability of wireless spectrum. A myriad of wireless technologies are poised to support IoT such as near field communication, zigbee, zwave, Bluetooth, wi-fi and others. As more and more devices are added to the IoT there will be an increasing amount of interference due to proximity of devices. This leaves just a few solution choices; either devices must become increasingly more resilient to interference, more spectrum must be added, or new protocols must be developed [21, 20].

The large number of devices deployed in the IoT will generate a mountain of data that must be collected, analyzed and responded in a timely fashion. This will create several challenges that will affect the future of IoT. First, big data analytics must mature to the point that this data can be processed in a timely fashion [9]. Second, data centers must be prepared to receive and store this data. Third, policy must be developed regarding the judicious use and retention of data that may be sensitive in nature [22].

The IoT must also be supported with standards in order to ease complexity involved in deployment of products and promote interoperability among vendors. These standards must be applied across the spectrum of capability to include policy, protocols, and architecture. Focus on the greater landscape of IoT must be achieved to maximize return on investment. Currently, research on IoT exhibits a fragmented approach with focus on single application domains and technologies [20]. Recent activity by the Federal Trade Commission and congress also highlights the need to address policy regarding security and privacy [22]. While IoT specific protocols have been developed it is likely that there is much work to be done to unify the field [23].

Privacy is a serious issue for the future of the Internet of Things. Through the technology employed IoT will collect mountains of data that are both mundane and extremely intimate in nature. In order to promote IoT adoption, vendors and service providers must exercise due care in developing and deploying technology. In addition, data that is generated by the IoT must be scrutinized to ensure that the appropriate access controls are in place, data is protected at rest and in transit, data is effectively anonymized, and that data is destroyed when it is no longer useful [22]. These concerns are underscored by recent data breaches at retailers such as Target, Home Depot, and Anthem [24]. To make matters worse, all of these requirements must be levied on hardware and software platforms that are typically resource-constrained [25].

Just as important as privacy is security for the devices that make up the Internet of Things. A lack of forward thought and attention to security leads to the types of breaches identified above. Hardware designers must ensure that their devices can support security enhancing features and that security is considered during up-front device design [25]. Software and firmware developers must likewise employ security best practice in design and consider the mechanics of vulnerability discovery and remediation. Finally, those deploying IoT technology must pay careful attention to ensure that sensors, devices, and services are installed with available security enhancing features enabled and properly configured [26].

Another challenge that accompanies security is cost. With a great deal of interest in the Internet of Things there will be a large amount of competition. Consumers (both individual and corporate) must be educated to understand the security differences between products. In many cases, purchase of a product comes down to cost comparison [19]. This behavior will likely be more prevalent in individual consumer purchases. When it comes to a commodity device like a light bulb the consumer may not look beyond cost in making a purchase. This brings a whole new aspect to the buying process as these devices will likely remain in service for an extended period of time with little or no support [27].

Current State of IoT Security and Privacy

Of all of the challenges identified above, none has a greater ability to influence IoT adoption than security and privacy [22]. Unfortunately, users seldom have a full understanding of the impact of security until after a breach has occurred. However, given recent security breaches that have led to compromise of privacy, consumers' appetites for poor security are waning. Unfortunately, there is an abundance of evidence to indicate that security in the IoT is lagging behind and in many cases repeating cyber security history [28]. This concern has become so great that Congress and the Federal Trade Commission have begun taking an interest in order to provide greater consumer protection [22, 29].

In recent security reviews conducted by the HP Fortify [30] and Veracode [31] teams, consumer-grade IoT devices have not fared well. In addition, research conducted by

Miller and Valasek [32] has indicated a great deal of vulnerability in modern automotive systems, which are projected to number 250 million by the year 2020 [6]. Finally, a session titled "The Internet of Fails" at the annual DEFCON conference in Las Vegas exposed a handful of these failures which has served to illustrate the pervasiveness of the problem [26]. One element that each of these studies have in common is that the security problems that are being exhibited are well known security issues that are present or have been eliminated in other more typical information technology domains. The problem is bad enough that the Open Web Application Security Project (OWASP) has created an Internet of Things Top 10 list of security oversights [33]. The findings of the HP Fortify report are directly correlated to this list [30].

"Internet of Fails" describes a confluence of several factors that has led to poor security in consumer-level IoT devices [26]. Low-cost development platforms such as Arduino and Raspberry Pi have increased accessibility for experimentation. These low-cost platforms typically require a minimum of skill to configure and program which has, in turn, led to a larger developer pool that is not typically familiar with secure device configuration and secure programming practices. These developers also may not understand the implications that lack of inherent security controls means for their potential user base.

In addition to typical revenue streams, such as venture capital, non-standard streams of revenue have appeared to answer the call for innovation. Crowd sourcing applications such as GoFundMe [34] and Kickstarter [35] have generated funding for a wide range of products. Since this funding is user-supplied much of the rigor of the risk-reward equation has been boiled down to functional demand. Where crowd sourced funding for a product is tight innovators must make trade-offs between cost, functionality, time to market and security. In this equation, security typically loses out. Especially when there is market competition and profit margins are slim [26].

Some of the basic security issues identified in the IoT studies above include the following:

- Support – It is projected that some IoT devices will be expected to be in service for up to 20 years [27]. With the burgeoning nature of the IoT market buyers must make wise investments in viable technology companies or risk having to purchase the same device multiple times. It is reasonable to expect that some IoT start-ups will fail over this period of time [26]. Without making this risk evaluation it can be expected that a number of devices will remain in service and unsupported. Reluctance to accept the end of life announcement for Microsoft Windows XP serves to illustrate resistance to replacement products despite increased risk when that product is still functionally capable [36].
- Maintenance – The internet of Things represents a vast expansion in the number and types of devices connected to the internet (directly or indirectly). As consumers and businesses adopt IoT technologies they must also consider the requirement to perform updates on these devices. While an auto-update infrastructure is desirable, this infrastructure carries its own security concerns such as the possibility for watering hole attacks and firmware modification in transit [26].

- Lack of Physical Device Security – Embedded systems, especially development platforms, have hardware debugging interfaces [26]. If these interfaces are not properly protected or physically disabled then malicious actors may be able to extract and reverse engineer firmware installed on the device. Since IoT devices must be cost conscious it is trivial for a malicious user to purchase these devices. Compromise of a single device may lead to device class level compromise due to commonality or the nature of the vulnerability.
- Lack of Encryption – In order to be useful, Internet of Things devices must communicate information. This information is typically transmitted to a gateway device or web service and in-turn viewed by the user using a typical computer or mobile platform. This can lead to a large number of communication paths that, if not properly secured, may be intercepted or manipulated by an attacker [30]. Even more important is protection of key material. The "Internet of Fails" DEFCON presentation identified situations where private keys could be extracted from firmware updates [26]. Use of hard coded key material in this fashion should be avoided at all cost. Once a key has been compromised communication should be presumed to be unprotected and subject to interception.
- Lack of User-Level Security – Users and their passwords have been the weakest link in security since the dawn of the internet. This concept remains true in Internet of Things devices. In the HP Fortify [30] report several of the devices that the team tested had a user interface that did not require passwords of sufficient length or complexity to adequately protect the users' information. In addition, "Internet of Fails" exposed passwords that were hard-coded in firmware that could be easily discovered in downloaded updates [26].

IoT Security and Privacy Concerns

If the current protective posture of IoT does not improve the internet will be rife with targets for attack and abuse. Many researchers are addressing difficult topics such as next generation capabilities to support Confidentiality, Integrity, and Availability [2, 20, 27]. However, a vast amount of vulnerability typically lies in the details of implementation, configuration, and administration. Due to the resource-constrained nature of IoT devices, it is likely that security will remain a variable in the time, functionality, and cost equation for some time to come [8, 25]. In addition, consumer-grade devices are likely to receive less rigor than commercial-grade devices from a security perspective [19]. This does not bode well because in the internet we have learned that a risk assumed by one is a risk to all. As illustrated in the Target breach, one compromise can lead to another where one party inherently assumes risk that another takes [37]. Many small businesses employ consumer-grade devices in their networks as a cost saving measure. This becomes increasingly important as more devices incorporate functionality to affect our physical environment.

Because of resource constraints, IoT devices will be particularly susceptible to Denial of Service (DoS) attacks [8]. These classes of attack serve to exhaust resources on a particular device in order to deny service to its operator. This can have a systemic effect in the IoT as other devices that rely on information produced by the targeted device will be denied this information. In turn, the information produced by upstream processors and sensors may therefore be denied or skewed based on the activity [30].

In addition, through compromise, IoT devices become excellent targets to stage a Distributed Denial of Service attack. While the IoT in general is expected to be largely heterogeneous there will be environments and classes of devices that are homogeneous or employ the same underlying technology. If an attacker is able to take advantage of this and compromise a large swath of devices they may be used to launch an asymmetric attack against a target entity and overwhelm it. The compromised devices may also pose a challenge to diagnose as they typically don't have a standard user interface and are expected to generate a large volume of continuous communication.

The Internet of Things also offers opportunities for re-envisioning attacks such as resource denial, resource exhaustion, physical safety, and pervasive surveillance attacks. While none of these concepts are new, the wide distribution of IoT devices and internet connectivity allows an attacker to pursue them from a distance and with relative anonymity and impunity. In addition, once vulnerability is found it becomes trivial to perform mass discovery thanks to services like Shodan HQ [38] which provides search engine functionality for finding internet connected devices.

Resource denial can be approached in the same fashion that recent banking Trojans have. In this situation, attackers may compromise and control access to devices or services in return for ransom from legitimate users. Once IoT devices have become integrated into an environment it may be impossible to continue operation without them. A recent example of resource denial is that of an IoT adopter who fully automated his home. One of the devices in his home automation system malfunctioned to the point that he could no longer control any of its constituent systems. It turned out that the culprit was a malfunctioning lightbulb that created an internal denial of service on his network [39]. A question to consider is whether a typical home user would be able to solve this problem. In addition, consider the types of resource denial attacks that might be carried out by a malicious actor. This could include access denial to automation systems or disabling smart meters delivering gas, water, or electricity.

A slightly different spin on resource denial is resource exhaustion. Instead of disabling service, though, the attacker may adjust set points on appliances such as heating, ventilation and air conditioning to waste energy. On a micro scale, the objective of this type of attack may be simply to burn resources or increase operating cost. On a macro scale, the attacker may target multiple businesses or homes within a specific geographical area with the objective of increased strain on the resource provider [19]. This activity could potentially result in infrastructure damage causing widespread outages such as the blackout of 2003 in the Midwest United States [40].

As we integrate more capability to control the physical world around us physical safety becomes an issue for the IoT. The Aurora [41] project and Stuxnet [42] worm have served to illustrate that vulnerability in cyber-physical systems can have dire consequences. A recent cyber-attack on a German steel mill caused massive damage by disrupting the control systems on a blast furnace. While there was no indication of injury, the potential was evident given that the blast furnace could not be properly shut down. Industrial control systems can be found across many industries employed in various safety critical functions [43].

Another potential threat to physical safety is integration of advanced sensing and controls within automobiles. Security researchers Charlie Miller and Chris Valasek demonstrated this type of attack through the on-board diagnostic port inside the vehicle. Their report illustrated the ability to command advanced vehicle control systems such as electronic steering, acceleration, and braking through this access method [32]. A follow-on report to their original 2013 work included an architectural review of a number of vehicles with the same types of features demonstrating the same types of vulnerabilities [44]. As mentioned earlier, Gartner expects 250 million vehicles to be connected to the internet by 2020. Implementations lacking security could allow these types of attacks to occur over the internet rather than requiring physical access to the vehicle.

Even if physical access is necessary, researchers have demonstrated other weaknesses that may grant easier access to the vehicle for implantation of malware. For instance, one researcher identified a flaw in the BMW smartphone application that rendered 2.2 million vehicles vulnerable to unauthorized access by way of unlocking the vehicle [45]. This research also revealed suspected dealer unlock codes that worked multiple times across multiple vehicles of the same make and model.

The prospect of physical access brings us to the connected home. Many home security systems allow the homeowner to control access to their residence through a smartphone application. Some systems provide the ability to not only alarm the home but control other physical aspects such as entry door locks, garage doors, lighting, and water [46, 47]. HP Fortify and Veracode security researchers surveyed several of these types of consumer devices and found an alarming number of vulnerabilities [30, 31]. The prospect of gaining physical access to a residence brings a new level of power to common burglary. Through sensors connected to these same systems attackers may be able to identify presence of the homeowner [19]. After presence is determined, an attacker may be able to take advantage of one of these vulnerabilities to obtain physical access to the premises with little risk over the internet.

The final concern that we will discuss is pervasive surveillance. Many researchers warn against the loss of privacy due to massive integration of technology into our environment. This concern is not without merit. With full adoption of the Internet of Things there will be an endless stream of data regarding our location, medical history, preferences, etc. from a vast array of devices that each may be used to uniquely identify us as individuals. Once a device is associated with an individual identity, it is likely that additional device associations can be inferred.

Some examples of current day privacy issues in the Internet of Things follow. Recently, Samsung received criticism over the privacy agreement for its smart television software. The privacy agreement warned users that any sensitive information discussed may be transmitted to a third party for translation [48]. This revelation startled users but these same people are likely surrounded by recording devices like microphones and cameras in many of the devices they own. These devices include common items such as laptops, smartphones, and televisions but may also extend to uncommon items such as children's toys and baby monitors [49].

In addition, it is possible to read unprotected RFID tag information without the owner being aware that the tag has been read or that it even exists [50]. This activity has been demonstrated by passively cloning devices such as passports and driver's license [51]. Once RFID tags have been used to identify the majority of consumer devices and embedded into clothing and documents privacy and attribution become a serious issue if not properly protected.

Conclusion

The Internet of Things holds a great deal of promise for improving our collective lives. Knowledge gained will allow us to realize efficiencies in nearly every aspect of human life. However, rapid adoption of Internet of Things technologies may lead to long-term problems given the current state of the industry. Unless standards, interoperability, and developer/user education and practices improve there may be significant negative consequences. In addition, there must be equality between consumer grade and commercial grade product offerings with regard to security.

The number of devices expected to be deployed to support the Internet of Things underscores the requirement for adequate security and privacy. IoT adoption represents an exponential growth in the attack surface of the internet and may bring with it new and unimagined attacks as a result. Since the IoT will also connect the virtual world with the physical world, security concerns turn into safety concerns.

Privacy in the internet of things is just as important and depends on adequate security measures to be in place. The implications of the Internet of Things may in reality be the trading of functionality and efficiency for the personal privacy that we have enjoyed as a free society. The sheer number of uniquely identifiable devices associated with an individual may mean that association of any single device with that individual may lead to further associations through simple observation. This may become so pervasive that privacy is unattainable. The result may be a surveillance society like something out of George Orwell's 1984.

Bibliography

1. Santucci G (2010) The internet of things: between the revolution of the internet and the metamorphosis of objects. [Online]. Available: http://ec.europa.eu/information_society/policy/rfid/documents/iotrevolution.pdf. Accessed Apr 2015
2. Leo M, Battisti F, Carli M, Neri A (2014) A federated architecture approach for internet of things security. Euro Med Telco conference 2014, Naples, 2014

3. Evans D (2011) CISCO Internet Business Solutions Group (IBSG). [Online]. Available: https://www.cisco.com/web/about/ac79/docs/innov/IoT_IBSG_0411FINAL.pdf. Accessed Apr 2015
4. I. o. T. i. 2020 (2008) European technology platform on smart systems integration. [Online]. Available: http://www.smart-systems-integration.org/public/documents/publications/Internet-of-Things_in_2020_EC-EPoSS_Workshop_Report_2008_v3.pdf. Accessed Mar 2015
5. Oxford Dictionary (2015) Oxford English Dictionary online. Oxford University Press, Oxford
6. Rivera J, van der Meulen R (2014) Gartner Newsroom, Gartner, 11 Nov 2014. [Online]. Available: http://www.gartner.com/newsroom/id/2905717. Accessed Feb 2015
7. Bryzek J, Cooper B (2013) TSensors Summits. [Online]. Available: http://www.tsensorssummit.org/Resources/TSensors%20Roadmap%20v1.pdf. Accessed Feb 2015
8. Covington MJ, Carskadden R (2013) Threat implications of the internet of things. International Conference on Cyber Conflict, Tallinn, 2013
9. Kott A, Swami A, McDaniel P (2014) Security outlook: six cyber game changes for the next 15 years. Computer 47(12):104–106
10. SRI Consulting Business Intelligence (2008) Disruptive civil technologies. United States National Intelligence Council, Washington, DC
11. Griffin J, Deuty S (2014) RFID arena. NORDIC ID, 15 May 2014. [Online]. Available: http://www.rfidarena.com/2014/5/15/rfid-shopping-cart-level-checkout-is-possible-with-technology-that-is-available-today.aspx. Accessed Feb 2015
12. CISCO Systems Inc. (2014) Internet of everything. [Online]. Available: http://internetofeverything.cisco.com/sites/default/files/pdfs/Hamburg_Jurisdiction_Profile_final.pdf. Accessed Feb 2015
13. Lakovidis V Intelligent buildings. Arqiva. [Online]. Available: http://www.arqiva.com/overviews/internet-of-things/facilities-management/. Accessed 08 06 2015
14. Kaplan M (2012) Intelligent elevators answer vertical challenges. ZDNet, 17 July 2012. [Online]. Available: http://www.zdnet.com/article/intelligent-elevators-answer-vertical-challenges/. Accessed Feb 2015
15. Zanella A, Bui N, Castellani A, Vangelista L, Zorzi M (2014) Internet of things for smart cities. IEEE Internet of Things Journal 1(1):22–32
16. James R (2014) The internet of things: a study in hype, reality, disruption and growth. Raymond James & Associates, Saint Petersburg
17. Greussner V (2015) Wearable device adoption revolutionizes patient monitoring. mHealth Intelligence, 29 April 2015. [Online]. Available: http://mhealthintelligence.com/news/wearable-device-adoption-revolutionizes-patient-monitoring. Accessed May 2015
18. de Medici L (2014) Top 10 implantable wearables soon to be in your body. WT VOX, 20 Oct 2014. [Online]. Available: https://wtvox.com/2014/10/top-10-implantable-wearables-soon-body/. Accessed Mar 2015
19. Koopman P (2004) Embedded system security. Embedded Computing Magazine 37(7):95–97
20. Miorandi D, Sicari S, De Pellegrini F, Chlamtac I (2012) Internet of things: vision, applications, and research challenges. Ad Hoc Networks 10:1497–1516
21. Kleeman M (2011) Point of view: wireless point of disconnect. Global Information Industry Center, San Diego
22. Federal Trade Commission Staff (2015) Internet of things: privacy & security in a connected world. Federal Trade Commission, Washington, DC
23. Schneider S (2013) Understanding the protocols behind the internet of things. Electronic Design, 9 Oct 2013. [Online]. Available: http://electronicdesign.com/embedded/understanding-protocols-behind-internet-things. Accessed Feb 2015
24. Granville K (2015) 9 Recent cyberattacks against big businesses. The New York Times, 5 Feb 2015. [Online]. Available: http://www.nytimes.com/interactive/2015/02/05/technology/recent-cyberattacks.html?_r=0. Accessed Mar 2015
25. Ukil A, Sen J, Koilakonda S (2011) Embedded security for internet of things. Emerging Trends and Applications in Computer Science, Meghalaya, 2011

26. Stanislav M, Lanier Z (2014) The internet of fails – where IoT has gone wrong. DEFCON Conference,24Aug2014.[Online].Available:https://www.youtube.com/watch?v=WHdU4LutBGU. Accessed Jan 2015

27. Abomhara M, Koien GM (2014) Security and privacy in the internet of things: current status and open issues. Privacy and Security in Mobile Systems, Aalborg, 2014

28. Lyne J (2015) Hacking the internet of things. Sophos Labs, 5 Mar 2015. [Online]. Available: https://www.youtube.com/watch?v=wKHDyhhgSXc. Accessed Mar 2015

29. Kelly E (2015) Congress sees security risk in 'internet of things. USA Today, 9 Feb 2015. [Online]. Available: http://www.usatoday.com/story/news/politics/2015/02/09/internet-of-things-house-caucus-senate-hearing/22927075/. Accessed Feb 2015

30. Smith C, Miessler D (2014) Internet of things research study. Hewlett Packard Fortify Team

31. Carlson J, Creighton B, Meyer D, Montgomery J, Reiter A (2015) The internet of things: security research study. 15 April 2015. [Online]. Available: https://www.veracode.com/sites/defafiles/Resources/Whitepapers/internet-of-things-whitepaper.pdf?mkt_tok=3RkMMJWWfF9wsRogv63BZKXonjHpfsX87+8tWKW+lMI/0ER3fOvrPUfGjI4IScdlI+SLDwEYGJlv6SgFTbnFMbprzbgPUhA=. Accessed Apr 2015

32. Valasek C, Miller C (2014) Adventures in automotive networks and control units. [Online]. Available: http://www.ioactive.com/pdfs/IOActive_Adventures_in_Automotive_Networks_and_Control_Units.pdf. Accessed Feb 2015

33. Open Web Application Security Project (OWASP). OWASP internet of things top ten project. OWASP. [Online]. Available: https://www.owasp.org/index.php/OWASP_Internet_of_Things_Top_Ten_Project. Accessed Feb 2015

34. GoFundMe. GoFundMe. [Online]. Available: www.gofundme.com. Accessed Feb 2015

35. Kickstarter. Kickstarter. [Online]. Available: www.kickstarter.com. Accessed Feb 2015

36. Pritchard S (2014) Windows XP: why is the enterprise so reluctant to let it go? IT Pro, 5 June 2014. [Online]. Available: http://www.itpro.co.uk/operating-systems/22409/windows-xp-why-is-the-enterprise-so-reluctant-to-let-it-go. Accessed Mar 2015

37. Krebs B (2014) Target hackers broke in via HVAC company. Krebs On Security, Feb 2014. [Online]. Available: http://krebsonsecurity.com/2014/02/target-hackers-broke-in-via-hvac-company/. Accessed 08 06 2015

38. Shodan HQ. Shodan HQ. [Online]. Available: www.shodanhq.com. Accessed Mar 2015

39. Hill K (2015) Internet of dumb things. Fusion, 3 Mar 2015. [Online]. Available: http://fusion.net/story/55026/this-guys-light-bulb-ddosed-his-entire-smart-house/. Accessed Mar 2015

40. Wald M (2013) The blackout that exposed flaws in the grid. The New York Times, 11 Nov 2013. [Online]. Available: http://www.nytimes.com/2013/11/11/booming/the-blackout-that-exposed-the-flaws-in-the-grid.html. Accessed Feb 2015

41. Schneier B (2007) Staged attack causes generator to self-destruct. Schneier On Security, 2 Oct 2007. [Online]. Available: https://www.schneier.com/blog/archives/2007/10/staged_attack_c.html. Accessed Mar 2015

42. Kushner D (2013) The real story of Stuxnet. IEEE Spectrum, 26 Feb 2013. [Online]. Available: http://spectrum.ieee.org/telecom/security/the-real-story-of-stuxnet. Accessed Mar 2015

43. BBC Technology News Staff (2014) Hack attack causes 'massive damage' at steel works. BBC, 22 Dec 2014. [Online]. Available: http://www.bbc.com/news/technology-30575104. Accessed Feb 2015

44. Valasek C, Miller C (2014) Survey of remote attack surfaces. [Online]. Available: http://www.scribd.com/doc/236073361/Survey-of-Remote-Attack-Surfaces. Accessed Mar 2015

45. Behrmann E (2015) BMW cars found vulnerable to being unlocked by hackers. 30 Jan 2015. [Online]. Available: http://www.bloomberg.com/news/articles/2015-01-30/bmw-cars-found-vulnerable-to-being-unlocked-by-hackers. Accessed Feb 2015

46. AT&T. AT&T digital life. AT&T. [Online]. Available: https://my-digitallife.att.com/learn/. Accessed Mar 2015

47. Cox Communications. Cox HomeLife. Cox Communications. [Online]. Available: https://homelife.cox.com. Accessed Mar 2015

48. Gibbs S (2015) Samsun smart TVs send unencrypted voice recognition data across internet. The Guardian, 19 Feb 2015. [Online]. Available: http://www.theguardian.com/technology/2015/feb/19/samsung-smart-tvs-send-unencrypted-voice-recognition-data-across-internet. Accessed Mar 2015
49. Needle D (2015) New threats range from 'dribbling breached data' to IoT and toys. E Week, 26 Apr 2015. [Online]. Available: http://www.eweek.com/security/new-threats-range-from-dribbling-breached-data-to-iot-and-toys.html. Accessed Apr 2015
50. Weber RH (2010) Internet of things – new security and privacy challenges. Computer Law & Security Review 26(1):23–30
51. Koscher K, Juels A, Brajkovic V, Kohno T (2009) EPC RFID tag security weaknesses and defenses: passport cards, enhanced drivers licenses, and beyond. ACM conference on Computer and Communications Security, Chicago, 2009

The Invisible War: The Convergence of Cyber and Electronic Warfare

Gus Anderson and Mark Hadley

Brief History of Networked Communication

As nations embraced new and evolving communications networks, the reliance on these systems brings with it an implied vulnerability – the network itself. Understanding the current paradigm and accurately forecasting the future of communications will provide militaries with clear advantage in this facet of warfare. In this chapter we will examine the networks currently employed, their development, how they might look in the future, and finally how they relate to the overall electronic battlefield of the next several decades. Having an idea of how communication and operations will look in the future will help us craft the next generation of disruptive techniques for use during wartime.

It is well understood that federated, planned and centralized systems cannot massively scale. This has certainly been the case as disruptive innovations have moved the first point-to-point telephony network to the Internet as we see it today. In the next 20 years we can expect this trend to continue.

Telephony Networks

The first telephony communication systems introduced in the 1800s where point-to-point (Fig. 1a). In these systems a subscriber would lease several pairs of handsets and have a lines constructed between them. As this infrastructure clearly could not scale

G. Anderson (✉)
Lockheed-Martin Advanced Technology Laboratories, Cherry Hill, NJ, USA
e-mail: Gustave.Anderson@lmco.com

M. Hadley
AFRL/RDMP, Albuquerque, NM, USA
e-mail: Mark.Hadley.1@us.af.mil

© Springer International Publishing Switzerland 2015
M. Blowers (ed.), *Evolution of Cyber Technologies and Operations to 2035*,
Advances in Information Security 63, DOI 10.1007/978-3-319-23585-1_3

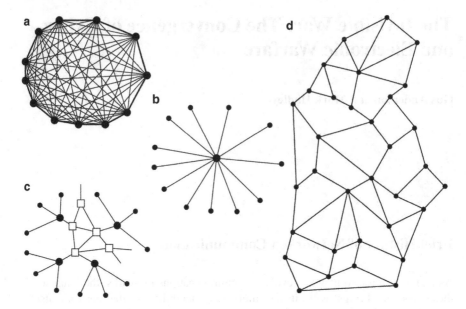

Fig. 1 Telephony networks (**a**) point-to-point networks, (**b**) star networks, (**c**) hierarchical networks, (**d**) packet-switched networks

Tivadar Puskas, in 1877, invented the telephone exchange [1] and the first commercial exchange was constructed by George W. Coy in 1878 [1]. This disruptive innovation represented the first significant shift in networked communications from a mesh of strictly point-to-point connections (Fig. 1a) to star network topologies (Fig. 1b) and later evolved to hierarchical networks (Fig. 1c). Unfortunately, these networks lacked resiliency, if any node in the end-to-end path fails the circuit breaks. Paul Baran in the 1960s, addressed this weakness with the advent of packet switched networks [2]. Rather than establishing a full end-to-end circuit where the entire data stream is transmitted over the same end-to-end path, packet switching breaks the data stream into blocks denoted as packets (Fig. 1d). The packets are then transmitted separately traveling different paths and rejoining into a whole when they were received at their destination.

Packet Switching

Packet switching enabled the development of ARPANET dissolving predefined architectures even further. One of ARAPANET's largest contributions allowed for the possibility of connecting almost any network to the ARPANET, independent of the local network's configuration (REF). This was achieved by creating a thin waist at the network layer of the protocol stack and the Internet protocol (IP) was born. In the following 30 years the ability to interconnect many heterogeneous networks through a common addressing scheme allowed for explosive growth and the beginnings of the Internet as is known today.

Mobile Communication

The Internet facilitated a fundamental change in the way we thought about communication. Traditionally, networks had focused on connecting one fixed location to another fixed location. However, with the Internet providing a user access to their data from any location (with access to the Internet) a new need arose. Users no longer only wanted access to their data at their home, office or Internet café, they wanted access at anytime, anywhere on their mobile device. This shift from fixed to mobile connectivity required another disruption and 3G cellular networks met this need.

Networked Communication in 2035

Each of the disruptive innovations provided a significant shift in the operation, organization and construction of network communications. In the next twenty years we can certainly expect this trend to continue. More recent trends have pushed communications towards a more dynamic and mobile model. In the next 20 years we can expect disruptive innovations to deliver a fully distributed heterogeneous network that is capable of dealing with dynamics of networks, communication channels (wired and wireless), content and users.

Current trends predict approximately 50 billion connected devices by 2020 and nearly 500 million to 1 trillion connected devices by 2035 [3]. At this scale centralized, planned and federated networks are going to become a thing of the past. We are even seeing the beginning of this trend today, as cellular providers cannot support spontaneous increased usage within small geographic areas. As a result cities requested request users to limit social media use at stadiums during large sporting events, as was the case with the Seattle Seahawks season opener in 2014 [4]. The reasoning behind these requests is that clogged cellular network could possibly prevent those in need reaching emergency services. Unfortunately, this was the case during the 2013 Boston marathon bombings [5]. Shortly after the first bombs were detonated, cellular service went down due to the heavy load of people trying to connect with their loved ones. An interesting side effect occurred providing us a window into what future networked communications may look like. Local residents began opening their wifi networks to allow connectivity and communications through an alternate medium [6]. In a similar fashion to the transition in the 1960s from circuit switched to packet switched networks to protect against byzantine failures users leveraged the multiple radios (wifi and cellular) on the mobile devices to maintain communications.

We can see how this trend may evolve in the next two decades increasing dynamic access while also increasing resiliency. For this to occur we will see new network architectures that relies on end user clients and devices to carry out a majority of the network operations including storage, communication and control [7]. The first feature we can expect is the locality of data in the network. Rather than data residing primarily in cloud data centers and delivered through the network upon request as it is today. We will see data residing at the edges of the network where it is most relevant. As an example, consider Netflix's Open Connect Initiative [8], where Netflix locates caching servers within Internet service providers (ISPs). These servers minimize video streams that traverse the Internet and maximize streams that are delivered to the user from a nearby caching appliance. Secondly, we can expect communication to reside primarily at the edges of the network rather than being routed over backbone networks. Natural extensions to current trends in the construction of resilient networks will allow for communication to not have to be routed through the cores of networks. Early examples include metropolitan mesh networks, vehicular networks and mobile ad-hoc networks (MANETs). Finally, we can expect to see control, configuration, measurement and management of networks to reside at edge nodes rather that primary control by network gateways or cellular cores. By no means is this a complete list of the evolutions we can expect in the next 20 years. It will be exciting to see the growth and development of dynamic networks fully capable of managing the dynamics of networks, channels, content and users.

History of Electronic Warfare (EW)

Electronic Warfare (EW) has grown into a whole realm of its own on the battlefield of today: Militaries continuously seek to overpower and nullify their opponents' ability to use this spectrum of warfare. Jamming, spoofing, and detecting – all major players in a modern military strategy. Use of the RF spectrum has grown significantly during the 100+ years since 1902, when the first intentional military jamming was employed in the Mediterranean [9]. As of 2015, the ability to perform these functions has improved exponentially, to the point where it is a significant factor in operations.

Information Operations (IO) has been part of military strategy for much longer, but with the advent of the electronic regime it also has grown in its use and importance. IO includes such functions as psychological operations, deception, operations security, and most recently – computer network operations. As the IO functions shifted to the electronic medium, it has been unintentionally melded with EW. What does the future hold for this merger? Beyond that, how will cyber operations affect either one?

Networked Communication and Military Operations

The relatively recent addition of networked systems opened the doors to this new realm of cyber – connected systems of systems, working off the backbone of high speed computers and networked connections. As the connections grow, so do the vulnerabilities to the system. This may well be the single-most important realm of warfare in the century to come: everything connected (including wireless) is vulnerable to attack.

We've seen this expansion even in civilian matters, as hackers steal identity and financial information from banks, cash machines – anything connected to the Internet. Where will the interconnections stop? What is the role of these entities in a global war?

Looking to the future of warfare, it may actually be an "invisible war." Imagine how one state actor might attack another and render kinetic attacks nearly useless? Or, would it be an on-going battle to inflict cyber "damage" to one-another before a shooting war ever starts? Predicting this interaction and how militaries should shape their forces will be a significant part of future warfare.

The changing landscape of communications will inevitably mean additional areas of capability, vulnerability, and attack. The years of transition to use of the electromagnetic spectrum for communication resulted in EW and IO that were never possible before; as the shift to advanced communications methods increases, so will the number of specialists required for operations – both day-to-day and during war.

Threat Surface

Combining these core functions of a military – EW, IO, and cyber – will be critical for maintaining both a political and military advantage in the future. We must continue to challenge the norm, seeking ways to leverage one area of operations with another. Already we see the emphasis and increased cyber capability of nations – nations that may not have had any significant influence on other countries before this increased reliance on network communications. Will they even need a physical military with kinetic weapons in order to influence rivals?

On the other hand, if you synchronize operations in each realm, what kind of effects could you produce? That's the goal of mission "packaging," in which aircraft or weapons of different types are launched/implemented together – to provide mutual support and increase the effectiveness of each player. These new realms of influence require new tactics to continue to influence the opposition, of which synergy will be essential.

As the communications backbone moves toward decentralized control, methods for attacking and defending networks will also continue to change; the question is, how? What will be the right balance between security and high-speed communications? The Internet has grown to be just that, linking nations who never before had such access to information or free communication.

Additionally, data that resides on the web will continue to influence the tactics. As the web moves to the completely meshed-network design, the data storage must follow to allow ease of access. Data will reside on devices and appliances connected to the Internet and move to where the information is most relevant. This locality of information will enable fastest response times. Through network encoding, the data requested may not even reside at the same location – it could be parsed across the web and recalled only when needed.

This increased-degree of connection brings new methods for influencing opposing forces. We've discussed the thought of increased cyber-attacks; maybe there are other methods that could be employed to disrupt these communications backbones. How will electronic jamming or other RF effects influence the total vulnerability? They may become irrelevant, due to increased use of fiber; or, alternatively, become increasingly powerful as the networks transition to wireless technology.

The move to wireless networks obviously will open the door to increased use of jamming or other EW methods. How would that construct influence military operations? Open-air architectures bring that realm of vulnerability to the network; combined effects of EW and cyber to disrupt communications and even operations will likely be a significant requirement for military forces of the future.

In conclusion, the combined effects of non-federated networks, encoded data on the network, increased use of wireless networks, and advanced in high-power jammers will continue to push the realm of cyber and electronic warfare. The growth in these two realms will undoubtedly continue, bringing changes to future warfare that will move the center of focus from kinetic operations to that of non-kinetic. The threat of over-powering cyber and EW forces will likely generate increased funding of non-kinetic research and a shift in operational mentality: Could this be the next Cold War? Or, just the Unseen War?

References

1. Patil VL (2015) "Historical Perspectives of Development of Antique Analog Telephone Systems." Journal of Telecommunications and Information Technology 3(70)
2. Baran P (2002) The beginnings of packet switching: some underlying concepts. IEEE Commun Mag 40(7):42–48
3. Coleman D (2013) Collaboration and the internet of things. Retrieved from http://www.cmswire.com/cms/information-management/collaboration-and-the-internet-of-things-022988.php
4. Soper T (2014) Clogged cell networks during big events: examining potential solutions to a serious problem. Retrieved from http://www.geekwire.com/2014/city-seattle-emergency-cell-phone/
5. Estes AC (2013) What happened to Boston's cell phone network after the marathon bombing? Retrieved from http://motherboard.vice.com/blog/officials-did-not-shut-down-bostons-cell-network-following-the-bombing
6. Ungerleider N (2013) Why your phone doesn't work during disasters – and how to fix it. Retrieved from http://www.fastcompany.com/3008458/tech-forecast/why-your-phone-doesnt-work-during-disasters-and-how-fix-it
7. Chiang M (2014) Fog networks. Retrieved from http://fognetworks.org/whitepaper/whitepaper3/
8. Netflix Open Connect. Retrieved from https://openconnect.netflix.com/
9. Kucukozyigit AC (2006) Electronic Warfare (EW) historical perspectives and its relationship to Information Operations (IO)-considerations for Turkey. Naval Postgraduate School, Dissertation, Monterey

Cyber in Space: 2035

Neil F. Bockus

A Taste of the Future…The Opening Moves of Operation Fuel Freedom

In spite of all the tension and nervous excitement, nothing could change the fact that it was 0103 local time, and Major Fred Brimmer felt drowsy staring at the screen during this Mid Shift. The opening steps of Operation Fuel Freedom were just kicking off the morning of 31 January, 2035, and concerns about theater ballistic missiles were high. Brimmer was sitting Mission Commander for the Space-Based Multi-Spectral (S-BAMS) Warning constellation. Cyberattack had been anticipated early on; it was just a question if the countermeasures would work as advertised.

The ops floor had a group of military in "space bags" – by design, it was akin to the missile blue suits, or pilot flight suits. The jet-black space operations uniform was adorned with the American Flag over the left shoulder, the livery of the squadron on the right. In the same color scheme, the name and space wings or "spings" were over the left breast pocket, with the command patch over the right. Contractors spotted the ops floor along with a few government civilians.

"We never did get that holographic globe, did we?" Captain Mueller observed, sipping coffee next to the Major.

"Too expensive, Jack. 'Sides, I think the projectors work just fine."

As S-BAMS Flight 3 crested the globe to begin coverage of the AOR, the Highly-Elliptical Orbiting satellite began to act strangely. Its artificial intelligence, running diagnostics against nominal state millions of times per second, began to recognize it was under attack. Someone was attempting to re-write the control protocols to force it to listen to another controller. 10 % of the "check copies," known good variants of the installed software, had been re-written. Using the remaining 90 %, the satellite initiated software self-repair, and utilizing its dedicated

N.F. Bockus (✉)
USAF, Operations Support Flight Commander, 22 SOPS/DOU
Schriever AFB, El Paso, CO, USA
e-mail: neil.bockus@us.af.mil

© Springer International Publishing Switzerland 2015
M. Blowers (ed.), *Evolution of Cyber Technologies and Operations to 2035*,
Advances in Information Security 63, DOI 10.1007/978-3-319-23585-1_4

defensive-cyber computers, compared the data streams, mission data, and likely attack vector. Bearing in its "mind" the known "last correct" configuration, S-BAMS Flight 3 initiated a warning to the SOC.
"Major! We've got a MCAV on 3!"
Malware/Cyber Attack & Vector...that's not good, but we were anticipating this.
"What type and where's it coming from?"
"Sir, the bird has identified the malware as a BURLAP SACK from within the AOR; the bird has localized it to three possible locations."
A BURLAP SACK; they're trying to re-write the command software to wrestle control from us.
"See if the Cyber Cell can't do anything about it, and have 'em check our own links! What's the bird's status?"
"3 is successfully combating the re-write. Currently, it's reporting 6 % of the check copies damaged, that's down from 12 % at worst reported about a minute ago."
It couldn't be as cutting-edge as we thought if the on-board defensive stuff recognized it that fast.
"Sounds like it's doing its job. Keep a close eye on it."
As the Cyber Attack Cell refined the localization data, they successfully began countering the attack, redirecting the attackers to ghosts and shutting down their connections. It would be a long night for them. S-BAMS flight 3 reported nominal about 2 minutes after the counter-attack began. Brimmer wasn't sure if a more elegant attack had happened or not during the more rudimentary BURLAP SACK, but the command center began receiving image data from the bird. About one minute later, the S-BAMS picked up a theater ballistic missile launch.
"That data flowing?"
"Navy's getting it now, probable target is the USS George H.W. Bush."
Brimmer heard Mueller begin the site report.
"Roger." Hopefully, the laser defense systems on the Bush were nominal. Major Brimmer didn't feel so drowsy anymore...

Space and Cyber Operations History

In government agency parlance, "space operations" encompass more than just satellites and their remote ground facilities (RGFs). Space operations are commonly broken down into four key mission areas: Space Control, Space Support, Space Force Enhancement, and Space Force Application, each of which are further divided into component parts. Each of the major space mission areas comprise a foundational element of space operations, with components or applications both inside the atmosphere, and in orbit, and cyberspace operations play a critical role in enabling each of the space mission areas (Fig. 1).

SPACE MISSION AREAS

SPACE CONTROL
OFFENSIVE SPACE CONTROL
DEFENSIVE SPACE CONTROL
SPACE SITUATIONAL AWARENESS

SPACE FORCE ENHANCEMENT
MISSILE WARNING
INTELLIGENCE, SURVEILLANCE & RECONNAISSANCE
ENVIRONMENTAL MONITORING
SATELLITE COMMUNICATIONS
SPACE-BASED POSITIONING, NAVIGATION & TIMING

SPACE SUPPORT
SPACELIFT OPERATIONS
SATELLITE OPERATIONS
RENDEZVOUS & PROXIMITY OPERATIONS
RECONSTITUTION OF SPACE FORCES

SPACE FORCE APPLICATION
INTERCONTINENTAL BALLISTIC MISSILES
MISSILE DEFENSE

Fig. 1 The space mission areas

There is a saying in the United States Air Force's Undergraduate Space Training, or "UST": "You can't have Space without Cyber." It may seem at first glance that the statement is untrue: to *put* an artificial satellite into space, all that is needed is a solid or liquid fueled rocket engine that can accelerate the payload to beyond escape velocity, and to altitude of about 100 miles above the Earth's surface. At this altitude and with a tangential speed of around 17,500 mph, the object will continuously free-fall around the Earth; the artificial satellite has achieved orbit.

If, however, a nation desires their artificial satellite to do more than simply orbit the Earth, to be able to track and communicate with the "bird," to be able to tell if it is alive, dead, in danger, etc., cyber operations enabled by computers and communication equipment becomes indispensable both on the satellite, and back on Earth.

Realistically, without the spacelift operations that fall under Space Support, space operations as a whole become a questionable concept. Spacelift is the gateway to all space operations, and without it, nothing can be put into space or passed through space. Without lift, there are no ballistic missiles, rendering missile warning moot. It is not possible to perform space control when there is nothing in space *to* control, and all of the services provided by Space Force Enhancement missions, such as navigation and communications, simply are not there. There needs to be a way to *get* to space, and this is what spacelift accomplishes.

Even in this most basic element of space operations, cyber effects rear their head. The rocket mentioned above must have the ability to guide itself, to launch in the proper direction, and when commanded, to rotate, jettison its various parts, and to deploy its payload at a given time and altitude to be successful. These various maneuvers and commands require two-way communication, and the rocket needs to "know" how it is flying, and if everything is nominal. Interpretation of various inputs, such as air density, heading from inertial navigation, and altitude requires both computers and communication links. On the launch pad, receipt of the rocket's collected state of health information requires communication to and from mission control, as well as the ability for operators to command the rocket and the satellite it is delivering. Each of these indispensable endeavors is entirely reliant on cyberspace, and a brief history of space operations will show how cyberspace operations have always been embedded in the exploitation of space.

Much of the space operations realm developed out of advances in ballistic missile technology. Sputnik-1, the Soviet Union's (and humanity's) first artificial satellite, was little more than just a silver ball that generated a ping that could be heard over a ham radio. It was a proof of concept: operationally the satellite payload could be replaced with a re-entry vehicle (RV) containing a nuclear weapon, and hit anywhere in the world – the Soviets had developed the technology for the first true Intercontinental Ballistic Missile (ICBM).

Some of the earliest U.S. space operations developments were for the Missile Warning (MW) and Space Track, later named "Space Situational Awareness" (SSA) missions that grew out of the frantic response to the Soviet technological leap. To be able to track either orbital or re-entering objects, and provide warning of an impending missile attack, the United States Air Force began development of the AN/FPS-49/50 Ballistic Missile Early Warning System, or BMEWS (pron. "bee-mewz"). The system was comprised of three to four massive mechanical surveillance radars, and a moveable mechanical dish tracking radar.

BMEWS was built at three different sites; Site I, located at Thule Air Base, Greenland, reached Initial Operational Capability (IOC) in 1960, Site II in 1961 at Clear Air Force Station, Alaska, and Site III in 1963 at Royal Air Force Station Fylingdales-Moore, England. In the event that these radars acquired a re-entering object, their crews would initiate a "Site Report" to warn of impending attack, along with the number of impacting objects being tracked, and time and location of first impact. The BMEWS data was sent back to the United States over data lines, providing about a 15 min warning from missile detection to impact.[1] This mission is still ongoing and has remained almost unchanged for the last 55 years.

Calculation of the track data to determine if the radar's target is a re-entering object, an orbital object, or if it is an aircraft or meteor requires major computing capability. If the object is a re-entering object, the computer needs to start estimating the location of launch based on the target's track data, and predict the most probable impact point based on the same. The data produced is known as Launch and Predicted Impact, or L&PI. If there are multiple impacting objects, the tracking radar needs to be capable of establishing a track on its current target, predicting the target's impact point, and then moving to a different detected target to establish the next L&PI. The computers need to calculate this data quickly to provide adequate warning in case of an attack, and in the case of the original BMEWS, to establish as many L&PIs as possible, given that the system's mechanical tracking dish could only establish one target track at a time.

Communications have always been central to the Space Track and Missile Warning missions; the BMEWS track data was useless unless transmitted to decision makers in NORAD. For missile events, the BMEWS crew would provide an analysis of the data to NORAD based on if the data was determined to be good, bad, or unknown by declaring it "Valid," "Anomalous," or "Under Investigation." The necessity for prompt and accurate communications in order to guard against transmission of false tracks, and potentially devastating consequences, highlights the absolute reliance this aspect

---

[1] Edited Extract from: Department of Defense Annual Report [1].

of space operations places on accurate computation and communication, and in turn its vulnerability to cyber effects. An example of an early cyber "bug" with BMEWS took place at Site I on 5 October 1960, when the Thule BMEWS computers interpreted radar returns from the moon to be a missile.[2] The radar never generated an impact point, and the situation was quickly defused by NORAD and Strategic Air Command.

By the late 1950s another technological effort was being born in parallel to the development of ground based surveillance systems such as BMEWS. Following World War II, the RAND Corporation had suggested building an artificial satellite for intelligence purposes, but no funding for such a project was available.[3] By the mid-1950s, however, with the continuing development of ballistic missiles and nuclear forces behind the Eastern Bloc's "Iron Curtain," satellite based surveillance became of prime strategic interest to the United States.

It was quickly realized that to support space based reconnaissance, the United States would require not only a satellite constellation, but a set of remote ground facilities (RGFs) to be able to command and control the satellites from launch to de-orbit. It was also found during this time, that aerial over-flights of the Soviet Union were becoming more and more critical for strategic intelligence, but for any number of reasons, be they from the legal standpoint of over-flight from space, the "space for peace" attitude of the administration at the time, or budget expenditure limits imposed,[4] problems persisted in finally getting a reconnaissance satellite into space.

Just as it had been critical to the development of BMEWS, the Soviet launch of Sputnik-1 on 4 October 1957 finally gave America's spy satellite programs the jump-start they needed.[5] The push for satellite reconnaissance was further advanced by the shoot-down of Francis Gary Powers' U-2 spy plane deep within Soviet airspace in 1960. In response to the increasing difficulty of airborne reconnaissance, two families of Low Earth Orbit (LEO) satellites were developed and launched; GRAB and Corona were Signals Intelligence (SIGINT) and photoreconnaissance satellite families designed to monitor countries of interest, such as the Soviet Union, from beyond the reaches of air defenses. Corona first flew in 1959, GRAB a year later. The programs were covered as scientific satellites; GRAB standing for Galactic Radiation And Background, while Corona was known to the public by the cover name "Discoverer." Corona carried a camera and a set of film canisters, after photographing an area of the target country the canister would be jettisoned at a predetermined point on the globe. The canister would re-enter the atmosphere and either be fished from the water, or caught mid-air by a modified cargo plane.

A set of RGFs were constructed and brought to operational capability between 1958 and 1961 at a variety of sites to enable Tracking, Telemetry and Commanding (TT&C) of the orbiting satellites. This Satellite Command and Control (SAT C2) mission is comprised of finding and following the satellite (tracking), receiving

---

[2] Wainstein et al. [2]

[3] Robert Perry [3], 2

[4] Perry [3], 7, 19.

[5] Perry [3], 24–25.

health, status, and mission data from the satellite (telemetry), and telling the satellite what to do (commanding). Some of the original RGFs in Alaska, California, New Hampshire, and Hawaii, built to support GRAB, Corona and other early ISR missions are active to this day as part of the Air Force Satellite Control Network (AFSCN), and each of these locations is reliant on cyber operations. Each of the RGFs may *enable* TT&C, but these sites do not tell the satellite what to do, when to activate, or where to drop its film canisters. Actual command and control of the satellite is done elsewhere, in what is known as a "Satellite Operations Center," or SOC (pron. "sock").

During the 1950s and 1960s, most intelligence satellites were placed in Low Earth Orbit – an approximate period of 90 min (that is: the satellite will accomplish one orbit of the Earth in 90 min.) Therefore, a single RGF couldn't be constructed – multiple RGFs were needed to talk to the satellite at different points in its orbit, but only a single SOC was truly necessary to house the command and control equipment for a given satellite. In order for the SOC to talk to its satellite, a network of computers and communications equipment was necessary. This network includes data lines, satellite relays ("sat-shots"), and ground based hubs, as well as additional computer equipment needed for the actual command and control of the spacecraft (Fig. 2). Early on, without other communications satellites for use in relays, the comm process was entirely intra-atmosphere over data lines and radio relays.

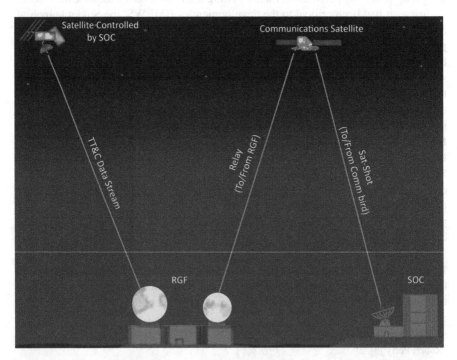

Fig. 2 Example of a "Sat-Shot" (not to scale). The communications segment doesn't necessarily start with a shot to a communications satellite, but this illustration shows an example when a sat shot is involved (Illustration: Author)

Fig. 3 AN/FPS-132(V)3 Upgraded Early Warning Radar (UEWR) at Thule AB, Greenland (Photograph: Author)

Other aspects of space operations evolved out of Launch, SAT C2, SSA and MW. Especially during the 1970s and 1980s, Missile Defense (MD) became a major focus with project SAFEGUARD and "Star Wars." While MW provides advanced warnings of a ballistic missile attack, MD is the mission to intercept those incoming missiles. BMEWS radars were replaced by phased array warning systems in the 1980s through early 2000s (Fig. 3). In turn, these radars were upgraded with more modernized computer systems, able to perform the MW and MD missions, as well as SSA missions such as Orbital Observations, Early Orbit Determination and Space Object Identification (SOI, pron. "soy"). Other radars, such as the Perimeter Acquisition Radar Characterization System (PARCS, pron. "parks") at Cavalier, North Dakota, also perform these various space missions. PARCS, originally just "PAR" was part of the original SAFEGUARD MD system from the 1970s.

But the missile trackers deal exclusively with LEO satellites, with a maximum range of around 3,000 Nautical Miles (NM) for the UEWR. A Geostationary (GEO) satellite, by comparison, is more than 23,500 miles away! To support the higher orbits that satellites utilize, deep space capable sensors and communication equipment are required as well, such as the Eglin Deep Space Radar, Millstone and ALTAIR radars, and Ground-based Electro-Optical Deep Space Surveillance (GEODSS, pron. "gee-oddz") telescopes are required as well. Additionally, resources such as the Space-Based Space Surveillance satellite provide on-orbit sensors used for SSA. Enabling TT&C with the various satellites in every orbit primarily falls to the AFSCN. As mentioned earlier, some of its sites continue to serve after more than 55 years, and each site has the ability to enable TT&C to satellites in any orbit around the Earth.

Satellites themselves evolved beyond photoreconnaissance and SIGINT alone, and now participate in other aspects of ISR, as well as just about every one of the space mission areas. Communications satellites provide aspects of SAT C2 by enabling comm links between the SOCs and RGFs. Others provide satellite communications for troops on the ground, or hikers away from cell phone towers, such as the civilian-owned Iridium constellation, or even space to ground communications as provided by NASA's Tracking and Data Relay Satellites (TDRS, pron. "Tee-dris"). One satellite family that should be immediately recognizable to the reader is the Global Positioning System (GPS) satellite family. GPS is used for more than just navigation; its timing is so accurate that it has become a standard for both military and civilian applications. It has such diverse uses as security applications, banking, timing and myriad others now taken for granted. Space-based missile warning began in the 1960s with the Missile Defense Alarm System (MiDAS) satellites, and continues to this day with the Defense Support Program (DSP) and Space-Based Infrared System (SBIRS, pron. "Siberz") satellites. Something that has not changed, and indeed has become even more critical over time, is the role of cyber in all of these space applications.

How does the UEWR discriminate between objects in track? How does a GPS receiver know where it is located? How is a TDRS asset told where to point its solar arrays? How does DSP return infrared images back to its control segment? Through computers and communication equipment – through cyberspace! And just as computers enable a radar to crunch critical data to warn of a missile attack, just as they make any satellite on orbit useful, they are also what make these assets vulnerable to cyber attack.

Current Cyber Vulnerabilities of Space Assets

By 2035, it is unquestionable that cyber warfare will have evolved significantly. That being said, history has shown that projections of future combat capabilities many times must be reigned in. As of 2015, the F-22 has not supplanted the over 40-year old F-15 as the USAF's front line Air Superiority Fighter, because too few were made – production was halted at 187 operational airplanes. US Army infantry are not equipped with powered armor, heads-up-displays (HUDs), or smart guns imagined in the 1980s and 1990s; they are still equipped with Kevlar® and ceramic plate armor akin to that first employed in the 1990s, and an M-16 family rifle designed out of the AR-15 of the 1950s. The Peace Keeper ICBM, once thought to replace the older Minuteman III, was retired 10 years ago while its predecessor runs strong. There are still mission critical applications and systems which run off of Microsoft Disk Operating System (MS-DOS), there is no holographic globe at the

Joint Space Operations Center (JSpOC, pron. "Jay-Spock") and there is *absolutely* no little red button to make a satellite perform a collision avoidance maneuver (COLA).

Despite this caution, the realm of cyber operations continues to push forward at an exceptionally fast rate, and cyber-attack is a particularly devastating tool when used maliciously today. Cyber-attack might be the ultimate weapon in modern combat, simply because nations have come to rely so heavily on cyberspace, and because computers and networks have been installed into everything feasible: from satellites, to fighter planes, to cars, to washing machines and refrigerators. No matter where they are installed, these computers are just as vulnerable to attack as your home PC, tablet, or smart phone.

As it was written in the introduction, cyber has been an aspect of space since operations began. For any purposeful operations in space, cyber processes are so integrated that distinction between the two arenas of action becomes blurred. The Data Processors which decide where to steer a phased array beam, the Command and Status processors which control RGF antennas to enable TT&C, and the systems which decide what needs to be done to keep a satellite flying are all deeply computerized. The question is not "which space systems have computers in critical, exploitable areas of operation?" but rather: "which space systems *do not* have computers in critical, exploitable areas of operation?" A search for such systems will be in vain. Computers and cyberspace are now and have been involved in every aspect of terrestrial and space-based space operations since before "cyberspace" was understood as an independent arena.

To illustrate cyber vulnerabilities to space assets, let's take a hypothetical satellite. Any useful satellite has two key components: the "payload" and the "bus." The payload is the system on the satellite which performs the satellite's operational missions; it is the purpose for which the satellite was launched. Satellite payloads include infrared imaging sensors to detect missile launches, positioning and timing antennas for navigation, communication arrays, and electro-optical cameras for imagery, be it military, civil, or scientific. The payload, however, cannot operate on its own. Simply throwing a camera into space does not allow the controller to operate that camera, to designate its targets, or to retrieve images from it. Additionally, the payload needs supporting structures and equipment to survive in the harsh space environment, maintain its electrical power level, and to perform its mission.

The bus is the portion of the satellite designed to support the payload. The bus provides power for the payload, cooling systems to vent heat, and heaters to warm the satellite as it passes through sunlight and shadow, attitude and orbit control subsystem (AOCS), engines and propellant to drive the spacecraft. The bus also includes the body and frame structures to hold the payload, and the communication and data handling subsystem (CDHS) which allows the satellite to communicate with and receive commands from its operators on the ground.

The CDHS is a series of computers, sensors, radios, and antennas which communicate with the various systems of the satellite and commanding SOC, enabling the bird to receive commands to perform its mission, and deliver back payload and system status data. The CDHS receives commands to carry out its mission, interprets

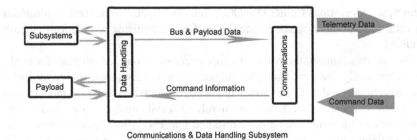

Fig. 4 Communications and Data Handling Subsystem (CDHS) data flow

and passes along those commands to the various subsystems to tell the satellite where it ought to be pointing, when to take a picture, if it needs to adjust its orbit or position, etc. The subsystems of the bus and payload configure themselves to accomplish the commands provided, and respond with data back to the SOC through the CDHS. Figure 4 provides an illustration of the dataflow.

To visualize how the entire set of subsystems function as a unified whole, think of the satellite as a car. The SOC is the driver. If the driver decides to turn, he or she will rotate the steering wheel left or right. In older cars, the connection was mechanical; rotating the steering wheel directly twisted gears and axles to move the car's wheels to accomplish a directional change. In a modern car, the mechanical linkages still exist, but are heavily reliant on computer interpretation to make minute corrections for a smoother, safer ride. If something is wrong, the car will illuminate a light or provide a warning; perhaps the antilock breaks are out, or the stability augmentation system (SAS) faulted. The driver will then have to consider hitting the brakes earlier, or taking a turn a bit slower.

If a SOC needs its satellite to turn to take a picture, its operators will send a command to the satellite to rotate. The satellite will receive the command through the CDHS, interpret the data and begin "talking" to the AOCS. The AOCS will communicate with its various systems to make the satellite point in the direction that the SOC operator has instructed by spinning reaction wheels or control moment gyroscopes. It may need to adjust the direction its solar panels are facing as a result of the rotation. If the operator requires the satellite to make an orbit adjustment ("Delta-V"), the satellite will be instructed to fire thrusters for the required span of time. In older satellites, some of these systems may be broken or partially capable of doing their job, and the operator needs to take these things into account, just like a driver losing antilock brakes or SAS.

Back to the car, what would happen if the car's brakes began actuating themselves on a highway without driver input? Or, if the throttle started opening up on the command of someone not inside the car as the driver approached their garage? The possibility of an accident, fatal or not, increases significantly. Just such a scenario was reported upon early in 2015, after DARPA revealed a cyber-attack capability that allowed a hacker to control those systems by hacking the car's OnStar® data link as an attack vector. Some consider this report to be fear-mongering of an improbable threat on the part of the media[6] while others consider it to be a serious, existing threat[7] that needs to be dealt with. Regardless of threat level, the capability has now been demonstrated. But, how strongly does this vulnerability correlate to our satellite?

The distance from ground to space does little to protect a satellite, and there are a number of possible cyber-attack vectors that could be utilized against assets in space. Being able to transmit directly to the target satellite within the spacecraft's "footprint" (that is, the area on the Earth for which the satellite is visible) is one possible vector against a satellite, but satellites listen for encrypted data, and will reject unauthorized signals, which would make such an attack difficult. The attacker would need to have an idea of how to command the satellite, and compatible commands to send to the bird as well. Perhaps most problematically, and most visibly, the means needed to transmit to the satellite include a large dish, knowledge of the satellite's two-line element set to know where to point that dish for data transmission, and a very powerful source of energy to get the signal out to the satellite, especially if the bird is in geosynchronous orbit.

So, while *technically* possible, a direct attack against the satellite itself is improbable. The operation would be noisy, easy to detect, and warrant a response. On the other hand, what if one were to launch a cyber-attack against the communications portion? Jumping into the command signal by attacking the RGF or the SOC, and implanting malware through the authorized signal could have devastating effect against a satellite. Sending false commands or readings to the CDHS, or adjusting how the satellite ought to respond if it gets into a certain attitude, altitude, etc. could cause loss of the space vehicle. Recall the automobile's accelerator and brakes – a false command resulting from an attack could suddenly spin up a control moment gyro. Or a thruster could be fired to tumble the bird. Alternatively, if the attacker were able to get in through the links and cause the primary payload to shut off, or maybe draw too much power and fail catastrophically, the satellite would become a multi-million dollar piece of space junk. There isn't much of a point to having a satellite on orbit if its payload is non-functional!

Ground-based radars, similarly, require computers to operate. These computers decide how to point the radar's RF energy beams, how powerful the beams need to be, and to process the radar returns by analyzing, formatting, and displaying the data of the targets in track. As described above, calculating a tracked object's orbit or trajectory to decide if it is an impacting object, and where it is most likely to land, has been part of the cyber aspect of missile warning since the very beginning. But, as phased array radars have replaced mechanical trackers, computers have become increasingly integrated into the decision of where and how a beam of RF energy needs to be steered to track an object. They are required to decide how much power the beam of energy needs to have so that the radar can see the object it needs to; an object with a smaller radar cross section (RCS) requires more power to track. The radar's data processors (DPs) handle all of these basic radar functions including management of

---

[6] Doug Newcomb [4]

[7] Staff of Senator Edward Markey [5]

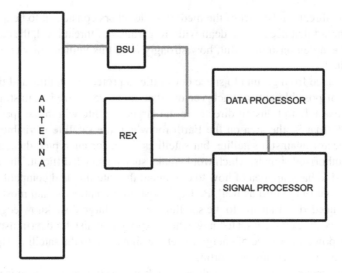

Fig. 5 Notional phased array operational flowchart. The Data Processor passes information to the Receiver/Exciter and Beam Steering Unit to generate and point the wave. The antenna shoots the wave into space and listens for a return. The return is passed back through the Receiver/Exciter, to the Signal Processor, and from there, the interpreted return is given to the Data Processor

the integrated systems of the radar to "tell" the system where to look, with how much power, and how it ought to steer its energy beams to perform its mission.

Upon receipt of radar returns, the Signal Processor (SP) processes and interprets the returning RF energy and passes the data back to the DP, which pays attention to the target's RCS, where the target is, where it is going, and where it likely was in the past (Fig. 5). In terms of the SSA mission, the radar produces Time, Elevation, Azimuth, Range, and Range Rate (TEARR, pron. "tear") data to keep a satellite's element set up to date. For an impacting object, the radar produces an L&PI (discussed earlier) for each object it tracks. This data is then communicated over data lines to a command center, such as JSpOC or the Missile Warning Center (MWC).

Like the satellite, which relies on communications to and from a complex of interconnected ground stations, cyberspace ties together a network of radars and electro-optical sensors for national defense. As with a satellite, getting inside of this network could allow an adversary to deliver devastating effects on the system's ability to operate, or alternatively, the command center's ability to receive data from each of its nodes. Depending on the type of cyber attack, individual systems within a radar could feasibly be shut down, provided false data, or be told to drop data, making it difficult or impossible to maintain track on threat objects, or cause the system to give false indications and warnings of an attack that isn't actually happening.

While space assets are a tempting target, most nations probably would not want to attack PNT assets like GPS or Russia's Global Navigation Satellite System (GLONASS, pron. "glow-nass"), due to both their civil navigation applications as well as for the destructive effect such an attack would have on timing standard generation, enablement of seamless dataflow, business transactions and more within the attacking nation itself. The most likely reasons for a nation to launch a cyber-attack against a strategic warning radar or overhead persistent infrared satellite is to deny missile warning ahead of an attack, or to corrupt a country's ability to maintain SSA. Either of these are most likely during direct conflict, and in the case of the former, a particularly long and brutal conflict from which no other option appears feasible to the losing side than mutually assured destruction.

Non-state actors, on the other hand, don't operate on the same motives as state governments. In the case of non-state actors, motivations of the individual or the group will drive the attack. For a terrorist organization, the more likely reason for cyber-attack is to harm people, economies, and perceived fighting abilities of a state, or for theft of money and resources to fund the organization's activities. As such, almost any space mission could be a target; it is just a question as to whether or not the group has the means to execute a successful cyber attack against the asset or its supporting network.

Future threats, however, could include malicious acts as recreational activity, or to show one's cyber prowess for prestige. A recent example of a cyber-attack "for kicks" took place around Christmas 2014, when a group of cyber ne'er-do-wells launched distributed denial of service (DDoS) attacks against Microsoft's Xbox Live® Network and Sony's PlayStation Network®, preventing users from connecting to either service. This was an attack on recreational networks, not military, civil, or scientific space networks to be certain, but there was no purpose for the attack other than to deny individuals who purchased the products relying on those networks their ability to use them as intended, and to claim credit for the attack. There was no monetary drive, nor political gain to be had; the attacks were done just because the group could do so.

In 20 years, if major advances in cyberspace render modern protective measures such as current-generation encryption useless, it wouldn't be too far-fetched for an independent operator or group to focus their efforts on a legacy satellite system or network with ruinous effect. In doing so, the group may well be making their attack effort to control or crash a satellite purely an endeavor to prove their own capability, or to receive kudos from like-minded members of the cyber community.

Space as an Attack Vector for Cyber

While it is the most obvious overlap of the space and cyberspace spheres, direct assault on space assets is only one concern for those worried about cyber defense. Another is the use of space assets to enable, or provide a vector for cyber-attack. Satellite communications and relays allow for international and intercontinental connectivity by enabling passage of data through space. In future conflicts, where cyber-attack will be a key component to seizing the initiative, space assets could be a major component for relaying a cyber-attack into a given area of conflict, or from a conflict area to anywhere else in the world. The question of whether or not international treaties and laws require change to allow for the utilization of space for cyber attack is a concern that needs to be wrestled with on the level of international treaties. These agreements are being challenged by the very nature of cyber weaponry if space is used as an attack vector for cyberspace (something of an inevitability for non-state actors), probing and very technical questions need to be asked about the code that the space segment is enabling. What is the code's potential? What was it designed to do? Is it being carried as part of the payload of the satellite, or is it travelling through the satellite from a control facility to a particular destination? Has cyberspace become a weaponized domain of operations? All of these directly impact existing treaties and their restrictions on the militarization of space.

For example, in accordance with the Outer Space Treaty of 1967, Article IV, it is illegal to have nuclear weapons or other weapons of mass destruction (WMD) on orbit around the earth, or installed on other celestial bodies in space.[8] Note that the OST does not state that *weapons* in space are banned, *only* nuclear weapons and WMD. If a satellite is being used to participate in a cyber-attack, it could be argued that the satellite is part of a weapon system, or weapon delivery system, which would be legal so long as the effect of the malware were to be considered less than a WMD.

An example of a legal WMD that utilizes space to reach its target is the Intercontinental Ballistic Missile (ICBM). ICBMs and shorter-range ballistic missiles are not affected by Article IV since they never achieve orbit; they do not attack *from* space, they attack *through* space. If a notional cyber-attack were being routed through a space asset to attack a nuclear power plant, with the intent of making the reactor go critical and spread nuclear contamination all around a given area, it could be argued that the code being used in that attack, when combined with the computers and controls it is targeting, is a WMD.

Although it would be unlikely for an agency to install such a specific bit of code onto a satellite and then launch the satellite into orbit with a nuclear power plant-attacking malware payload ready and waiting for initialization, this is a notional example of what could be considered a WMD on orbit without any physical nuclear, biological or chemical component. The malware and means to transmit it accomplish nothing without the intended target, but when employed against that target, the amount of suffering and devastation that could be caused is on the same level or possibly worse than a dirty bomb.

If the malware, however, is sent from a ground facility and utilizes a satellite relay to get the code to its intended target, and then the satellite relays the malware to reach its target *through* space, it could then be argued that the satellite is not operating in violation of the OST. The satellite used in the attack relay may have many different uses, and was never expressly designed to deliver that malware to its target. The satellite is merely an accidental component of the vector chosen to make the attack, one not necessarily explicitly chosen by the attackers. Additionally, the malware is never permanently stored on the satellite for the express purpose of attack.

---

[8] Outer Space Treaty [6]

This aspect of using space to enable cyber-attack also highlights the potential use of civilian satellites as relays and assets for strategic military or political purposes. If a civilian satellite is used as a relay to launch malware or other cyber-attacks against military targets, that civilian satellite may be considered a legitimate target for counter-attack if it could be positively identified as a participant or component of the attack vector. Currently, however, it is difficult to attribute a cyber-attack to a specific person or nation, and it may be equally difficult to attribute a specific satellite or constellation as a participant in cyberspace operations.

If future technology allows quick and certain knowledge as to the origin and vector of an attack, it could open space assets to retaliatory assaults. If a satellite was found to be a link enabling a cyber-attack, there may be justification for countering that satellite with either kinetic or non-kinetic counter-attack (ASAT, jammer, counter-cyber, etc.).

Under the current treaties and customary international law, the legality of the use of space assets for cyber-attack is greatly up to interpretation. Just as the example was provided above of what *might* be interpreted as a WMD on orbit through a very specific malware payload, a counter argument could just as easily be made that the code and transmission capabilities mean nothing without their precise target. Whereas a nuclear warhead on orbit could be deployed anywhere and always have the same yield and effect, the malware *only* works if it can effectively penetrate the security of a nuclear power plant, which relies on not just transmission, but successful evasion of defensive cyber measures. As such, even with its malicious intent, the code on the satellite is not a WMD on its own.

Cyberspace operations have become a critical component in not only our day to day lives, but in military operations as well. Given this, the treaties, agreements and laws that govern military operations in space should be reviewed for potential impacts both on and from cyber applications in space. Even in the single example before, having malicious code either aboard a spacecraft or relayed through one is quite a bit different than having a nuclear warhead aboard, and yet by enabling a cyber-attack vector, could have very similar results.

Will Space Become a Huge Vulnerability?

Space today is a highly contested and congested environment. Over 16,000 objects are tracked every day by the United States Strategic Command's Space Surveillance Network, and there are exponentially more objects too small to detect. A paperclip (~1 g) travelling at 17,500 mph (7,823.2 m/s) has tremendous energy, and can strike a satellite with 20 times the energy of a rifle bullet. The collisions of satellites, such as the Cosmos-Iridium crash of 2009, and ASAT tests high above the atmosphere, such as China's 2007 direct-ascent test, more and more objects clog the various orbits around the Earth.

By the year 2035, space will unquestionably become even more contested and congested. As new nations make efforts to place objects on orbit, rocket bodies, boosters and payloads will continue to increase in number, making collisions more likely. Dead satellites carelessly left on orbit will become more and more dangerous as the number of space objects increases.

The Cosmos-Iridium incident created thousands of new, uncontrolled objects in space due to the extreme velocity at which the satellites collided. China's ASAT test was done at "high altitude" for Low-Earth Orbit, and created a cloud of debris affecting many LEO satellites. In 2015, a Defense Meteorological Satellite Program (DMSP) satellite exploded on orbit, creating a debris field in low-earth orbit. As of March 2015, 43 new objects were identified in orbit due to the satellite breaking up.[9] By the 2030s, collisions and anomalies like these could be much more devastating to space capabilities in general.

Cyberspace operations become a chief concern as the number of orbiting objects increases at an accelerating rate. If an unauthorized user were to make an attack on space systems, they could potentially affect not just the targeted system, but the whole array of satellites trying to maneuver through the jammed space environment of 2035. This raises the troubling concern that space assets themselves are becoming speeding cyber vulnerabilities, mechanisms for physically disrupting other orbital objects. Thus, for example, a satellite with few cyber defenses could be taken over and utilized kinetically against a more cyber-hardened satellite, with second- and third-order effects across its orbiting altitude, to include debris fields and damage or destruction of other non-target space assets.

The Future – Disruptive Innovation

The previous exposition discussed space operations today and in the near future. Twenty years from now, however, the playing field will have changed dramatically. Bearing in mind the caveats mentioned above, some of the major disruptive innovations have the capability to directly affect space operations in 20 years include advances in quantum computing, adaptive space technology, active cyber defense, and characterization and recognition of threats through advanced artificial intelligence.

Offensively, one of the biggest vulnerabilities which quantum computing could be applied to exploit is encryption. With the potential for solving much more complex equations applied to the field of cryptography, significant advances in quantum computers over the next 20 years could cause a revolutionary ability to defeat current-generation encryption rapidly. Recall the discussion about encrypted and authorized signals that satellites listen for. If, using a quantum computer, an encrypted signal were broken down and cracked, an adversary with knowledge of another nation's space systems could feasibly use their own TT&C assets to control, exploit or destroy that nation's satellite systems.

Given current trends, it's a good bet that radars, secure satellite communications, PNT, and just about every other space or space-enabled system will become

---

[9] Mike Wall [7]

increasingly vulnerable. Much more advanced countermeasures would need to be employed; potentially using technologies like quantum computers in the Defensive Cyber role to create equations of much greater complexity, though this would only delay the inevitable. Alternatively, a quantum computer's extraordinary processing power could be used to endow cyber-agile capabilities into space systems, such as significantly faster phased and cycling cyber-coordinates over communication links and ports, causing an outside attack to become much more difficult.

Another major innovation that will help defend space assets from certain cyber-attacks is "adaptive space technology;" that is, the ability for a space asset to be able to withstand a cyber-attack and not only survive, but recover to full or near-full mission capability. Like quantum computers, self-adaptive technologies are in their infancy, but research has begun in the realm of smart phones to be able to re-write or patch damaged code in response to abnormal activity.[10]

Recall that every space system is largely a series of computers which communicate to a variety of hardware components to perform a given mission, and return information to operators (be it processed radar returns, electro-optical images, signal characteristics or otherwise). If an adversary were monitoring their cyber-attack against a space asset and believed themselves to be successful, moving onto the next target, only to have their former target recognize the damage and begin self-repair, the adversary attack would be, in effect, be nullified.

In 2035, it is quite possible that this innovation will have evolved several steps further. The current concept is early in the experimentation phase and 20 years is a long time in the realm of cyberspace. If a space asset were endowed with this technology, and also provided attack characterization, recording, and trace capability, the asset which had been attacked could provide its operators with near real-time battle damage assessment, attack characteristics, malware signatures and possible attack vectors, while still surviving the adversary's attack and leaving them none the wiser.

At its extreme, this technology would allow an asset which had been rendered completely inoperable by an attack, to repair itself and come back to life. This would hinder follow up attacks and require re-assessment as to why the cyber-attack was unsuccessful. In the meantime, the attacker will have exposed their Tactics, Techniques and Procedures (TTP) inadvertently, while failing to defeat their target. Thus the "Blue side" operators would get insight into their enemy's decision loop, and give probable information on how to defend future attack vectors, targets, and method of attack, while providing possible opportunity for offensive retaliation. A technology like this would have to work very quickly to recognize that its asset is under attack, as the physical results of this attack (such as firing thrusters, moving gyroscopes, angling the solar panels, etc.) could have extremely negative impacts to the space vehicle in short order.

Knowing where an attack originated would enable another disruptive innovation: overt active defenses. With how cyber operations have been trending, it seems inevitable to the author that offensive cyberspace operations will eventually become a

---

[10] Alexander Kott [8]

commonplace component of military operations in the future. Currently, offensive cyberspace operations are very cloak and dagger. Cyber-attacks have been going on for a very long time, but state-backed cyber-attacks are still taboo to mention.

Akin to the "spy games" between the East and West during the Cold War, cyber-attacks are difficult to attribute, devastating when successful, and deniable if they are discovered. Thus nation states, and other perpetrators of cyber espionage and attack easily, and commonly plead innocence. The change which will likely happen by 2035, and which will be clearly disruptive in nature and potential, is the draw of military and state cyber operations out of the "black" world where they currently reside. This will enable active defenses – attacks to counter attacks in order to deny, disable, or destroy an opponent's cyber-warfare capabilities. Characterization and recognition of adversary cyberspace capabilities and likely courses of action may be one of the best means to decide whether or not to make a cyber-attack against a given nation, or source of cyber-attack located within that nation.

Considerations: Unchecked Innovation and Countermeasure Development

That which was true of atomic weapons is especially true of cyber weapons: new technologies and weaponry can very quickly be turned on their innovators. Something to consider for developments now and 20 years from now is the question: "How could this be used against me?" It is a question that isn't always asked, perhaps because the innovator doesn't care, perhaps because they are of the mindset "who would ever use this technology for evil?" or perhaps they are concerned with the needs of the present, rather than what could happen in the future.

It is not only the obvious attack vectors that will become increasingly vulnerable over the next 20 years; unforeseen ones will crop up as well. For example: the concept of the Wi-Fi house seems very convenient. A refrigerator which knows its own contents and what needs to be re-stocked, a washing machine, heaters and air conditioners which can be turned on by telephone, door locks which can be actuated from work; who wouldn't want such conveniences? The problem is that once each of these pieces of technology are networked, they become a vulnerability. Each piece is interconnected to the other, and if an attacker can get into the washing machine, they can pivot to other appliances, computers, tablets and smart phones on the network. These in turn are talking to the increasingly interconnected components of a modern car, which consistently talks to satellites via datalinks. Thus, in the future, an attack on a space asset could begin with an attack on a toaster! As these interconnections grow, the attack surface grows. This is the true danger of the 2035 world, an attack may originate anywhere, for any reason, and have dreadful results.

As we develop technologies that have the capability to disruptively change either the battlefield, or our personal lives, we need to ask ourselves the questions: "How could this be used for nefarious means?" "What does this technology enable, and how can it be exploited?" Perhaps most importantly: "If it were ever exploited against us, *how do we counter it?*" If we ask these questions on the front end, even so much as consider them and have a basic "playbook" on how to defeat our technology if it were ever turned against us, we will be much better off when the technology inevitably falls into the hands of our adversaries, be they state or non-state actors.

One needs not look back more than 100 years to find examples of this happening. The Atomic Bomb was America's trump card for all of 4 years. The AIM-9 Sidewinder air-to-air missile became a lesson in guided missile technology for the Soviet Union when one failed to detonate in its target. The missile was removed upon landing, exfiltrated and exploited to develop a near-identical copy, the R-3/AA-2 "ATOLL" air-to-air missile. ARPANet and its TCP/IP protocol established the framework for what would become the Internet; a means by which to share information, make business transactions, communicate, and steal information wholesale. What about the interconnected house…?

In the realm of space, we must consider the disruptive innovations of the future. We must remember that our space assets are, by their very build and function, cyber assets. We must recognize that advances in cyberspace will render our current cyber-defense capabilities obsolete, and that cyber-agility, cyber-survivability, and countermeasures will become much more important in the future as cyber-attack capabilities continue to evolve, and that to secure space access and operations in the future, we will rely more and more on cyberspace advances, innovations, and TTPs.

References

1. Department of Defense Annual Report [FY 1960], July 1, 1959, to June 30, 1960 (1961) USGPO, Washington, DC. MDA, http://www.mda.mil/global/documents/pdf/1960%20BMD%20extract.pdf
2. Wainstein L et al (1975) The evolution of U.S. strategic command and control and warning, 1945–1972. Institute for Defense Analyses, Arlington, p 218
3. Perry R (1973) A history of satellite reconnaissance, vol. I, Corona. National Reconnaissance Office. Chantilly, Virginia
4. Newcomb D (2015) 60 Minutes joins car hacking hype. Forbes, 29 Feb 2015. http://www.forbes.com/sites/dougnewcomb/2015/02/09/60-minutes-joins-car-hacking-hype/. Accessed 29 Mar 2015
5. Staff of Senator Edward Markey (2015) Tracking & hacking: security & privacy gaps put American drivers at risk. http://www.markey.senate.gov/imo/media/doc/2015-02-06_MarkeyReport-Tracking_Hacking_CarSecurity%202.pdf
6. Outer Space Treaty (1967) Article IV. http://www.unoosa.org/pdf/publications/ST_SPACE_061Rev01E.pdf. p 4
7. Wall M (2015) Power system failure eyed in US military satellite explosion. Space.com, 3 Mar 2015. http://www.space.com/28713-military-satellite-explosion-dmsp-f13.html. Accessed 4 Mar 2015
8. Kott A, Swami A, McDaniel P (2014) Security outlook: six cyber game changers for the next 15 years. IEEE Comput Soc 47:105

Future Trends in Large Data Handling

Hiren Patel

Introduction

Large data processing has been happening throughout evolution. Target recognition in large-format persistent surveillance systems is easily accomplished when the human eye tracks an object in a distant landscape. The flood of visual data entering the 130 million neurons [1] is quickly pushed up the Data, Information, Knowledge, Wisdom (DIKW) pyramid to information using past experience with that object. All of this is performed in real-time, with a computing system (the brain) that uses a fraction of the energy required in today's modern data farms.

Historically, data collection from sensors or other sources required reducing it down initially into information via feature generation. For example, intelligence analysts would be trained to spot what a military tank looks like by paying attention to certain details such as a long tank barrel. Then in a photograph, they would look for this feature to quickly identify a target tank.

The recent explosion in Big Data technology jumps the DIKW chain by using advanced data analytic tools to skip the information level of the DIKW pyramid. A 2008 essay makes the argument that Big Data analytics make the scientific method obsolete [2]. These tools along with significant computational resources, can sort and analyze vast quantities of raw data directly and determine trends that can enable predictive analysis. The additional advantage with this method is that the original data can be left intact allowing future study if needed. These benefits have encouraged the collection of data from all factors of day-to-day life.

In the proceeding sections, we will discuss data analytic tools and resources, followed by applications if Big Data analytics. We will highlight several current and future challenges in this area and finally suggest emerging technology enablers.

H. Patel (✉)
US Air Force Research Laboratory
e-mail: hiren.patel@us.af.mil

© Springer International Publishing Switzerland 2015   59
M. Blowers (ed.), *Evolution of Cyber Technologies and Operations to 2035*,
Advances in Information Security 63, DOI 10.1007/978-3-319-23585-1_5

Big Data Technologies and Tools

The term Big Data is an often over-generalized term used for the processing of data that is so large, it is time-prohibitive to transfer or copy it. Subsequently, new technologies were developed to process data in-place, versus transferring it to the customer or researcher location. The 2000 U.S. census data set is 200 GB is size, the Human Genome data set is 210 GB, and the Common Crawl Corpus data set of web crawl information is an incredible 541 TB in size. All are freely available through Amazon Web Services (AWS). These and other data sets are stored and made available via various data analytic services such as AWS, Microsoft Azure and IBM Big Data services. These companies also offer cloud storage and computing services to business users who want to store and process their own collected data, such as data collected from websites.

Many companies also house large data sets that they use for their own commercial benefit, such as Facebook, Google, and Twitter. The storage of vast quantities of data along with the computing power to supply it to users requires massive facilities. Facebook's two Prineville Oregon data centers are each 330,000 square feet in size and in 2012 used 153 GW of power [3]. The facilities have grown since then.

With such large data sets, the emphasis is on data reduction to just what is needed to gain meaningful insights. Various tools have been developed that utilize batch processing where common instructions can be performed across numerous computing cores over different pieces of data in parallel. The MapReduce Function in Hadoop for instance can perform the task of finding the largest value in a large data set by splitting up the data set into smaller parts and searching for the largest values in each of these parts in parallel, and then iteratively performing smaller searches on the previous search result's winners [4]. Once the basic functions such as sort and search can be performed for large scale data, complex data mining tools such as neural networks can be employed to develop a predictive model. Leo Breiman stated in [5] that there are two cultures in statistics. One assumes the data are generated from a stochastic model. The other allows the data to determine the statistical model. Big Data processing methods follow the latter statistical culture. The number of applications that are benefiting from such data analysis is growing quickly. The demand for data scientists has vastly increased in recent years and many colleges and universities have added degrees in this area [6]. In the following sections, we will describe some of the areas in which data analytics have had great success.

Medical Data Analysis

The field of statistics has always found application in medicine. Causation and correlation research of drugs and therapies to diseases are what doctors rely upon to make diagnoses for their patients. Pharmaceutical companies also rely on statistics to determine real effect of their drugs on combating diseases. In the past, the number of trials was limited by location and the amount of data that could be processed and store. However, with Big Data technology, many more variables about each patient can be stored and processed. In addition, health data can now be stored from different patients over a long period of time and this historical data can provide a larger sample set from which to draw insight and meaningful diagnoses. For instance, in [7] an attending physician was able to create a database for childhood lupus by making boxes of medical records electronically searchable. With this tool created, she correctly administered an anti-coagulant treatment based on recorded medical history of past patients. The digitization of medical records mandated by the Affordable Care Act will increase the amount of information available for medical research. Although there are many justified privacy concerns for pooled medical data, the opportunities for medical progress cannot be denied.

Another field of medical research that is benefiting from data analytics is genetic research. The human DNA consists of 3 billion base pairs. While the Human Genome Project took an army of computers, $3 billion in funding and 13 years to complete, current projects funded by the US National Human Genome Research Institute (NHGRI) are close to achieving the same feat for $1000 per person in much reduced time [8]. Genetic research holds the promise of designer drugs that can be tailored to the specific person rather than the average person as is currently done. Also, new research advances in cancer treatment, Alzheimer's disease [9], and others are depending on the analytical capabilities of Big Data technologies. With companies such as Human Longevity promising to sequence as many as 40,000 genomes per year [10], the amount of genomic data will quickly accelerate in size. Big Data analytics will serve to identify the effects of the various genes on the human body. Several research efforts have already started in this field and offer promising roads toward future development [10, 11].

One of the barriers to data analysis is incomplete or incompatible data records. Medical records collected from one hospital are likely not available to other hospitals. In addition, several medical record software vendors exist, none of which are completely compatible with each other. Thus, although more medical data is being collected than ever before, most of it is not collectively searchable. However, as benefits of data analytics reduce costs by increasing early detection and correct diagnoses rates, insurance companies are highly likely to require standardization in record keeping. As new drug therapies are developed more accurately and quickly with data analytic research, pharmaceutical companies are also likely to drive standardization. Government participation may also help. In April 2013, the National Institutes of Health (NIH) announced the Big Data to Knowledge (BD2K) program to address Big Data challenges such as lack of appropriate tools, poor data accessibility, and insufficient training [12]. Among the goals of BD2K is to facilitate the broad use and sharing of complex biomedical data sets. Among the 2014 awardees are projects to create centralized data hubs for nuclear receptor data, cardiovascular research and fMRI-based biomarkers. Each of these projects will seek to encourage data sources such as hospitals and universities to contribute and populate respective joint databases where all partners can then collaborate on furthering medical research.

Big Data and Image Processing

The recent trend towards higher resolution images via greater megapixel cameras has vastly increased the amount of necessary data storage necessary. Higher resolution video formats such as 4 K video only exacerbate the issue as these video files store 8 MB images at 30 frames (images) per second. Despite these daunting file sizes, some companies have found methods to extract useful information. Google's Picasa software and Facebook can both scan images uploaded to their software and perform facial recognition to a surprising degree of accuracy. In addition, they can analyze images to gain the context in which it was taken to better provide personalized advertisements to the user. It is estimated that Facebook users post an average of 300 million images per day resulting in many petabytes of stored information that is routinely processed and analyzed [13].

Medical imaging from MRI systems offer unprecedented views of the human body, but also require in some cases 15 TB of data per year [14]. Projects such as the Cardiac Atlas Project (CAP) [14] have started foundational research into using machine learning techniques to perform image recognition of abnormalities in 3-D medical images. These images consist of data cubes of millions of pixels of information, and therefore can benefit from Big Data processing methods.

The field of target recognition in imaging systems has been around for many decades. The US Air Force's Gorgon Stare consists of 9 different cameras, can send 65 different video feeds, and according to Maj Gen James O. Poss, "will be looking at a whole city" [15]. The challenge however is to sift through the mountains of data that systems such as these generate. If machine learning systems can pre-process data with sufficient accuracy before sending it to the intelligence analyst, the operator workload can be vastly reduced. In addition, simple tasks such as moving target tracking or even scene change become very difficult when dealing with such large data files. Current Big Data tools along with pattern recognition methods can greatly help, if only on an offline capacity as the data would need to be processed on high-end servers. The Air Force Distributed Common Ground System (DCGS) consists of 27 geographically separated networked sites for the collection and processing of intelligence information collected from a variety of sensors [16]. This system can process imagery information with both data analytics and human operators to help turn Data into Knowledge for the military commander. The problem of real-time processing remains however as much of the imaging files are much too large to allow in-place processing.

Big Data and Computer Security

In 2010, the DARPA CRASH program sought proposals for computer systems that mimicked the human immune system [17]. The goal was to design a system that could survive a cyber-attack by learning about the malware even as it was being attacked and relay that information to other systems that could learn and harden their defenses before they were attacked. Although the program had a 4 year life cycle and was focused on single or networked computer systems, the same theory can be applied to cyber defense on a grander scale. Already, anti-virus companies find signatures for new cyber threats and convey them to all systems using their software via new virus definitions. However, these systems rely on the capability of the anti-virus company to see the total threat space, something that is an NP-complete problem. A much more reliable method would be for the attacked system itself to convey details of its attacker to all other systems. New data analysis tools will have to be developed to parse through the mountains of data generated from log files from millions of connected computing systems and determine what constitutes a true threat. Information from log files, abnormal behavior of the system, duration and effects of the attack provide inputs to a cyber security model that can correlate symptoms to attack effects. This view was echoed by Gartner Research Director Lawrence Pingree at the Intel Security FOCUS conference in 2014, where he likened security threats to police All Points Bulletin (APB) where the criminal's description is conveyed to all police officers to maximize coverage. For security suites such as Intel's Threat Intelligence Exchange, once a system identifies that it is being attacked, symptoms of the attack are sent to a central repository which then informs all others [18]. IBM also has a system that pairs its QRadar Security Intelligence with Big Data analytics to determine abnormal behavior and events over years of activity [18]. Such long range assessment is invaluable in detecting stealthy malware that does not produce overt effects on a system, but can only be determined by analyzing system behavior for extended periods of time before and after the attack.

In the January 2013 RSA Security Brief [19], the benefits of Big Data towards cyber security are further highlighted. Authors cite two main risk factors in the coming years: the first is the dissolution of network boundaries, where distributed private networks are expanded to include more customers and items and take advantage of cloud storage and computing. The larger and more decentralized the network, the more vulnerable its nodes can be to attack. The second is more sophisticated adversaries. Today, sophisticated hacking attacks that are reported weekly come in two flavors: large scale very public attacks such as those on Target., Home Depot, Sony and other companies where their websites were shut down or customers' information stolen. The other is covert attacks that secretly and continuously steal and transmit the victims' information. These attackers have found and exploited vulnerabilities even in systems with sophisticated protection suites.

Upcoming Challenges for Big Data

Big Data analytics have yielded some stunning benefits and there is no sign that we are near the end. Engineers are using insights gleaned through data mining to optimize assembly lines, discover new medicines, protect computer systems and perform anomaly detection. However, as Big Data's popularity increases, so do the unique challenges that are associated with it. In this section, several upcoming challenges are described.

The Internet of Things

The number of connected devices is set to increase dramatically with a recent push for the Internet of Things (IoT). Through the IoT revolution, various devices that we use in day-to-day life will be connected to the internet and have the capability of conveying information. This is of great interest in building automation and control where the closed/open status of a door or window can be tracked. Faulty machinery components of sophisticated systems can be identified by monitoring the health of key components. Health of a warfighter on the battlefield can be monitored and automated messages sent to centralized repositories that can provide accurate information on battle casualties.

With this increased data collection comes the burden of collecting and archiving the data. Apple, Amazon, Facebook and Google have all built massive data centers based on predictions of their data storage needs. However, the amount of data required is a monotonically increasing problem – there will always be more data that needs to be stored. With IoT, the increase in data that needs storing will go up significantly to where even current data centers may not suffice. New low-cost and low-power storage technologies are needed to keep up with the cost of storing information.

The only way around ever-increasing data storage requirements is to make a determination on which data needs to be archived and which does not. Choosing to discard information is a difficult problem. Although data today may seem uncorrelated to an effect, new data mining tools such as deep learning may find a connection in the near future. There is the option to store only the usable features generated from the raw data instead of the data as a whole. For instance, in the case of persistent surveillance, if the user only wishes to know the time in which an event happened, only the time stamp can be recorded and the image need not be stored. However, if later the user wishes to determine what the event was, then that data would not be available as the images were never stored.

Security and Privacy

A 2014 report from the White House on Big Data and Privacy [20] shows that over 80 % of respondents to a survey stated that they were "very much concerned" about proper transparency and oversight for data practices. It is well known that internet companies such as Google, Facebook, Microsoft and others collect and store information on their users' for commercial benefit. This may be only slightly irritating when an ad for a product you searched for on Amazon follows you when you are trying to read your Gmail. Many of these companies have data handling policies in place to protect user identities. However, the fact remains that these companies are collecting vast amounts of personal data and the users have little to no say on how their data is used. In addition, even though in most cases identifying information can be removed from the collected data, techniques like data fusion can piece enough information from different sources so as to identify the person related to a particular data. Also, "de-identifying" information in this way can in some cases remove its usefulness for predictive analysis.

Closely related to privacy concerns are the security concerns of adequately protecting vast amounts of personal data from falling into the wrong hands. Having data from various sources stored in centralized locations turns these locations into big targets for malicious cyber-attack. The challenges of cloud security include protection and trust of hardware, facilities, operators, code and companies using the data [21]. Often times, many of these layers are not known to the subject whose data is being gathered. Even for a company engaging in Big Data analytics, it is difficult to establish a fully trusted data flow system whereby they can truthfully ensure their users that their data is being well guarded. Some larger companies such as Google, Facebook and Apple have established their own data centers to improve their level of trust by using their own hardware, however this too does not assure security [21]. These Data centers must be physically secured, access to massive computation systems must be physically restricted, and theft detection systems should be well established. Many Software-as-a-Service (SaaS) applications that collect data from users run in internet browsers which places the security risk on both ends: at the user terminal where it may not be known if even basic security measures such as anti-virus, firewall, or routers are being used; and at the receiver datacenter whose the security measures are not usually known to the user.

Technical Challenges

The scale of Big Data is what sets it apart from previous generations of data analytics. Data sets that are an order of magnitude or more larger than previously useable data are now routinely being processed. The storage requirements are only predicted to increase over time. The most apparent technical challenge in the near-term is the need for more dense memory and faster processors. In [22], data size in kB/day were shown to increase exponentially from 2003 to 2011. In 2010, enterprises and data users stored over 13 exabytes of new data. While data archiving technology such as tape drives exist [23, 24], these are typically only allow sequential access which is very difficult to work with for Big Data analytics. New low-power, dense and random access memory technologies are required for the next generation of data analytics.

In addition to data storage, there is a need for the next generation of computer processors. It is well known that computer processors have been following Moore's law for many decades, doubling computer processing power every 18 months. However, as incoming data increases exponentially, new architectures will be needed to keep up with demand. Processors built inherently for large data distributed processing are needed, that can sort and process data in parallel but also be able to combine information from multiple locations to draw insights.

Finally, there must be continual development in the Big Data analytical software. Machine learning and pattern recognition have had a cyclical nature of research, where there was intense interest in certain decades and lack of interest in others. Currently, there is an uptick in research in these algorithms due to the many Big Data success stories. However, for every improvement in classification accuracy by a next-generation classifier, there must also be a corresponding development in software that can use these classifiers in parallel over massive data centers and spatially separated data sets. Next generations of data retrieval and indexing software will also need to be developed for such massive data sets.

Future Trends in Large Data Handling

The processing of massive data sets has yielded many significant results, the benefits of which more than offset the need for improved technologies in the years to come. With the many challenges for Big Data in the near and long term future, there has been a corresponding increase in research and development in this field. Technology is being developed on multiple fronts to allow the successes achieved through the processing of massive data sets to continue in the future years.

Dr. Michio Kaku writes that we are rapidly entering the stage of computer commoditization, where computing power can be sold as a commodity [25]. Seeing the rapid rise of Big Data facilities and services such as Amazon AWS cloud computing and storage, this is very true. In most circumstances, companies using Big Data will only need large computational resources for a relatively short period of time after which these systems will remain idle. Multiple methods of computer resource commoditization are available now, such as SaaS, Analytics as a Service (AaaS), and Infrastructure as a Service (IaaS). These service models allow businesses to only pay for what they need. And to complement computational resource commoditization, there are various cloud services that allow data storage on third party data centers. These third party facilities save companies cost by consolidating IT personnel and resources.

With the increasing amount of information being collected, the need for more advance storage will outpace the need for more compute power. Therefore much research is being generated in the fields of next generation storage technologies. A good example is the non-volatile Resistive Random Access Memory (RRAM). As transistor size decreases, the effect of electron leakage becomes significant and can affect the stored value in adjacent memory cells. RRAM seeks to replace the traditional transistor-based memory model with an alternative method that lowers leakage current while reducing size and increasing endurance. RRAM uses a switching material sandwiched between two electrodes to represent a memory cell. The motion of electrons under the influence of an electric field causes a measureable change in resistance, which is readable as a memory value. A company named Crossbar has recently announced commercialization of 3-D stacked RRAM which increases memory density [26]. Crossbar has indicated that the first application of their technology will be in high-capacity enterprise systems. Other memory technologies are also being developed such as Magnetoresistive RAM (MRAM) and Phase-Change Memory (PCM) in an effort to find a suitable replacement to traditional DRAM and NAND based memory architecture. Commercialization of these technologies in the coming years will help significantly to improve storage.

The current trend toward mobile computing has increased the need for low-power compute and data storage technology. As previously mentioned, large data centers consume very high amounts of power. New lower power processors with smaller transistor sizes will help to bring the power requirements down. In addition, real time data analytics are now possible with these low power processors. Instead of sending the raw data to the data center for processing on massive compute servers, the data is sifted in real time at the source for useful information and only that data is sent to the central repository for storage. Further, certain processors are being developed that change the traditional architecture of a microprocessor from a serial nature to a parallel one. The GPU manufacturer Nvidia has developed a programming interface called Compute Unified Device Architecture (CUDA) that allows programmers to take advantage of the large number of parallel processors in a GPU. Nvidia believes that there is great potential in fields of machine learning and has developed a deep learning library cuDNN to decrease processing time [27]. In some cases, speedup of 14x versus a 12 core CPU were realized when training on an image dataset with a neural network.

GPU computing's Achilles heel has always been memory transfer. GPUs can only store small amounts of memory on board and the latency of transferring memory back and forth between the GPU and CPU often makes them unusable for Big Data applications. However, recent work in MapD architecture has shown that GPUs can be used in data sorting and produce significant time savings. In [28], the author generated a hierarchical memory structure similar to that in the classical CPU architecture, with hard drives at the lower level, main memory buffer pool in the middle and GPU memory at the top. Similar to memory cache behavior, data is read and stored in chunks and if the required data is not in the cache, it is searched for at the next lower memory level. With this memory framework in place, the author was able to achieve speedup of over 1,000,000 times from using the algorithm on the GPU versus an in-memory CPU implementation. Real-time twitter search throughout the entire United States for particular words is now possible with sub-$1000 systems, which can be useful in a variety of ways to sense words that are trending on social media and correlate them to points on a map [28, 29]. By knowing what is popular among users in a particular location, an estimate of the collective emotions in the area can be predicted. This can be useful for marketing the right product for the correct audience, but also for allocating appropriate crowd control resources in volatile situations.

Conclusions

Many benefits have been realized with Big Data analytics and cloud computing resources. Data that is an order of magnitude or more larger than previous generations can now be routinely analyzed to discover hidden patterns. Fields of medicine, cyber security, image processing and defense can benefit by tracking collected information and drawing conclusions based on bigger data sets than were ever previously available. Future progress in Big Data technology will depend on research needed to overcome significant technological, security and policy barriers. However, Big Data takes advantage of a generalized rule in statistics: in most cases, more data will generate better statistical models. With the aid of these better models, the potential exists to more accurately draw Wisdom from Data.

Bibliography

1. Hecht E (1998) Physics: algebra/trig. Brooks/Cole. New York
2. Anderson C (2008) The end of theory: the data deluge makes the scientific method obsolete. Wired. Wired Mag., 23 Jun 2008. Web. 3 Feb 2015. http://archive.wired.com/science/discoveries/magazine/16-07/pb_theory
3. Rogoway M (2014) Facebook says its Prineville data center construction created 1,500 Oregon jobs. The Oregonian, 21 May 2014. Web. 23 Jan 2015
4. White T (2012) Hadoop: the definitive guide. O'Reilly Media, Inc. Sebastopol, CA
5. Breiman L (2001) Statistical modeling: the two cultures (with comments and a rejoinder by the author). Stat Sci 16(3):199–231
6. Lipman B (2014) Universities increasing programs for data scientists. Wall Street and Technology. Information Week, 29 Dec 2014. Web. 3 Feb 2015. http://www.wallstreetandtech.com/careers/universities-increasing-programs-for-data-scientists/d/d-id/1318139
7. Frankovich J, Longhurst CA, Sutherland SM (2011) Evidence-based medicine in the EMR era. N Engl J Med 365(19):1758–1759
8. Hayden EC (2014) Technology: the $1,000 genome. Nature 507(7492):294–295
9. Biffi A et al (2014) Genetic variation of oxidative phosphorylation genes in stroke and Alzheimer's disease. Neurobiol Aging 35(8):1956.e1
10. Dorrier J (2014) Genetic big data: what it means. The World Post. The Huffington Post, 17 Nov 2014. Web. 3 Feb 2015. http://www.huffingtonpost.com/2014/11/17/j-craig-venter-genetic-big-data_n_6159046.html
11. Strobl C et al (2008) Conditional variable importance for random forests. BMC Bioinf 9(1):307
12. Margolis R et al (2014) The National Institutes of Health's Big Data to Knowledge (BD2K) initiative: capitalizing on biomedical big data. JAMIA 21(6):957–958
13. Tam D (2012) Facebook processes more than 500 TB of data daily. CNET. n.p., 22 Aug 2012. Web. 3 Feb 2015. http://www.cnet.com/news/facebook-processes-more-than-500-tb-of-data-daily/
14. Fonseca CG et al (2011) The Cardiac Atlas Project—an imaging database for computational modeling and statistical atlases of the heart. Bioinformatics 27(16):2288–2295
15. Nakashima E, Whitlock C (2011) With air force's Gorgon Drone 'we can see everything'. Washington Post, 2
16. Air force distributed common ground system (2009) U.S. Air Force, 31 Aug 2009, n.p, Web. 3 Feb 2015

17. Kenyon H (2012) DARPA's CRASH Program reinvents the computer for better security. Breaking Defense, n.p., 21 Dec 2012. Web. 3 Feb 2015. http://breakingdefense.com/2012/12/darpa-crash-program-seeks-to-reinvent-computers-for-better-secur/

18. Marko K (2014) Big data: cyber security's magic bullet? Intel makes the case. Forbes Magazine, n.p., 9 Nov 2014. Web. 3 Feb 2015. http://www.forbes.com/sites/kurtmarko/2014/11/09/big-data-cyber-security/

19. Curry S, Kirda E, Schwartz E, Stewart WH, Yoran A (2013) Big data fuels intelligence driven security. RSA Security Brief, Jan 2013. http://www.emc.com/collateral/industry-overview/big-data-fuels-intelligence-driven-security-io.pdf

20. Big data: seizing opportunities, preserving values (2014) Executive Office of the President, May 2014. Web. 3 Feb 2015. http://www.whitehouse.gov/sites/default/files/docs/big_data_privacy_report_5.1.14_final_print.pdf

21. Fernandes DAB et al (2014) Security issues in cloud environments: a survey. Int J Inf Secur 13(2):113–170

22. Jagadish HV et al (2014) Big data and its technical challenges. Commun ACM 57(7):86–94

23. Sony develops magnetic tape technology with the world's highest areal recording density of 148 Gb/in2 (2014) Sony Global, n.p., 14 Apr 2014. Web. 10 Feb 2014. http://www.sony.net/SonyInfo/News/Press/201404/14-044E/index.html

24. Sekiguchi N et al (2014) The development of perpendicular magnetic recording tape by roll-to-roll in-line sputtering. IEEE Trans Magn 50(11):1–4

25. Kaku M (2012) Physics of the future: how science will shape human destiny and our daily lives by the year 2100. Random House LLC

26. Mearian L (2013) A terabyte on a postage stamp: RRAM heads into commercialization. Computerworld, N.p., 5 Aug 2013. Web. 10 Feb 2015. Toronto, Canada http://www.computerworld.com/article/2484619/data-center/startup-pits-rram-against-dram-and-flash-storage.html

27. NVIDIA cuDNN – GPU accelerated machine learning. Nvidia, n.p., Web. 10 Feb 2015. https://developer.nvidia.com/cuDNN

28. Mostak T (2013) An overview of MapD (massively parallel database). White paper, Massachusetts Institute of Technology, Cambridge, MA

29. Rudder C (2014) Dataclysm: who we are (when we think no one's looking). Crown. New York

The Application of Virtual Reality for Cyber Information Visualization and Investigation

Garrett Payer and Lee Trossbach

The Not So Distant Future of Cyber Analysis and Interactivity

A defensive cyber analyst logs in for her working day, pulls her issued virtual reality (VR) headset over her head and logs into a cyber-defense virtual platform.

Shortly after putting on the VR headset, she is surrounded in virtual space by virtual monitoring tools and displays from network sensors around the world. In the virtual environment created for her, she can see panels of related information surrounding her in a starscape-like fashion. Peripheral indicators can be viewed with a quick look, and primary indicators and active windows are ahead of her in a windshield-like interface.

The system she monitors manages intelligence information, providing intelligence analysts the ability to view, monitor, interact with, or modify the information. She's been assigned specifically to defend the system, not just against attacks, but from adversaries intent on extracting information. Adversaries have vested interest in sensitive or classified intelligence information, not only for its own potential value, but also to derive the techniques used to collect the information in the first place. If intelligence information pertaining to current locations and objectives of analysts fielded overseas is placed in the wrong hands, many of her colleagues active in the field may find themselves compromised.

She physically gestures an open hand and motions her arm from right to left "swiping" an active window into view. Her VR headset detects the motion instantly, presenting this morning's most pressing indicators of malicious activity. She verbally asks the panel "Computer, sort the indicators in chronological order", causing the panel to automatically rearranges the indicators. The panel automatically rearranges the indicators. As she swipes through the list of indicators, she concentrates

G. Payer (✉) • L. Trossbach
TMS, ICF International, 7125 Thomas Edison Dr #100, Columbia, 21046 MD, USA
e-mail: garrett.payer@gmail.com; garrett.payer@icfi.com; lee.trossbach@icfi.com

© Springer International Publishing Switzerland 2015
M. Blowers (ed.), *Evolution of Cyber Technologies and Operations to 2035*,
Advances in Information Security 63, DOI 10.1007/978-3-319-23585-1_6

on those showing excessive output activity from any monitored network; searching for clues alluding that information is being pulled out of a network asset. While this isn't out of the ordinary, excessive amounts of information being pulled from the system can indicate an adversary may be attempting to exfiltrate data.

"Computer, identify any sessions where data transmitted from a system node to a foreign node exceeds one gigabyte. Also display if the sum of the data received in under an hour exceeds the amount of data transmitted," the analyst requests. The list of indicators shrinks, displaying only those with attributes she has selected. As she begins working through the list, she notices that a few unique sessions appear to have high data transfer rates at specific intervals. Uncertain as to whether the identified sessions are related, she drags the session indicators directly over and creates a virtual pile next to the active window. Once tens of indicators have been identified, she swipes away the active panel. She holds her palm outward facing towards the pile of indicators, and then spreads her fingers widely apart while moving her arm inward. The pile spreads out in front of her in an array, she is able to look between them simultaneously to discern any patterns of behavior. A few of the indicators catch her eye as they have similar network traffic patterns and seem to be in sync with each other. She points her finger toward the indicators matching the pattern and slides them over to her right to create a refined pile of evidence that can be formally referenced later in her investigation.

"Computer, create a 3D line graph with the x axis being the amount of data transferred and the y axis being time in 10 minute increments. Plot the indicators I have selected on this graph." The graph appears, showing a time series of peaks and troughs representing each sessions and the amount of information transferred over time. She reviews the graph, and the relationships presented indicate that someone is using a node (a workstation) inside one of the monitored networks to transmit data every hour to different nodes registered to foreign IP addresses located in possibly unfriendly territory. Unsure as to whether these historical transmissions are of actual malicious intent, she feels that in order to determine the nature of this behavior, she will need to capture more raw data.

"Computer, based on the characteristics of these indicators create an alert of this same behavior pattern based on a time interval of an hour. Set the confidence of match to 90 %." Knowing that the system will alert her to behavior matching the pattern she discovered, she continues with the rest of her routine.

While she reads over the recent reports filed by her fellow analysts, an audible alarm sounds. She physically gestures holding a box in front of her and motions as if she sets the box to the side and the entirety of what's displayed in front of her is visually moved aside accordingly. What remains is an alert panel showing a blinking alert image. She points to the image and it expands, she sees it is the transmission she set up earlier. "Computer, display our logical network map, overlay and highlight known hosted services." All other displays seemingly fade away, and what looks like something similar to an engine or large piece of machinery with multiple parts appears in front of her. Each piece of the machine is made up of what appears to be a number of different glowing spheres, each indicating a node on the network. Some nodes are notably brighter in accordance with her alert request. The pieces, and their form, are an expression of the relationship or model of how these nodes function within the connected system.

She passes her hand through part of the model, and various pieces of thread appear. Each thread connects between two different nodes representing a network session between them. Many nodes have several thread connecting between them, indicating many sessions have taken place. Some threads also become thicker or thinner based on data volume in a single session. In rare cases some threads abruptly disappear and reappear, indicating network connection issues. Looking across the entire picture, her experience indicates the sessions appear to be exhibiting normal behavior. "Computer, highlight the session that set off the alarm." The picture in front of her enlarges as it appears that she is diving into the system in order to observe the interactions at a much smaller scale. The scene zooms in on a particular node with a thread that spans towards what looks like a cloud. This thread seems more like a pipe as it's appears to be several orders of magnitude bigger than all other surrounding threads.

"Ah, there it is," she whispers. Then, she grabs the thread, and performs a tearing gesture, opening the thread, causing a number of windows with textual and visual information to continuously spew out. As they go by, she notices they seem to be related. "This appears to be information pertaining to our missions out west." She grips the pipe and squeezes to stop further information windows spawning from the thread. "Well, let's slow this down so I can investigate further." She pinches the pipe sized thread. As she pinches the thread it becomes smaller and smaller until it's closer to the size of the other threads within the system. She thinks to herself, "Alright, I've dynamically limited the throughput of that session for now, let's see what's happening on our node."

Using her two index fingers, she points in front of her and slowly moves them apart, zooming in on the node in question. As she places her hand on the node, a number of windows appear around the node. One window displays a list of indicators associated with the node, providing a history of anomalous node activities. Another window displays the currently running processes. Finally, all of the threads associated with that node become red; while other threads of the system change to a pleasing blue.

"Wow, that's sure a lot of connections" she notices. The colored threads appear to connect to most of the data storage nodes. She thinks to herself, "This is clearly abnormal, as other nodes of this type have significantly less threads attached to the storage nodes." Considering the amount and type of traffic traveling from the node to a foreign entity, and the fact that it's connected to significantly more data nodes, she believes that this may be a successful exfiltration. She speaks, "Computer, show me the difference in processes between this node and this other node" as she simultaneously points to what appears to be a similar node. A window appears with a single item displayed. "Ah, this might be the culprit." The process is named virusscan.exe. She knows that current virus scanning software in use does not utilize this executable. She grabs the window, and places it on her evidence pile.

"Computer, show me what files this process has accessed in the last hour." A window appears with a list of recent file accesses, including whether it was to read or write to the file. She glances at the window for a few seconds, and it appears that the process seems to accessing only executable files. "Seems to be very interested in the executables. I wonder if this process might be attempting to establish some level of persistence within the system." She shrugs knowing that she has probably discovered the culprit, but she will enlist the help of the counter threats team in determining the motive and capabilities of this threat. She swipes this information into the evidence pile.

She then flicks her wrist to cause the destination node for the exfiltration to become visible. "So, this is where the data is being sent to over the internet?" As she hovers over this node, a number of information windows appear. One of the windows catches her eye. "Ah, that makes sense!" The country of origin for the IP address in question appears to contain a number of known bad actors. "This goes in the pile," she determines, as she swipes the window over to the evidence pile. Another window catches her eye.

"Known threat IP addresses?" The window in question is a list containing related threat items from various threat feeds where the IP address was cited. "Hmm, this includes many matching indicators from a known bad actor that has compromised similar organizations as ours. I'm going to say, based on the evidence I've collected, that there is a high degree of probability that this exfiltration is targeted malicious activity," as she simultaneously swipes this data to her evidence pile. "Clearly, one of our nodes was compromised, and is now being directed by an attacker to scour our data and to send this information back on a regular interval."

Pointing her index fingers and slowly moving them closer together, she zooms out to the original node in question. She reaches out and touches it twice. A pause symbol, similar to what one would use to pause a song on a music player or smartphone app, appears over the node. The threads established with the node abruptly disappear. "Computer, bring up the honey pot network and prepare to transfer this compromised node in real-time." The overarching illustration of the intelligence system falls away and is replaced with a similar, albeit simpler, version of the intelligence system. The thread color has shifted from red to purple, denoting that the node's communications are now being observed to derive threat intelligence. "All right little guy, you won't be performing any malicious activity on our real networks." She drags the compromised node into the model, near similar nodes, and taps it twice. The threads that had disappeared reappear, and the thread connected to the foreign node begins to expand again.

She grins knowingly. This environment contains disinformation and decoy binaries containing Trojan horses. This could allow an individual to establish a foothold in the attacker's infrastructure. "Boy, will the attacker get a surprise if they start snatching up those binaries. This problem now belongs to the counter threat team." She glances over to the pile of evidence she had gathered to make her determination of the observed behaviors as being malicious. She sighs. "It's going to take me at least ten minutes to generate a report from this data. I guess I'd better get cracking." She begins by separating the information gathered in her evidence pile. Once sorted and displayed in accordance with their relative start times, she draws lines to establish relationships, essentially linking observations in time series. Once she creates and disseminates this report, she is ready to reset and continue her day. "Computer, back to observation mode", the displays and windows that were available when she first entered the VR environment phase into view and surround her again.

At the end of her day, she disengages from the system and removes her VR interface. As she stretches for a moment before leaving, she notices someone left the storage closet open again. She smirks at the piles of 30-inch 4 K (4,096 by 2,160 pixels) monitors, keyboards, and mice collecting dust. She cannot imagine how those before her ever did the job.

Introduction

Being a data analyst can apply to a wide variety of career fields. Examples include NASA operators and scientists, stock market brokers, meteorologists, system or network administrators, and newly coined cyber professions [1]. Cyber analysts observe the behaviors of monitored networks and systems they protect to determine if there are indications of malicious behavior. The behaviors can include network activity as well as activity within hosts on the network such as file access and login information. Malicious behavior can be as diverse as Denial of Service (DoS) attacks [2], to unauthorized access, to destruction of the system. This chapter about visualization using novel methods will focus more on network and cyber related professions; specifically network management, and network security. It details how the principles of locality and spatial reasoning can be supported by technology such as the Oculus Rift (OR) [3] and reduces the cognitive burden on analysts as they perform their investigations. Despite our focus on network and cyber professions as the medium to discuss data visualization, the methods described in the following sections would be of value for a number of other professions, including those mentioned above.

The Cyber Analyst

Whether analysts perform their duties in a security operations center of CYBERCOM, maintaining global networks, or performing cyber operations, analysts primarily use a physical computer monitor that provides the surface in which information about the behaviors of the system they are to protect is presented. Identifying and responding to network attacks requires analysis of vast amounts of data within shrinking timelines of viability; the time in which the data is useful in preventing malicious behaviors. The key to assisting analysts with interpreting and understanding ever-larger amounts of information is facilitating the use of more intuitive visualizations and analysis software with capability consideration primarily designed around human performance. Often, analysts interact with data using a combination of both graphical user interfaces (GUI) and command line interfaces (CLI). Many modern commercial tools related to network operations and cyber operations are GUI tools with tabular interfaces (similar to tabs in a spreadsheet application). CLI tools allow the use of scripting languages such as Perl [4] or Python [5], and are often used to supplement provided commercial GUI tools. While both commercial and custom applications could technically provide a GUI or CLI as the primary interface, there is a tendency for commercial-off-the-shelf (COTS) products to leverage a GUI. Analysts will often leverage their GUI tools and CLI tools in tandem (with personal preferences toward one or another) to maximize analysis capabilities and efficiency.

Visualization: A Big Data Solution?

Being stuck between a rock and two hard places, analysts need to analyze more data but while major efforts [6–8] are underway to solve the big data computational problem, analysts lack the physical devices to view and interface with it in a reasonable manner. The data they already have is often presented in such an unrefined manner that it can be overwhelming. To offset the amount information an analyst must observe, additional or larger monitors are added to workstations. With larger screen real estate, more intuitive data representations can be utilized by analysts. Even if analysts had more intuitive visualization tools, increased screen space is still limited by physical space and budget.

As the amount of information available on the Internet is increasing exponentially [9] as are size and complexity of the systems needed to access this information [10]. As these systems become more complex, and the amount of information continues to grow, an analyst becomes faced with the problem of analyzing significantly more security data in order to determine if malicious behavior is present let alone discerning additional details such as the attack vector used or goals of the behavior. In the future we may find that interacting with such large amounts of security data may be difficult or impossible using existing tools and software.

With VR technology such as a VRH, the space for visualizing different information and data pertaining to cyber events becomes almost limitless. The information being displayed is no longer specifically restricted to a few small rectangular displays but instead is perceived to be as a space as wide and far as the eye can see. VR technology allows the canvas in which information is to be visualized to be completely software defined. Not only will a VRH provide an analyst nearly infinite space in which to display data, but a VRH opens the door to new and innovative visualization techniques in order to assist analysts in identifying malicious behavior. The rest of the chapter will present our current research efforts at transforming the data that a cyber-analyst typically sees using a normal computer monitor into information to be displayed within a virtual environment rendered on a VRH.

Today's Analyst Workstation

The current state of a common workstation, and the number of monitors utilized by those with data analyst roles, such as the network management and network security analyst, is not significantly different from the workstation of any other computer-based job in the modern workplace. Some of the key differences are related to an analyst being in an operations center where there are large wall-mounted monitors supporting entire teams with heads up display (HUD) and dashboard-like information applications [11]. A common occurrence for an analyst is to have a set of monitors per computer that is being utilized. For those professions related to the Department of Defense (DoD) for example, an analyst may be utilizing multiple computers simultaneously when required to perform tasks on computers operating at different classification levels, which gives the illusion of a larger usable workspace than what is actually available. At the end of the day, the real life experience in an operational center for either type of data analyst is that many individuals will be in an environment designed to maximize seating space, and analysts must conform to the assigned tools, both hardware and software, provided to them [12], and they are expected do their best with what is provided.

More inspired concepts of what would make a vibrant and, one hopes, more efficient network or cyber operational center could be for researchers and developers to reach into the many various worlds presented in science fiction (sci-fi) shows and novels for inspiration. Many of the devices we take for granted today started as concepts within sci-fi. Historic examples of the imagination presented in sci-fi becoming reality include the very large concepts such as space craft and space stations, as well as palm-sized computers including smart phones and tablets. One notable operational sci-fi- inspired space that has been known for many years is the so called "Star Trek" room [13] that is reportedly utilized by the Army at Fort Belvoir, where it is said the Army has a strong cyber presence. Despite the Star Trek room being interesting from a design perspective, most of the pictures shared by the media demonstrate the common analyst workstation still having a few monitors per station on average – not significantly different than other common workstation in less inspired environments. While one can assume working in such a unique space may provide additional motivation to succeed for analysts working in that space, given enough time the novelty will wear off, and the same issues regarding the lack of innovation in how analysts interact with their data will continue to persist despite analysts appearing to work in a futuristic environment.

The Analyst Workflow

There are many jobs listed on websites such as Monster Jobs [14] in the DoD, Department of Energy (DoE), and other government and private entities that gives the reader a sense of the day-to-day requirements of a data analyst from either the network management, or network security perspective. By perusing a few postings and their requirements, one can observe similarities in titles and requirements where traditional network monitoring and management responsibilities may overlap with positions that require cyber data analysis. The requirements of analyst can include understanding the TCP/IP stack, familiarity with popular communication protocols such as HTTP, IRC, SMTP, SSL, and skills including network packet inspection. Furthermore, desired experience with particular tools and vendors such as Cisco, Dell, Juniper, Microsoft, Redhat, Sourcefire, Snort, Arcsight, and Splunk are often listed.

While a few tools and vendors are listed more often than others in these job postings, there is no specific set of data analysis tools used by analysts in similar work environments. This is largely due to tools having a specific niche combined with one of the following enterprise network features specific to the company or organization: vendors often have tools designed to work with their already installed network appliances; various provided primary enterprise domain tools such as Microsoft or Linux (Red Hat); the many types of logs to be managed (enterprise domain, network devices, and installed software on servers and desktop computers); various status management tools related to network appliances and network provided services (both internal and customer based); multiple IDS or other network security or policy based solutions; and Security Information and Event Management (SIEM) tools to help administrators and analysts both deal with all of these cumulative sources of data.

To those readers that are interested in a better grasp of all of the overwhelming choices of tools that support these jobs (and the differences or lack thereof), you are encouraged attend an IT technical- or cyber-focused trade show, which is quite often tied to conferences provided by organizations such as IEEE, RSA, and AFCEA. During these conferences, vendors compete to sell individual appliances, related tools, and/or tool suites. Vendors attempt to out-market each other with large, fancy booths, eye-catching advertisements, and visualizations (that may or may not actually be a part of their product). Competition is, of course, expected between vendors, but it makes the task of choice daunting and possibly overwhelming. At the end of the day, data analysts are often not included in the decision on what is used on network they are responsible for monitoring. Analysis tools are often inherited or chosen for them and analysts have to adapt. However, by touring conferences for oneself given the opportunity, you can see how each product (or set of products) in a particular niche is going to compete for maximum attention on monitors utilized by data analysts in the network management and network security professions.

The numerous tools available in environments that are often a mix of vendor devices and solutions indicates that both network management and network security data analysts will need to monitor and actively leverage several tools from various vendors to perform key elements of their positions. These job specific tools will be utilizing the same monitor space in addition to the more commonplace enterprise and office-related software common to any desktop in the workplace. Commonly installed software in the workplace would include day-to-day activities such as email, company specific databases, data store and retrieval, an office suite (word processing and spreadsheets), video or chat conference software, and web browsers. In either a personal or professional environment, any computer user has particular techniques and methods for interacting with their machine, techniques and methods they have developed as habit or best practice over time. The concept of utilizing either one primary window or several smaller windows spread throughout the reader's monitors, at home or in the workplace, would make the issue of "what works best" very familiar to the reader. How a user chooses to arrange application windows and information on their monitor/s usually comes down to preference combined with what the options are, (e.g. if one has a larger monitor at home and two smaller monitors at work, there are likely differences in the ways in which those virtual display spaces are utilized).

Common key functions for both network management and network security analysts is to monitor, detect, report, and mitigate issues discovered in their relative area of responsibility. Network management is more often dealing with the availability of key resources of the network itself (public-facing web servers, domain servers, and virtual private network (VPN) nodes) being online and functioning properly. Network security is more often dealing with attackers and trying to mitigate attacks that are on the verge of (or already) causing compromise on the network. There are certainly many other responsibilities that are required for both professions that one will notice in looking at job requirements for either role, but the noted example above accounts for one of the primary objectives whereby both professions will be leveraging many tools to accomplish their jobs. Note that based on job descriptions, assume for the purposes of this chapter that the data analyst for either role is qualified for the job and hence is familiar or has been trained in the tools or scenarios considered throughout the chapter.

If the reader has not previously seen some of the dashboards related to network management or network security, performing a Google image search for terms like "network management dashboards", "network management tools", "cyber operations dashboard", or "network security tools" will provide the reader with many examples of dashboards that could be of use to one of our data analysts. The reader may notice that there are many different display options due to differences in vendor and data presented. However, some of the information displayed will have a level of commonality; many tools will display warning alert indicators, such as network traffic volume, common ports, speedometer-like network indicators, line graphs and pie charts of network activity.

One of the most common themes in dashboards is that they compete to be the one tool that is front and center to our data analysts and or data analysts teams most of the time. Previously we referred to network operations center examples of the large screens at the front of network operation centers; these dashboards would be displayed on those screens for reference by teams. However, they can also be intended for monitoring by analysts at their workstations. The difference in one vs the other (or combinations thereof) is in the policies, procedures, and expectations between one organization and another. As noted previously, there exists a slight overlap between the roles of network management and network security. Most attacks on computers are accomplished through networks [15] there are many tools that are useful to both roles A rather large sample of the top 125 common tools can be found on SecTools.org [16], which provides names, descriptions, and updates of the most common, popular, and worthwhile tools very common to both professions.

The Current State of Analysis

Consider the two following scenarios for a network management-based data analyst and a network security-based data analyst. Their jobs include a similar work flow, a similar reliance on many tools isolated to a common workstation setup between them, and each having two monitors. Some of these concepts and techniques are technical in nature, and if the reader is unfamiliar, the key takeaways are not the functions of the tools themselves, but how the data analyst has to juggle active windows. For readers familiar with the tools and professions, these scenarios will hopefully provide a somewhat entertaining read that is relatable to your environment and daily challenges.

Scenario 1

A network management data analyst has a required dashboard portal that displays a full-screen list of world-wide key servers and network paths on one monitor. Most nodes are showing green for nominal behavior, indicating that sessions established between the nodes and data transferred between them are within acceptable tolerances based on mid-day averages during the business week. Some nodes are yellow to represent "caution", indicating above average load balances that could lead to failure, but each node indicated in yellow has already been assigned a tracking ticket for senior support to take a closer look. On the other monitor, the analyst has their enterprise email full screen in the background so he can watch for emails that require his attention, as well as a web browser with a tab open to a network management blog displaying the latest trends in network management success stories and a weekly report compilation tool open in another tab.

Sometime in the afternoon, the network management data analyst notices several email indicators appear, indicating trouble with a network node. While quickly reading the email, the analyst notices a flash on the dashboard. The icon relating to the troubled node turns red, indicating a critical issue, and flashes with an alarm of no connectivity. The data analyst drills down into the dashboard and is presented with some minimal information, and discovers the last check-in was a half hour ago and it stopped reporting health. Up until then, the node was green, therefore indicating nominal behavior. As our data analyst is looking into this basic information and determining more analysis is warranted, he has to minimize his dashboard to get to his troubleshooting tools, which were behind the dashboard on standby. Note that the analyst has the option of minimizing the dashboard or moving it to another monitor. Either way is fine for the purposes of the narrative. The point is that the dashboard is just in the way when he needs to leverage other tools.

The analyst moves the dashboard and brings his network trouble shooting tools to the foreground, which will provide the evidence needed to move forward with a solution, or enable him to determine if this is a false positive. As he moves the dashboard to the other monitor, his troubleshooting tools begin to take over his attention. However, as he is nearly completed with moving the dashboard over, he sees a high importance email from his boss. He moves the dashboard back and reads the email. His boss provides a screen shot from the dashboard indicating the red node and asking what is being done about it. He pauses even longer in order to fire off a "working it" email response to his boss, goes back to adjusting the dashboard, and engages with his network troubleshooting tools.

He decides to run a ping command in one window to test connectivity to the node, and a traceroute to validate the network communication path in another. After typing the commands, as the results start coming back, he pulls up his log management tool to see the last several lists of logs that were sent back before the disconnect. The tools are responding to his queries that the network communication path seems ok, but the node does not respond. Though he is able to ascertain through logs that just before the node went down, it indicated it had started using the uninterruptable power supply, which could indicate a malfunction or power issue at the site. He pulls up his chat window from behind his email client to engage with a local network administrator on site who indicates that they are not experiencing power issues. The data analyst has enough information to generate a trouble ticket, so he pulls up the reporting application over top of all of his trouble shooting windows and fills out the required fields. He toggles back and forth between windows to make screen shots, include log information, and record the actions he has taken. He sets the priority to high and submits the ticket so that the local network administrator can start hands-on trouble shooting with the network node in the administrator's network data center.

Having accomplished his task, the data analyst closes or minimizes all windows no longer in use, brings his dashboard back up, and responds to the email from his boss noting the ticket number. Looking at his Windows task bar, he can see he is juggling no fewer than 15 active applications and many tabs in the web browser, and he wonders where the third monitor is that he requested.

Scenario 2

A network security data analyst has her Security Information and Event Management (SIEM) tool up and displaying alerts from the companies' many intrusion detection sensor (IDS) tools feeding it. Also, on another monitor, she is reading a security blog and has her enterprise email up and running. During her shift, the SIEM tool dashboard has shown nothing but false positives from the IDS tools. Eventually there is one alert that catches her eye as different from the other false positives she had been reviewing. She saw one like it last week, and it was confirmed as indicating a compromise. She selects the alert in the SIEM and the SIEM display brings up the alert message. Some basic information is provided in the message and it mirrors her recollection of the event last week. Unfortunately, the SIEM is only showing her some basic indicators and not enough raw data. Therefore, she will need other tools to facilitate a thorough network forensic investigation.

She moves her SIEM tool to her other monitor and brings up a graphical user interface (GUI) for network packet inspection, as well as several command line prompts to facilitate back-end access to raw data and security logs. Using her GUI packet analysis tool she can now see more raw data from the session. She observes primary indicators that match the command and control protocols in the malicious software that was installed on a company asset last week. She pulls up her command line tool in a separate application window and performs network flow analysis and packet analysis. Looking at the asset in question, she could follow the network traffic and observe where a user had been browsing a website forum and had inadvertently been redirected to some other unintended website. In pulling the network packets up from the redirect and following the packet trail, she can see that the user was confronted with a pop up to install software in order to continue reading an article. It appeared as though the user clicked yes, which led to the installation of a virus on the workstation.

She then wants to validate her findings against the previous incident details to confirm the current activity indicates the presence of the same virus. She pulls up the incident response ticket system on top of her analysis tool applications, pulls a search for the previous incident, and matches the traffic going to a hostile IP, observing in the process that the hostile IP is the same in both cases.

Satisfied with the evidence, she opens a new ticket and begins to fill out the required fields. She alt-tabs between windows and moves her cursor between monitors to take related screen shots and paste relevant packets and flow data into the ticket. She submits this information to her senior support for mitigation. She saves the trouble ticket and closes the window for the ticketing system. She sees in her email that her ticket successfully went out, when she suddenly received several related emails from other analysts seeing the same activity. She minimizes her forensic tool application windows and brings her SIEM back up. It becomes clear why the other data analysts are asking her questions. Five more alerts are displaying now in the SIEM from when she started. She pulls up her chat window and starts a group session to get everyone on the same page, she looks at her toolbar and notices she has no less than 20 applications open. She wonders if she will get the extra monitor she asked for weeks ago.

Analysis: A Process That Can Use Improvement

One could read up to this point and determine that the solution to the information overload is the use of more and larger monitors. As we will discuss, much of the data analysis process data can be improved with the introduction of additional display real estate; however, as we've shown, many environments will not support using the amount of real estate necessary to reduce the cognitive load of switching back and forth between panels. In addition, there are challenges of increasing data volume due to the presence of more and more network devices (such as bring your device to work) combined with the growing popularity of using cloud for services (such as online storage). The cognitive load on analysts, can cause them to context switch too often. Analysts are at risk of losing track of information as larger numbers of windows are being utilized during an investigation.

The conventional solution of more and larger monitors would only be providing the data analyst more buckets or larger buckets to work with, but not a true sense of freedom whereby they can maximize and utilize any sense of space for visualization. They are still held to the containers (display devices) provided to them whereby each configuration provides the data analyst with different, but limited options.

The above scenarios are a far cry from the scenario described in the beginning of the chapter. Much of the work performed by the analyst is entirely manual. Context clues are often missing from existing visualized data, and there is very little interoperability between security tools as well as how information from these tools is presented in a holistic manner. The action of switching between information displays involves toggling between windows, which becomes inefficient when trying to view multiple pieces of information to establish context and relationships. An analyst may take days in some cases, rather than minutes or seconds, in order to connect the dots. In order to strive for the future described in the beginning of the chapter, the way analysts visualize and interact with information will need to change. Much of the work performed by analysts should be assisted or driven by computers, freeing the analyst to provide an understanding or explanation of the observed behavior within their system.

Augmenting the Analyst's Sensemaking Ability

Computers are capable of identifying patterns in activity; however, they do not possess the ability to understand why an activity is considered malicious. Rather, this ability is achieved through an inherently human process –sensemaking. Sensemaking is the ability to look at large, and often disparate and incomplete, information to derive an understanding [17]. While behaviors can be detected that seem similar to actions associated with past malicious activity or indicators, a human analyst is still needed to conceptualize how these indicators are related and how that pattern can be determined [18].

Indicators can be provided through a number of sources including a wide variety of cyber tools, each utilizing a disparate interface that leverage and provide access to the following: network packet captures, audit logs on systems that record user actions, and performance characteristics of systems. All of this information can provide an analyst with a much larger understanding of the nature of the systems they are defending. For example, once an anomaly, policy violation, attack, or compromise has been discovered, analysts can examine the network packets that traveled to and from the systems under investigation to determine if there are any specific features within a packet that can indicate compromise, such as a specific sequence of bytes meant to exploit a network (or host-based) service on the target machine. The byte sequence can then be encoded as an IDS signature for an IDS solution such as Snort [19], which inspects individual network packets. With this signature deployed, a multitude of packets traveling across the network can be checked for this same network indicator by sequence at a much faster rate than a human could perform alone.

Discovery of the byte sequence or compromise aren't generally spontaneous events that analysts just happen to stumble upon when examining low level information such as packet data. The analyst generally starts either by examining data associated with anomalous activity within the system, or from external sources such as threat or vulnerability information from outside organizations. As an example, when Microsoft releases a security update for their web server, IIS, an analyst can filter through the information to specifically look at network traffic destined for the organization's web servers. By filtering the information, an analyst can quickly identify network traffic destined for these web servers from unfamiliar sources. This is an indicator of potential malicious behavior, but not a confirmation of malicious activity. Since this can be attributed to new clients connecting to the organization's services, additional indicators will be needed to confirm that this is malicious behavior.

An analyst must continue to investigate and find additional evidence to provide further context for unusual connection activity. Additional evidence can be found by identifying additional indicators of malicious activity, such as network traffic sourced from the compromised asset to known attacker command and control servers. Using this information, the analyst can piece together an understanding of how a compromise may have occurred and determine a pattern of behavior that can be used to identify future attacks.

This understanding is achieved through an analyst's skill in sensemaking. The process of sensemaking begins when an analyst examines external data and information. Typically an analyst will be limited to a computer with two to three monitors of varying levels of resolution. When performing their investigation, analysts will not only need to view information in various forms, but also by viewing external information such as threat data from threat feeds. Furthermore, they will reference material such as service and protocol characteristics, operating systems, and application versions. This process may result in analysts having tens of different tabs containing needed information in the web browser application alone. This collection of tabs is positioned on top of GUI and CLI interfaces providing the various views of the information they are examining.

Even with multiple monitors, keeping track of all of this information becomes a large cognitive load. An analyst will expend a significant amount of effort simply tracking relevant information across these tabs and windows. Switching windows and tabs represents a significant context switch for analysts and can cause them to lose their place or lose their organization, ultimately disrupting or completely stopping the analyst's process of sensemaking. For the process of understanding and determining patterns, limiting analysts to using a number of rectangular panels makes them significantly more inefficient. Much more efficient mechanisms to display system behaviors and information are possible with the introduction of virtual reality (VR) technologies.

As we've discussed, analysts are inundated with large amounts of data and utilize a number of tools in an attempt distill this data into actionable information. Worse yet, depending on the necessary tools an analyst utilizes to perform their functions, they spend much time and effort on juggling various windows on multiple displays, which results in cognitive strain and a reduction in the analyst's efficiency. In many processes, interoperability between tools and other information is difficult or impossible, burdening the analyst with additional inefficiencies and forcing them to keep track using more manual processes, thus causing further cognitive burden. Rather than forcing the analyst to continually tab among various windows to mentally or physically note relevant information and then exert effort to recall that information, much of this information can be expressed using more intuitive visualizations.

When discussing visualizations for cyber security, many individuals will associate situational awareness and sensemaking with mapping or "viewing" cyberspace, in an attempt to perceive the cyber battlefield similarly to a kinetic battlefield [20]. A great example of this is the company Norse's IPViking [21] which shows a world map with "attacks" being "fired" at specific targets. This visualization provides a high level view of worldwide attacks, including their sources and targets. Other examples would include network or system maps indicating relative health defined either by anomalous behavior or aggregate state of vulnerability.

The purpose of these visualizations is to provide the viewer with a single-glance understanding of the state of their systems providing instant information of the ongoing progress of activities such as vulnerability mitigation, or assessing current malicious or anomalous activity. This type of information can be very useful for battlefield commanders, policy makers, stakeholders and leadership. For analysts charged with determining which behaviors constitute inadvertent, malicious, and benign actions, these visualizations are only a single step, and usually the first step, in performing their functions.

Intuitively, it would make sense to move the existing analyst process to a VR environment. At the very least, moving all of the windows that an analyst uses during their investigation to a VR environment would be a good step. However, due to the seemingly limitless ways the information can be displayed and interacted with, additional focus on how VR can be utilized to display information and provide a more intuitive experience for analysts performing investigations will also be needed. These experiences can be broken down into two major ideas of providing intuitive modeling through the use of locality and augmenting the analyst's existing sensemaking abilities.

VR has been around, in one form or another, for decades [22]. The idea is that an individual can be transported to a virtual world through the use of technology, typically through a headset or perhaps through direct electrical stimulus to the nervous system. Almost as old is the idea of applying VR for the use of cyber offensive and defensive capabilities as portrayed in science fiction movies. This would typically involve mentally transporting an individual to a virtual world where the objects rendered correspond to virtual representations of network nodes. The point of this exercise would be to allow an individual to interact with these objects as if they were physical objects. While there are a number of advantages to this level of interactivity, these concepts would be stretched to the point of ridiculousness. As an example, an attacker could interact with a firewall in virtual reality being perceived as physical touch, however, the act of applying "physical" force to the firewall should not remove its protection. The act of "punching" a firewall will not break its functionality.

The idea that attackers or defensive teams will virtually patrol the perimeter of their networks and do battle wielding physical actions tied to cyber capabilities within a cyber-domain will have to remain in the realm of science fiction. Future attacks and defense mechanisms will be opposed, possibly entirely, by other automated tools and processes since they operate at significantly faster speeds than humans. Even now, while analysts search through network packets to identify key indicators for malicious behavior, this action is only in support of generating and testing a hypothesis. When a pattern is found, an analyst will describe this pattern as a signature and utilize a tool such as Snort to search packets at network speeds, an act that could not be accomplished using humans alone.

While virtually defending the perimeter within cyberspace is not practical or feasible, the use of virtual reality can augment an analyst's capability in understanding and sensemaking when analyzing and processing large amounts of information. While the normal workflows of analysts revolve around manually shifting information on two or more monitors, the use of a device such as a VRH would provide nearly infinite display space for visualizing different information and data pertaining to cyber events. The information being displayed would no longer be restricted to a few small rectangular displays but instead would be perceived by the analyst to be as wide and far as the eye can see. The use of a VRH allows the manner in which information is visualized to be completely software-defined. Not only will this VR environment provide an analyst nearly infinite space in which to display data, but it opens the door to the research and development of new and innovative visualization techniques in order to assist analysts in identifying malicious behavior.

Sensemaking and Spatial Reasoning

When analysts use a set of large panels, providing a larger physical view and high resolution workspace, one of the first uses of this larger workspace is to provide a larger view of multiple pieces of information. Instead of having multiple tabs within a single web browser, an analyst is free to utilize multiple windows that can be situated through the workspace. This large space can provide a degree of spatial awareness that can be associated with information.

One of the most intuitive methods of utilizing spatial awareness on large displays is clustering related data or information in the same or physically close location. When investigating indicators or alerts, they will usually examine the current alerts, threat intelligence, and latest vulnerability information. This information will provide further context when the analyst examines cyber data in order to determine the actions taken on the systems that the analyst monitors. Information about a new vulnerability may take the form of a webpage displayed through a browser window. This can then be placed in a space on the display. As an analyst begins to query the data for possible indicators that may be related to this vulnerability, this information in the form of terminal or perhaps browser windows will be placed adjacent to or layered on top of the information about the vulnerability. As an analyst investigates further, related panels or windows can be layered over top of those already existing. Relationships between pieces of information can be described by the location and distance of the window or panel that contains a specific piece of information relative to other present data. This intuitive organizing principle is similar to how people who are given a lot of paperwork may sort related papers into different piles based on their properties.

The use of higher resolution and large panels enables analysts to utilize more intuitive methods of sensemaking in order to identify patterns of behavior within data. The example we provided in the previous section discussed the importance of how space can assist with cognitive processes. Increasing the amount of workspace that is provided to analysts prompts a move from virtual navigation – changing around a number of tabs and windows – to that of physical navigation, which is the ability to glance at peripheral information on demand in regards to its spatial organization. While it's certainly possible to increase the amount of usable screen real estate for analysts, in some organizations this can become an issue because competition for space and money make these resources, or the ability to implement more or larger monitors, difficult.

From this perspective, the simplest goal of a virtual reality interface is to be able to interact with data to expand the workspace an analyst can use from several monitors to a near infinite plane. This frees the analyst from the virtual limits imposed by normal displays and brings to bear the normal physical visual limits that would be at their disposal if handling real world objects. However, unlike the real world, the visual experience can be 100 % dictated by software. Not only will this allow for interaction with virtual objects much the same way they might be interacted with in the real world, but also computer aided functions such as quickly searching for words in a document are now accessible.

One of the major challenges when reviewing alert data is establishing the context in which the alarm was triggered. Having an alarm may not actually indicate malicious activity, and the alert information itself may not be enough to conclude malicious activity. One of the major advantages when using VR is that information can be overlaid with existing information that is being viewed by an analyst. Relevant information such as configuration information or threat data indicating that a particular domain was used as part of a malware trend recently can all be displayed over top of information that an analyst is sifting through.

The use of hardware such as existing VR head-mounted displays, which can track head movements, which makes identifying what the user is looking at much easier. When examining an alert with a number of IP addresses included, an analyst can look at those IP addresses and superimpose knowledge base or configuration information over top of these addresses. An analyst can make an easy determination that despite the alert indicating a web exploit was sent to these IP address, the overlay presenting the information about the IP addresses can clearly indicate that, for example, one IP addresses belongs to a backup web server that is currently not hosting a web service, and the rest of the IP addresses are desktop computers (also not hosting web services); thus allowing an analyst to determine incident response does not need to be activated.

One of the major issues when analysts use visualizations is that the visualizations are packaged to only look at specific sets of data and have little to no flexibility in how information is presented. While one can argue that humans are really geared to understand information visually, command line tools and tabular formats provide the easiest mechanisms in which to query, filter, and manipulate data. This flexibility is a necessary part of the cognitive process when data is examined for evidence, and the associated patterns of behavior that can be described, can also be generated. Without this flexibility, visualizations for information will continue to be shunned or used in specific cases.

A successful case of the utilization of visualization in a cyber-context is in the use of monitors with high resolution. Similar to the process described above in which analysts could use the larger workspace for spatial relationships, high resolution screens also allow for more granular detail in visualizations.

On normal screens, a graph may provide a summarized view of a network diagram or traffic characteristics, but an analyst can discern greater detail in the summary with higher resolution by moving closer to the monitor. Points on the graph can be much more detailed and indicate specific sources of information, providing additional context for analysts in the investigations. Normally, the process of drilling down into the finer details would require interacting with the visualization with the mouse, clicking on points to discern specific information such as the IP address responsible for a spike in bandwidth utilization. Drilling down in this manner would often skew the original summary graphic, requiring analysts to virtually navigate between the information, thus placing a larger cognitive burden on them.

Final Remarks

When discussing our objective the use of VR technology for the use of data analysis throughout this chapter, the main goal of leveraging this disruptive technology is to enable an analyst to focus on investigation of behaviors on the systems they are monitoring. Analysts should interact with the data in an intuitive manner in order to discern patterns of behavior that indicate problems such as innocuous network anomalies, unexpected service degradation, through and including malicious intent and compromise. An analyst should not focus on finding known patterns but rather discover new patterns, leaving the heavy lifting of pattern recognition to the computers. Increasing screen real estate can allow for additional intuitive investigation techniques through spatial reasoning, but analysts would still be restricted to a specific window of information presented in front of them.

As we described in the beginning of the chapter, one of most intuitive ways to provide an analyst with an interface to perform these functions is the use of VR. The adjacency of information is what comes naturally to humans when forming relationships or patterns of behaviors. This adjacency can be better presented by using the limitless display space provided by VR technology to allow for larger areas to perform sensemaking, and to bring up additional information as separate windows in order to provide context to the observed behavior that is currently under investigation.

Information systems can be modeled in a number of unique ways including nodes that have their communications rendered as threads that may be interacted with by merely touching them. Changes on these systems can be performed by touching nodes or pinching threads, or swiping parts of the model to different spaces. These spaces can be rendered as actual physical locations or based on other aspects of locality.

Through the use of VR technologies, it's possible for analysts to focus on interacting with and the investigation of systems across a vast and immersive virtual space, rather than spending their time manually reviewing data to find existing patterns. Without a change in the current behavior of analyst investigation techniques, the influx of data increasing year after year will make analysts less and less efficient in today's common workstation environments. While humans can't scale well for these tasks, the information can be analyzed and presented in more dynamic and intuitive ways so that it won't be necessary for them to struggle against what is ultimately an impossible task.

References

1. Singhal A (2007) Data warehousing and data mining techniques for cyber security, vol 31. Springer Science & Business Media, New York
2. Mirkovic J, Reiher P (2004) A taxonomy of DDoS attack and DDoS defense mechanisms. ACM SIGCOMM Comput Commun Rev 34(2):39–53
3. Oculus VR (2015) Oculus VR. [Online]. Available: https://www.oculus.com/. Accessed 30 Apr 2015
4. Perl (2015) Perl.org. [Online]. Available: https://www.perl.org. Accessed 30 Apr 2015
5. Python (2015) Python Software Foundation. [Online]. Available: https://www.python.org/. Accessed 30 Apr 2015
6. XDATA. Defense Advanced Projects Research Agency. [Online]. Available: http://www.darpa.mil/program/xdata. Accessed 2 June 2015
7. Cyber Security Analytics. Terra Data. [Online]. Available: http://www.teradata.com/Cyber-Security-Analytics/. Accessed 2 June 2015
8. IBM security intelligence with big data. IBM. [Online]. Available: http://www-03.ibm.com/security/solution/intelligence-big-data/. Accessed 2 June 2015

9. Kallinkikos J (2007) The consequences of information: Institutional implications of technological change. Cheltenham, United Kingdom: Edward Elgar Publishing

10. Hague BN, Loader B (1999) Digital democracy: discourse and decision making in the information age. London, United Kingdom: Pyschology Press

11. An inside look at AT&T's operations center, and its security strategy (2013) Infosecurity Magazine, 13 May 2013. [Online]. Retrieved from http://www.infosecurity-magazine.com/news-features/an-inside-look-at-atts-operations-center-and-its/. Accessed 30 Apr 2015

12. Vergun D (2015) Cyber chief: Army cyber force growing 'exponentially'. United States Army, 5 Mar 2015. [Online]. Available: http://www.army.mil/article/143948/Cyber_chief__Army_cyber_force_growing__exponentially. Accessed 30 Apr 2015

13. Kelly MB (2013) Here's the 'Star Trek Command Center' that NSA Chief Keith Alexander used to woo politicians. Business Insider, 17 Sept 2013. [Online]. Available: http://www.businessinsider.com/the-us-army-star-trek-command-center-2013-9. Accessed 30 Apr 2015

14. Monster Jobs. Monster. [Online]. Available: http://www-classic.monster.com/. Accessed 30 Apr 2015

15. Hansman S, Hunt R (2005) A taxonomy of network and computer attacks. Computers & Security 24(1):31–43

16. Fifield D (2014) SecTools.Org: top 125 network security tools. Nmap Security Scanner Project. [Online]. Available: http://sectools.org/. Accessed 30 Apr 2015

17. Klein G, Moon BM, Hoffman RR (2006) Making sense of sensemaking 1: alternative perspectives. IEEE Intell Syst 21(4):70–73

18. Bowen BM, Devarajan R, Stolfo S (2011) Measuring the human factor of cyber security. IEEE international conference on technologies for homeland security (HST), IEEE, Waltham, MA, USA: 2011, pp 230–235

19. Roesch M (1999) Snort: lightweight intrusion detection for networks. In 13th Large Installation System Administration Conference (LISA99)

20. Pellerin C (2015) Rogers discusses cyber operations, ISIL, deterrence. U.S. Department of Defense, 2 Mar 2015. [Online]. Available: http://www.defense.gov/news/newsarticle.aspx?id=128278. Accessed 30 Apr 2015

21. IPViking – Live. Norse Corp. [Online]. Available: http://map.ipviking.com/. Accessed 30 Apr 2015

22. Tweedie S (2015) See how strange and trippy virtual reality was 20 years before the Oculus Rift. Business Insider, 21 Jan 2015. [Online]. Available: http://www.businessinsider.com/virtual-reality-before-the-oculus-rift-2015-1. Accessed 30 Apr 2015

Quantum Information Science

Erik Thoreson

> *Physics as we know it, will be over in six months*
>
> *– Max Born, 1928*

Quantum Information Science

Introduction

The intended goal of this chapter is to provide an operational picture for the future use of quantum technologies in the approximate period between 2025 and 2045. This chapter is intended to inform the generalist familiar with wargaming. It is not intended to be a detailed discussion of the technology, a description of the pitfalls, or a listing of the technology hurdles. In order to provide an operational picture, this manuscript assumes the engineering difficulties will not impede enabling the technology by the 2025–2045 period.

Any new technology must overcome a variety difficulties resulting from market, financial, engineering, and political pressures [1]. These combinations of factors are what makes forecasting the actual use of the technology nonlinear. In the final report, "Persistent forecasting of disruptive technologies" [2], the authors describe that the value of forecasting technology is not accurately predicting the future, but minimizing surprises. Akin with that process, this manuscript aims to provide a potential alternative future – one in which quantum technologies are commonplace, and a universal full-scale quantum computer is operational.

You may or may not be aware, but you are currently receiving the benefits of quantum physics in one way or another. For instance, the photoelectric effect enables digital

The views expressed in this article are those of the author and do not reflect the official policy or position of the US Air Force, US Department of Defense, or the US Government.

E. Thoreson (✉)
USAF, Dayton, OH, USA
e-mail: Erik.Thoreson@us.af.mil

cameras to operate [3]. The discovery of the transistor – an electrical component needed for modern computers – required the understanding of quantum physics [3]. Nuclear power [4], Higgs Boson [5], lasers [6], and many others all required some understanding of quantum physics during the early development stage.

Before further discussion, I would like to define quantum technology. So, what is new about the things called quantum technologies? There is an untapped aspect of quantum physics known as "entanglement", and these new quantum technologies exploit or manipulate this feature called "entanglement". The description of this term can take some time to develop, requires much thought, and can be quite confusing to understand. Thus, if you are really interested in knowing more about entanglement then I suggest you consult these references [7–10]. These references are likely more eloquent about describing entanglement than I will ever hope to be for this manuscript.

I have defined a quantum technology – a device or component that exploits or manipulates entanglement, but what is quantum information science? Quantum information science represents the combination of quantum physics with information science. Quantum computing and quantum communications are applied disciplines within quantum information science. Quantum information science is the study of information science as applied to systems that operate via the laws of quantum physics. The study of harnessing entanglement is "to dramatically improve the acquisition, transmission, and processing of information" [11]. Additionally, entanglement is what enables the exponential speed up in calculations on a quantum computer [12], the ability to detect eavesdroppers, low probability of interception, and theoretically unbreakable secure communications [13–15].

Now let us flashback to 1983. If you are a science fiction (sci-fi) fan, you have likely watched "War Games". This fictional movie was about a teenager who hacks the US Department of Defense's war gaming and simulation computer called, "WOPR (War Operation Plan Response)" [16]. Little did this cyberpunk realize that he was controlling a military simulation of global thermal nuclear war nor did he fathom that the system had an adequate amount of artificial intelligence to launch an actual nuclear war. In the end, the cyberpunk was the hero of the story. The hero was the only one who could force the machine to think about the consequences of its action – total destruction of the earth.

Other movies have had a similar theme – computers gone mad with controlling or destroying humans: Colossus: The Forbin Project [17], 2001: A Space Odyssey [18], and The Terminator [19]. Great movies for the sci-fi enthusiasts, but why mention it here? I believe these films represent a standard depiction of an alternative future for computing technology – computers gone crazy. The presentation of alternate futures can seem like sci-fi. However, if you compare the past knowledge about computing with the current trends of computing you will find that the sci-fi movies have many exaggerated truths, but in other ways are good predictors of the future trends. For instance, War Games assumed that all computing and control devices were connected via networking technology, and today we see many different internet-connected devices like lights, phones, tablets, doorbells, and others. Thus, the aim of this chapter is to provide an alternate future somewhere between pure science fiction and just a commonly observed trend.

In the rest of this chapter, I present my alternative view of the future based on working quantum technologies. I will describe some past case examples of technologies employed during WWII and technologies that rapidly developed during the 1980's. These examples will highlight how the use of immature technologies can affect the strategic outcomes for war. In addition, these examples show a trend, technologies developed 20 years from now might not even be conceived for another 15 years. Next, I will describe the three phases of quantum technology development. Lastly, I use a fictional narrative to convey the perspective of an individual living in the 2025 to 2045 timeframe to describe how these technologies are impacting the world in that timeframe.

WWII Innovative Technologies

The empires of the future are the empires of the mind – Winston Churchill, 1943

The purpose of this section is to describe examples of innovative technologies that did not exist prior to employment during WWII, but did develop in little to no time. The utility of these WWII technologies drove technology development for the next 70 years. The National WWII Museum has a website [20]. On their website, they have a downloadable poster. The poster lists the 12 major innovative technologies from WWII. These technologies shaped not only the war, but also shaped the development of technologies for years to come. They were, also, quite immature at the start and during the war [21]. The National Museum of the US Air Force also has a number of aircraft deployed during WWII on display [22]. The number and types of aircraft deployed throughout the 40-year history leading up to WWII are staggering. However, the museum provides a good snapshot of how technology evolves in time.

WWII Optimization Problems The Allies needed a way to coordinate large forces. A significant algorithmic or mathematical advancement was the use of techniques developed in the field of operations research (OR). OR is the study of how to mathematically organize troops, logistics, and troop deployment. These techniques enabled the Allies to hunt German U-boats and hold D-Day (aka. Operation Overlord [OO]).

OO occurred on June 6, 1944 and was an Allied attack on the fortified Axis location on the beach in Normandy, France. The Allies used five landing beaches (UTAH, OMAHA, GOLD, UTAH, JUNO, and SWORD) to attack the Germans. This was one of the largest force-on-force operations in history consisting of 8 allied countries, roughly 18,000 vehicles and approximately 328,000 personnel. OO happened without alerting the Germans to the assembly of the Allied force [23, 24]. One of the key advancements was the employment of OR in coordinating this large-scale attack.

WWII Artificial Harbors The Allied forces needed to invade through the shore at Normandy – a location without ports, but it did have deep-water harbors. The deep-water ports would be ideal for supporting a land invasion by sea. To accomplish an attack at Normandy, the Allies constructed two artificial ports (codenamed Mulberry A and B) in England. The Allies then towed these world's first artificial harbors to the Omaha and Gold beaches. There was no long coordinated research and development effort. Someone conceived the ability to do this, and the allies went into action; this was very disruptive. Who would have predicted that the Allies would create ports that did not exist prior to June 6, 1944 to move 12,000 tons of supplies per day [25]?

WWII Missiles WWII was the first war to use rocket-powered missiles – a weapon developed by the Germans during the war called the V2 rocket. Germans used the V2 rockets to terrorize England and kill thousands of people. In 1944, no one else in the world had these type of weapons. The V2 rocket was 12 tons, could carry a 1-ton warhead, and flew at 4000 mph; all at a time when the fastest Allied aircraft flew at about 400 mph. Luckily, these weapons were newly developed and suffered some problems that limited the damage they could have done, because, otherwise, they were impossible to intercept [26]. However, this technology was foundational to the US achieving a successful landing on the moon 25 years later in 1969 via the Apollo 11 Mission [27].

WWII Jet Aircraft In April of 1944, the Germans first used the Messerschmidt ME-262 fighter jet in combat. Again, no one else in the world had this technology. The ME-262 could carry two 550 lb. bombs, fly at 540 mph, and had a 30 mm MK 108 cannon in the nose of the aircraft. However, it had some serious engine problems because the mean time to failure of the engines was about 12 h or less [28]. This first combat use of this jet aircraft caused a revolution in military and civilian aircraft that we still reap the rewards for today.

WWII Code Cracking Computer The Bombe: the mechanical computing machine that enabled the cracking of the German Enigma code. In 1942, Joe Desch, National Cash Register, Dayton, Oh, was tasked with developing and building a less elegant, but faster and more reliable version of the British Bombe that he designed. By 1943, 120 of these machines had been installed, and the US had taken over the task of breaking the majority of the German Naval Enigma traffic [29].

Remotely Piloted Vehicles (RPV) / Unmanned Air Vehicles (UAV)/Precision Guided Munitions (PGM) The Allied forces needed a method to attack the research, development, manufacturing, and launch sites for the V-weapons – like the V2 [30]. One such method was developed by the US included the re-purposing decommissioned B-17's. Under Operation Aphrodite, the US gutted and stripped B-17's of the standard armaments, and retrofitted them with the ability to control them remotely, and thousands of pounds of explosives / bombs. People flying in a nearby CQ-17 Mothership then guided these retrofitted B-17's to their targets [31]. This operation started with pilots just parachuting out of the cockpit in August 1944. The operation ended in January 1945 with remotely controlled airplanes; all conceived, developed, and deployed in a little less than 5 months during the war. We are still to this day using this concept, but with far more advanced machines.

This section illustrated that when the need arises, as it did in WWII, new technologies were developed and deployed in less than the duration of a major world war. In the 4-year period during WWII, the world conceived, designed, developed, and deployed many technologies that drove the development of civilian and military technologies for the next 70 years.

This book aims to describe a picture of what 2035 might look like, but keep in mind that most, if not all, 2035 technologies do not exist, yet. Thus, we can only describe the future based on what we know now. As illustrated by WWII, if a major world war were ever to happen again, you can expect that there is likely to be a similar genesis of new technologies [32, 33]. Thus, predicting the accurate use of technologies is futile. However, we can prepare for the future by estimating the type of expected technologies that will then result in minimizing surprise [2].

Quantum Technologies Leading to 2035

Something unknown is doing something we don't know what. – Sir Arthur Eddington, 1927

Prior to 1900, physics was in theoretical peril. Physicists at the time knew the classical form of the behavior of blackbody radiation as a function of wavelength from the Rayleigh-Jeans law. However, the law was only valid for large wavelengths. If you calculated the law at small wavelengths, the equation predicted infinite energy at zero wavelengths, called the "Ultraviolet Catastrophe". This catastrophe was a real problem because it appeared to violate the law of total energy conservation and observed measurements [34]. In 1900, Planck resolved this issue by making a wild assumption that energy from a black body emitted only "in certain finite chunks" or "quanta". After making this assumption, he was able to derive a form of blackbody radiation that matched measurements and resolved the "ultraviolet catastrophe" [35]. The significance of Planck's assumption was that it started the quantum revolution. Within 20 years, Planck and Einstein won the Nobel Prize in physics (1921, photoelectric effect). In approximately another 10 years, Heisenberg, Schroedinger, and Dirac (1933) won Nobel Prizes for development of the quantum and atomic theories. In another 10 years, contributions by these scientists and many others ultimately lead to the most disruptive technology in humankind – the atomic bomb and nuclear power plants [36, 37].

We are now on the verge of another revolution in quantum technologies. This first phase has already happened. This first phase involved the development of the theory, and corresponding experimental techniques to generate quantum states, and to control them [38]. J. P. Dowling and G. J. Milburn describe the world as undergoing a second quantum revolution by the end of this phase. They described the first revolution as the development of the new quantum rules. Whereas, the second revolution included the development of new quantum technologies based on the new quantum rules of physical reality at the quantum level. I posit that we are still in this second quantum revolution, and will be there until about 2025. Sometime before or during the 2025–2045 period, we will enter into the third quantum revolution – a time where quantum technologies are commonplace, and many new technology advances are occurring rapidly. The pace of development will be as fast as the time during WWII, between 1939 and 1945, but these events will characterize the technology trend for at least another 100 years, and into the twenty-second century.

In the rest of this section, we will fast forward to 40 years later from the first use of the atomic bomb. I will split the recent past, current, and future development of quantum technologies into three phases. I will describe the accomplishments of the first, second, and third phases. Lastly, I will cast these technologies into an operating picture, with the goal of describing a strategic view of the third phase.

1985 – 2005: Kicking Off the Second Quantum Revolution

Someday we'll all have phones as portable as the 11-pound Mobira Talkman. Until then, NTT is making things a little easier with the "Shoulder Phone"… – Engadget, Bulletin Board System, 1985 [39]

The year is 1985. Commodore just released the Amiga 1000 that sold for approximately $1,300 (without the monitor), and the NSFNET was in the process of linking the first five university supercomputers [40]. Bill Gates wrote a letter to Apple suggesting that they should license their hardware and operating system out to other companies [41]. The cell phone was introduced in 1983, and in 1985 the cell phone saw great success with the shoulder portable phone version. By 1987, there were 800,000 cell phone users in the US conducting business, and in general increasing every user's productivity [42]. Thus, the personal computer, the internet, and cell phone was in its infancy in 1985. By the end of Phase I, Youtube was founded, Shop.com had coined the phrase "Cyber Monday", Google Maps launched, Pandora Internet radio service launched, and Star Wars III: Revenge of the Sith was released (every clone trooper costume was computer generated) [43, 44]. The lesson from these 1980's developments is that within 20 years, the computer, cell phone, and internet fundamentally changed the way we as a society communicated and interacted with one another.

In the rest of this section, I will provide a brief history of quantum communications and quantum computing. All of these subjects have many books written about them. Thus, this chapter assumes that the reader is at least familiar with them at a rudimentary level. If not, for quantum communications, please see these references: [45–53]. For quantum computing, see these references: [54–58].

Quantum Communications – History In 1983 Bennett, et al. proposed a method for unforgeable subway tokens [59]. Also prior to 1985, Gilles Brassard and Charles Bennett developed the first quantum key distribution (QKD) protocol, called "BB84," which transfers cipher keys theoretically secure from an attack by a hacker. The security of the key transfer guaranteed by the laws of physics; hence, the name "quantum key distribution". I am skipping significant detail from history on the development of QKD, but it is better read from one of the creators of the first QKD protocol [see reference [60]].

However, throughout the entire 1980's no one took quantum cryptography / QKD seriously until they demonstrated a prototype in 1989 over the open air [60]. In 1991, Arthur Ekert reinvented the BB84 protocol [61]. In 1993, the first fiber optic demonstration occurred at the University of Geneva [62]. In 1997, D. Bouwmester et al, experimentally demonstrated a critical technology for developing quantum computation networks [63]. By 2001, ID Quantique (IDQ) was founded – the world's first commercial QKD company [64]. In 2002, IDQ offered the world's first QKD commercial system. Finally, at the end of this phase, DARPA developed and demonstrated a quantum network via collaboration with BBN Technologies, Boston, and Harvard Universities [65].

Quantum Computing – History In 1982, Richard Feynman suggested that there are classes of quantum mechanical problems that not easily simulated on classical computers; however, these problems would be ideal for simulating on quantum computers [42]. In 1985, David Deutsch provided the first blue print for building a universal quantum computer [66]. In 1994, Peter Shor published a paper that discussed a quantum algorithm intended for a "universal" quantum computer could factor large numbers exponentially faster than any classical computer [67]. In 1995, Lov Grover published a paper describing a quantum algorithm for searching a database (like phone numbers) faster than a classical computer [68]. In 2000, David DiVincenzo published an article describing the criteria for building a quantum computer [69]. Also in 2000, Edward Fahri et al. published a paper describing a quantum algorithm for solving a particular type of optimization problem using a quantum computer [70]. This period -between 1980 and 2000- initiated the foundational development of a new science, called quantum information science (QIS). QIS combines thoughts and concepts from quantum computing with concepts from information theory.

D-Wave Inc.'s, founded in 1999, goal is to be the first commercial company to sell and market a quantum computer. After extensive research on the best method, they down-selected a type of quantum computer based on the ideas from Fahri et al. [71]. There is much scientific debate about whether D-Wave's quantum computer is faster than a classical computer, but it is thought to not be a universal quantum computer [72]. Thus, the D-Wave approach to quantum computing is called quantum annealing, which is good for solving certain types of optimization problems [73]. D-Wave lists the applications for their machine as water network optimization, radiotherapy optimization, protein folding, machine learning, object detection, labeling news stories, video compression, and Monte Carlo simulation [74].

Summary – Quantum communications and computing In this "Second Quantum Revolution", the foundations of quantum communications (or quantum key distribution) and quantum computing solidified into real tangible devices that could be developed and demonstrated. Thus, as we move forward in the quantum development time, the use of these technologies will need factored into the future operating picture. Even though the "Second Quantum Revolution" has not yet resulted in fully realized quantum technologies, lessons from the technology development during WWII taught us that immature technologies were effective during wartime. In addition, like WWII, the technologies deployed for a hypothetical future war in the 2025–2045 timeframe have not been conceived, yet [75].

2005–2025: The Second Revolution in Process

The enemies have a brain, they watch what we do, they make adjustments. – Donald
Rumsfeld, 2006 [76]

The current year is 2015, and we are midway through the Second Revolution.
The "quantum [communications] space race" is in full swing. There are already
many commercial vendors offering quantum key distribution systems: ID Quantique,
SeQureNet SarL, MagiQ Technologies, Quintessence Labs Inc., Raytheon BBN
Technologies, IBM, Nippon Telegraph and Telephone (NTT) Corporation, QinetiQ
Group PLC, Toshiba Corp., and Nucrypt LLC [51]. Thomas Jennewein estimated
the market for quantum cryptography would develop through four separate target
markets. These markets, in order from first to last, are: (1) governments, militaries,
and research institutes; (2) financial institutes and large corporations; (3) public
utilities and small/medium enterprises; (4) other uses [57].

In this part of the "Second Quantum Revolution", we are now starting to see
emerging applications in new fields of QIS. For instance, a 2007 proposed application using quantum physics or "entanglement" enables a technique called quantum
imaging [77]. The proposed advantages of this method is that it can observe blocked
or obscured objects, and promises spatial resolution beyond the diffraction limit
[59]. In 2011, Marco Lanzagorta proposed a quantum radar, which is the quantum
analog to the classical radar [78]. For quantum communications, in 2014, Travis
Humble introduced a type of "software defined quantum communications system"
[79]. This year, in 2015, we start to see the emergence of practical applications, like
the protection of critical infrastructure [80, 81] and quantum clock synchronization
[82]. However, there are also more exotic applications. These applications include:
the ability to transfer quantum information without transmitting physical particles
[83], quantum authentication [84], quantum-advanced encryption standard (Q-AES)
[85], and quantum unclonable functions for authentication [86].

In addition, as mentioned in the previous section, there are also emerging applications
for optimization problems using the quantum annealing approach. Examples include:
mission planning, logistics, systems validation and verification, pattern recognition,
anomaly detection, network science, machine learning, material science, risk modeling,
trading strategies, financial forecasting, and energy exploration [87]. However, the function and claims of the D-Wave machine are the source of much controversy and scientific discussion, but "universal quantum computing of non-trivial size still seems out of
reach" [88].

Summary – Putting it all together The Second Quantum Revolution involves the
development and demonstration of new devices and systems, and the continued
creation of a multitude of new theoretical and practical applications in quantum
communications and computing. This Second Quantum Revolution also involves
the development of entirely new technologies based on the control and manipula-
tion of entanglement (e.g. quantum sensors). In the next section, I will describe the
next revolution, dubbed the "Third Quantum Revolution."

2025–2045: The Rise of the Third Quantum Revolution

I think there is a world market for maybe five computers – Thomas Watson, Chairman of IBM, 1943

The start of this phase begins 10 years from now, and scientific advancement will continue to happen. Daniel Kilper, et al. describe the future of the internet using projected statistics [89]. They estimate that the number of Internet-connected devices will be 6.5 times the world population by 2020. The data needs will grow exponentially, and the growth of energy efficiency devices is not enough to meet the projected demand. This need for energy efficiency for devices will, in part, drive the development of optical networking and the need to make data transfers within colossal data centers more efficient. They expect that by 2017 metropolitan traffic to and from local data centers will surpass long-haul traffic. Of greater concern is that "optical [data] channels are approaching their physical capacity limits…" They further estimate that the demands of the near future will require a higher level of parallelized fiber optic channels, cognitive and real-time optimization, and optical systems that are programmable and virtualizable [51].

In 2011, Amin Vahdat et al. estimated that a data center with over 100,000 servers each operating at 40 Gb/s would require an internal bandwidth 4 petabits/s or $4*10^{15}$ bits per second [90]. This bandwidth is equivalent to transferring approximately 1 million files that are 4 Gb in size every second. However, a hypothetical single quantum computer with 100,000 logical qubits would be capable of executing $2^{100,000}$ operations in a single execution step. If it took one second for that single execution to complete, the quantum computer would have calculated more steps than the simple calculator on my computer can handle. Thus, a large-scale universal quantum computer will be capable of making calculations that will make a large data center computational capabilities look prehistoric. Understand that there are still many significant technical hurdles to overcome, and there are caveats on specific uses for the quantum computer.

In 2013, Rodney Van Meter wrote a book on quantum networking in which he proposes the "quantum recursive network". This new type of network will function as more than just an information transfer network, but it would also function as a "general-purpose distributed quantum computing system" [91]. In 2014, S. B. Sadkhan et al. wrote a book on information security and included a chapter on quantum key distribution networks. In that chapter, they proposed a method called Quantum Secure Socket Layer (QSSL). This new QSSL method extends SSL to the quantum realm to allow quantum key distribution networks to integrate within the current internet security architecture [92].

Summary – Putting it all together Sometime during the 2025–2045 timeframe, we will experience the shift into the Third Quantum Revolution. This phase of development will involve the realization that quantum communications and quantum computing technology are commonplace. This will be responsible for an accelerated technology development phase akin to the development just after WWII, and will likely drive technology development for the next 100 years. However, the uniqueness of this phase is that the number and scale of fundamental new scientific discoveries will increase by at least tenfold. In addition, these developments will spawn multiple new fields of science and engineering that will solve some of the hardest problems currently facing the scientific endeavor.

2025–2045: Quantum Operating Picture

"[Remember the lesson from WWII] Freedom is not free." – An undisclosed Navy D-day WWII vet, 2015
The National WWII Museum has an exhibit on wargaming where patrons can use WWII miniatures for educational purposes. The goal is to play through "historical battles or armies in hypothetical situations" [93]. The museum states that the purpose for educational wargaming is to teach: social skills, critical and strategic thinking, accuracy, and creativity [94]. These attributes require thinking through the various possible combat resolutions by asking the three central questions: (1) "What weapons are being used?" (2) "What percentage of chance do they have to affect the target at range?" (3) "What are the different possible effects that can be created?" [95]

Developing the operating picture for the year 2035 is akin to wargaming in that it requires much creativity. However, it is significantly different in that there is no history to rely upon and the future operating picture is likely not accurate. Like referenced earlier, the goal of looking into the future is to minimize surprise by making educated guesses about what the future might look like [2]. Also mentioned earlier, if you have ever watched science fiction movies, you have seen someone else's wild guess about the military, technological, social, political, and economic situation in the distant future. Storytelling is an effective medium for conveying thoughts about what the future might hold. Therefore, in the rest of this section I will present a fictional monolog aiming to minimize surprise, but not intending to be accurate.

The Operating Picture for the Third Quantum Revolution This is the personal journal of H. M. Edward the III, a quantum scientist. Well, I used to be a quantum scientist, but now I am a quantum engineer. This is not a dig at engineering. It is an example of how the quantum computer has evolved and has lost its science appeal. It has now been 10 years since the development and discovery of the first universal quantum computer, and most of the discoveries have resulted from quantum computers. However, the fundamental advances in quantum computing are more akin to basic engineering. Quantum communications has been around for 20 years; since I was in grade school. My father was a quantum physicist when the field started evolving rapidly, and so I used to hear about the latest and greatest advance – it was a very exciting time. These advancements inspired me to follow his example.

There are now multiple global networks operating based on quantum principles. Quantum communications still exist, because, once a universal computer was working, some smart people figured out ways to by-pass post-quantum cryptographic algorithms using a modified universal quantum computer. However, teleportation based quantum communications networks still exist because they have been able to entangle data at distant data centers. These networks are also able to operate as a distributed quantum computer; capable of shifting resources between data centers if one goes off-line. For approximately $200/year, individuals can purchase the resources of the quantum cloud, which includes secure data storage, transmission, and computation. If you are independently wealthy, you can purchase a brain implant that allows direct access to the quantum cloud without the need for a smartphone or other device. The price you pay is the loss of freedom and independence because you always have to stay relatively close to a functioning quantum node.

I am the Chief Technology Officer for my quantum technologies company. We have some military contracts but by far the largest revenue stream comes from materials development and medical use. We have designed a material that is two or three atoms thick, stronger than titanium, but harvest's about 85 % of the energy from the sunlight impinging on the material. We also have a quantum computer placed at 90 % of the hospitals in America, which are used for developing tailored drug or gene therapy. An individual goes to these hospitals and gets a full diagnostic workup, and the quantum computer then searches for the tailored combination of drugs or gene therapy that will remove any ailment. Virus epidemics are next to zero because the quantum computer can link to all hospitals in the country and solve biochemical reactions at a quantum level thereby helping to determine the needed antibodies for any organism. We make a lot of money from computer maintenance contracts and upgrades.

The military contracts represent a small percentage of our overall business, but they are significant in that we are doing our part to help ensure the American and Allied population remains safe from oppressive aggressors. We no longer have the need to put people in harm's way. Since machines wage war, and few people get killed or injured, the threshold for going to war is a lot lower. Thus, the winner is determined by how advanced the fighting machines are and how many machines are expendable. Additionally, the military quantum computer network can solve a large number of logistics, planning, materials, and technology problems further aiding in the use of machines to wage war.

Our company's quantum computer enabled this advancement in the ability to wage war through machines. Using our quantum computing machines, we have been able to develop an enormous number of materials and devices hardened for operation in multiple environments. Our military can hold any adversary at risk globally through any domain: air, space, ground, water, or cyberspace. For the most part space was an enabler for war but is now commonly a place to wage war; particularly at nearby planets and moons where we still fight over territory and indigenous resources.

By far, the six most enabling military technologies to wage machine war resulted from using the quantum computer to:

1. develop ultra-small clean energy sources;
2. develop new materials, capable of withstanding the battlefield wear and tear;
3. optimize software for autonomous operation;
4. develop small clean propulsion systems;

5. design a capability for the machines to link securely back to the quantum cloud through teleportation based quantum communications networks; and
6. design quantum sensors that operate in GPS-denied environments [96] and detect obscured targets [97].

There have been significant advances in weapons systems too; however, large destructive weapons are not needed to wage effective war. The quantum computer can calculate the best targeting solution across all domains, weapons type, and sensor suites. The result is a top five list of the most practical actions, with the top option being the best option with the least amount of destruction required. Thus, the commander has the option to choose the option based upon the political intent of the action or the required reaction to an aggressor, without concern about collateral damage. The best action will always include the least force required to achieve the military objective. Only a quantum computer can perform the calculations needed to ensure the most probable solution that is also the least likely to cause unwanted second, third, and fourth order effects. -H.M. Edward, 07 Dec 2045

References

1. Townes CH (1999) How the laser happened: adventures of a scientist. Oxford University Press, New York
2. Committee on Forecasting Future Disruptive Technologies, National Research Council (2009) Persistent forecasting of disruptive technologies. The National Academies Press, Washington, DC
3. Muller RA (2010) Physics and technology for future presidents: an introduction to the essential physics every world leader needs to know. Princeton University Press, Princeton
4. Greenberger D et al (2009) Compendium of quantum physics. Springer Science & Business Media, Dordrecht/New York
5. Focus: Nobel Prize – why particles have mass. https://physics.aps.org/articles/v6/111. Accessed 07 Apr 2015
6. What is quantum mechanics good for?. http://www.scientificamerican.com/article/everyday-quantum-physics/. Accessed 07 Apr 2015
7. BruÄŸ D (2002) Characterizing entanglement. J Math Phys 43:4237–4251. http://dx.doi.org/10.1063/1.1494474
8. Plenio MB, Virmani S (2006) An introduction to entanglement measures, arXiv:quant-ph:0504163v3. http://arxiv.org/pdf/quant-ph/0504163.pdf
9. van Enk S (2011) TUTORIAL: entanglement and quantum information theory. In: Frontiers in optics 2011/Laser Science XXVII, OSA Technical Digest (Optical Society of America, 2011), paper FWN2, San Jose
10. Zeilinger A (2000) Quantum entanglement and information. In: Quantum electronics and laser science conference, 2000 (QELS 2000). Technical Digest 163, 12–12, San Francisco
11. Quantum information science (1999) http://www.nsf.gov/pubs/2000/nsf00101/nsf00101.htm. Accessed 07 Apr 2015
12. Jozsa R, Linden N (2002) On the role of entanglement in quantum computational speed-up, arXiv:quant-ph:0201143
13. Hurst C (2015) The quantum leap into computing and communication: a Chinese perspective – Analysis. Jt Forces Q 77:44–50
14. US Air Force Chief Scientist (2011) Technology horizons: a vision for Air Force science and technology 2010-30. Air University Press

15. Titterton DH (2015) Military laser technology and systems., Artech House, pp 432–435
16. War Games. http://www.imdb.com/title/tt0086567/synopsis?ref_=tt_stry_pl. Accessed 07 Apr 2015
17. Colossus: The Forbin Project (1970) http://www.imdb.com/title/tt0064177/. Accessed 07 Apr 2015
18. 2001: A Space Odyssey. http://www.imdb.com/title/tt0062622/. Accessed 07 Apr 2015
19. The Terminator (1984) http://www.imdb.com/title/tt0088247/. Accessed 07 Apr 2015
20. The National WWII Museum. http://nationalww2museum.org. Accessed 16 Apr 2015
21. The war that changed the world: how science and technology of World War II influences your life today. http://nnwwiim.org/image/sci-tech-wii-poster.pdf. Accessed 16 Apr 2015
22. WWII Gallery. http://ww.nationalmuseum.af.mil/exhibits/airpower/index.asp. Accessed 20 Apr 2015.
23. D-Day (1944), http://www.pbs.org/thewar/detail_5217.htm. Accessed 16 Apr 2015
24. World War II: D-day, The Invasion of Normandy. Http://eisenhower.archives.gov/research/online_documents/d_day.htm. Accessed 16 Apr 2015
25. Mulberry Artificial Harbors – Normandy, WWII. http://worldwar2headquarters.com/HTML/normandy/mulberries/mulberry-harbor.html. Accessed 16 Apr 2015
26. Germany conducts first successful V-2 rocket test. http://www.history.com/this-day-in-history/germany-conducts-first-successful-v-2-rocket-test. Accessed 16 Apr 2015
27. Apollo 11: First landing on the moon. https://www.youtube.com/watch?v=RMINSD7MmT4. Accessed 16 Apr 2015
28. ME 262. http://www.warbirdalley.com/me262.htm. Accessed 16 Apr 2015
29. Bombe. http://www.cryptomuseum.com/crypto/bombe. Accessed 16 Apr 2015
30. Operation Crossbow. http://self.gutenberg.org/articles/Operation_Crossbow. Accessed 20 Apr 2015
31. Operation Aphrodite. http//www.self.gutenberg.org/articles/operation_aphrodite. Accessed 20 Apr 2015
32. Civil War Technology. http://www.history.com/topics/american-civil-war/civil-war-technology. Accessed 20 Apr 2015
33. WWI: technology and the weapons of war. http://ncpedia.org/wwi-technology-and-weapons-war. Accessed 20 Apr 2015
34. On the law of distribution of energy in the normal spectrum. http://axion.physics.ubc.ca/200-06/Planck-1901.html. Accessed 16 Apr 2015
35. Black Body Radiation. http://www.cv.nrao.edu/course/astr534/BlackBodyRad.html. Accessed 16 Apr 2015
36. All Nobel Prizes in Physics. http://www.nobelproze.org/nobel_prizes/physics/laureates. Accessed 16 Apr 2015
37. Baggott J (2011) The First War of Physics: The Secret History of the Atom Bomb, 1939-1949. Pegasus Books, New York
38. Dowling JP, Milburn GJ (2003) Quantum technology: the second quantum revolution. Philos Trans Royal Soc London Series A Math Phys Eng Sci 361(1809):1655–1674
39. Cell phones. http://www.engadget.com/2005/08/22/engadget-1985/. Accessed 16 Apr 2015
40. 1985 Computer History. http://www.computerhistory.org/timeline/?year=1985. Accessed 16 Apr 2015
41. In 1985 bill gates pitched apple to make macintosh into windows. http://www.cultofmac.com/148548/in-1985-bill-gates-pitched-apple-to-make-macintosh-into-windows/. Accessed 16 Apr 2015
42. Mobile telephones for all occasions. Http://www.nytimes.com/1987/09/23/business/mobile-telephones-for-all-occasions.html. Accessed 16 Apr 2015
43. Computer History – 2005. http://www.computerhope.com/history/2005.htm. Accessed 16 Apr 2015
44. Star Wars: Episode III – Revenge of the Sith; trivia. http://www.imdb.com/title/tt012766/trivia. Accessed 16 Apr 2015

45. Clavis 2 whitepaper. www.idquantique.com/wordpress/wp-content/uploads/clavis2-whitepaper. pdf. Accessed 16 Apr 2015
46. Gisin N, Ribordy G, Tittel W, Zbinden H. Quantum cryptography, arXiv:quantph/0101098v2. http://arxiv.org/pdf/quant-ph/0101098v2.pdf
47. Langer T, Lenhart G (2009) Standardization of quantum key distribution and the ETSI standardization initiative ISG-QKD. New J Phys 11
48. Elliott C, Colvin A, Pearson D, Pikalo O, Schlafer J, Yeh H (2005) Current status of the DARPA quantum network, arXiv:quant-ph/0503058. http://arxiv.org/pdf/quant-ph/0503058v2.pdf
49. Hoi-Kwong L (1999) Will quantum cryptography ever become a successful technology in the market place? arXiv:quant-ph/9912011v1. http://arxiv.org/pdf/quant-ph/9912011v1.pdf
50. Al Natsheh A, Gbadegeshin SA, Rimpiläinen A, Imamovic-Tokalic I, Zambrano A (2015) Identifying the challenges in commercializing high technology: a case study of quantum key distribution technology. Technol Innov Manag Rev 5(1):26–36, http://timreview.ca/article/864
51. Jennewein T, Choi E. Quantum cryptography: 2014 market study and business opportunities assessment. Institute for Quantum Computing, University of Waterloo, IQC-QPL-R-1403001, Rev. C, 9 July 2014
52. Weinfurterq, et al. Quantum key distribution and cryptography: a survey, http://vesta.informatik.rwth-aachen.de/opus/volltexte/2010/2361/pdf/09311.AlleaumeRomain.Paper.2361.pdf. Accessed 16 Apr 2015
53. Stuhler J (2015) Quantum optics route to market. Nat Phys 11(4):293–295
54. Nielsen MA, Chuang IL (2010) Quantum computation and quantum information. Cambridge University Press, Cambridge/New York
55. Steane A (1997) Quantum computing, arXiv:quant- ph/9708022. http://arxiv.org/pdf/quant-ph/9708022v2.pdf
56. Kok P, et al (2006) Linear optical quantum computing, arXiv:quant-ph/0512071v2
57. Google and NASA's Quantum Artificial Intelligence Lab. https://www.youtube.com/watch?t=32&v=CMdHEuOUE. Accessed 16 Apr 2015.
58. Nielsen M. Quantum computing for everyone. http://micahelnielsen.org/blog/quantum-computing-for-everyone. Accessed 16 Apr 2015
59. Bennett CH et al (1983) Quantum cryptography, or unforgeable subway tokens. In: Advances in cryptography. Springer, Boston
60. Brassard G (2006) A brief history of quantum cryptography: a personal perspective, arXiv:quantph/0604072v1. http://arxiv.org/pdf/quant-ph/0604072v1.pdf
61. Ekert AK (1991) Quantum cryptography based on Bell's theorem. Phys Rev Lett 67:661
62. Clavis 2 white paper. www.idquantique.com/wordpress/wp-content/uploads/clavis2-whitepaper. pdf. Accessed 16 Apr 2015
63. Bouwmeester D et al (1997) Experimental quantum teleportation. Nature 390:575–579
64. ID Quantique Company Profile. http://www.idquantique.com/about-idq/company-profile/. Accessed 16 Apr 2015
65. Deutsch D (1985) Quantum theory, the Church-Turing principle and the universal quantum computer. Proc R Soc Lond A 400:97–117. doi:10.1098/rspa.1985.0070.Published8July1985
66. Steane A (1997) Quantum computing, arXiv:quant- ph/9708022. http://arxiv.org/pdf/quant-ph/9708022v2.pdf
67. Shor PW (1995) Polynomial-time algorithms for prime factorization and discrete logarithms on a quantum computer, arXiv:quant-ph/9508027. http://arxiv.org/pdf/quant-ph/9508027v2. pdf
68. Grover LK (1996) A fast quantum mechanical algorithm for database search, arXiv:quant-ph/9605043. http://arxiv.org/pdf/quant-ph/9605043v3.pdf
69. DiVincenzo DP (2000) The physical implementation of quantum computation, arXiv: quant-ph/0002077v3. http://arxiv.org/pdf/quant-ph/0002077.pdf
70. Fhari E et al (2000) Quantum computation by adiabatic evolution, arXiv:quant-ph/0001106v1. http://arxiv.org/pdf/quant-ph/0001106v1.pdf
71. D-Wave company website. http://www.dwavesys.com/our-company/meet-d-wave. Accessed 16 Apr 2015

72. Is D-Wave quantum computer actually a quantum computer? http://physicsworld.com/cws/article/news/2014/jun/20/is-d-wave-quantum-computer-actually-a-quantum-computer. Accessed 16 Apr 2015
73. An introduction to quantum annealing (2007) http://dwave.files.wordpress.com/2007/08/20070810_d-wave_quantum_annealing.pdf. Accessed 16 Apr 2015
74. D-Wave Applications. http://www.dwavesys.com/quantum-computing/applications. Accessed 16 Apr 2015
75. This is an example that quantum technologies will continue to evolve creating new opportunities in "finance, defense, aerospace, energy, and telecommunications": UK National Technologies Programme: National strategy for quantum technologies, Quantum technologies strategic advisory board, March 2015. https://www.epsrc.ac.uk/newsevents/pubs/quantumtechstrategy/. Accessed 01 May 2015
76. Transcript of Donald H. Rumsfeld, US Secretary of Defense Farewell Speech. http://www.washingtonpost.com/wp-dyn/content/article/2006/12/08/AR2006120800850.html. Accessed 28 May 2015
77. Shih Y (2007) Quantum imaging, arXiv:quant-ph/0707.0268v1
78. Lanzagorta M (2012) Quantum radar. Morgan & Claypool, San Rafael
79. Humble TS, Sadlier RJ (2014) Software defined quantum communication systems. Opt Eng 53(8):086103
80. Karol M, Zyczkowski M (2015) Quantum technology in critical infrastructure protection. Saf Secur Eng VI 151:109
81. Hughes RJ et al (2013) Network-centric quantum communications with applications to critical infrastructure protection, arXiv:1305.0305. http://arxiv.org/pdf/1305.0305v1.pdf
82. Tavakoli A et al (2015) Quantum clock synchronization with a single qudit. Sci Rep 5:7982
83. Guo Q et al (2015) Counterfactual quantum-information transfer without transmitting any physical particles. Sci Rep 5:8416
84. Luo YP, Hwang T. Authenticated semi-quantum direct communication protocols using Bell states, arXiv:quant-ph/1503.08967. http://arxiv.org/pdf/1503.08967v1.pdf
85. Jasim OK et al (2015) Evolution of an emerging symmetric quantum cryptographic algorithm, arXiv:quant-ph/1503.04796. http://arxiv.org/pdf/1503.04796v1.pdf
86. Roberts J et al (2015) Atomic-scale authentication using resonant tunneling diodes, arXiv:quant-ph/1502.06523
87. http://www.dwavesys.com/quantum-computing/industries. Accessed 16 Apr 2015
88. Troyer M (2015) Beyond Moore's law: towards competitive quantum devices, 46th annual meeting of the APS division of atomic, molecular and optical physics, Columbus
89. Kilper D, Bergman K, Chen VWS, Monga I, Porter G, Rauschenbach K (2014) Optical networks come of age. OSA Opt Photon News 25:50–57
90. Vahdat A, Liu H, Zhao X, Johnson C (2011) The emerging optical data center. In: Optical fiber communication conference/National fiber optic engineers conference. OSA Technical Digest (CD) (Optical Society of America, 2011), paper OTuH2
91. Van Meter R (2013) Quantum networking. Wiley, Hoboken
92. Sadkhan SB et al (2014) Multidisciplinary perspectives in cryptology and information security. IGI Global
93. Educational WWII wargaming. http://www.nationalww2museum.org/learn/educational-wwii-wargaming/index.html. Accessed 16 Apr 2015
94. Choosing wargames. http://www.nationalww2museum.org/learn/educational-wwii-wargaming/choosing-wargames.html. Accessed 16 Apr 2015
95. About wargaming. http://www.nationalww2museum.org/learn/educational-wwii-wargaming/about-wargaming.html. Accessed 16 Apr 2015
96. MoD creates coldest object in the universe to trump GPS. http://www.telegraph.co.uk/technology/news/10833087/MoD-creates-coldest-object-in-the-universe-to-trump-GPS.html. Accessed 16 Apr 2015
97. Meyers RE (2010) Diffraction free light source for ghost imaging of objects viewed through obscuring media. No. ARL-TR-5095. Army Research Lab, Adelphi MD, Computational and Information Sciences Directorate

Dark Web and the Rise of Underground Networks

Tim Singletary

What Is the "DarkNet"

When you think of the "DarkNet" as it is commonly referred to, you must first understand the "Internet".

The Internet

There is quite a bit of debate over who exactly created the Internet these days. Determining if it was Xerox, ARAPNET, Vincent Cerf and Robert Kahn, Steve Jobs or Philip Emeagwali is irrelevant. It is here, an intertwined network within a global network comprised of computers of every range, size and capacity.

Those making claims of creating (or co-creating) the Internet almost all had grand visions of global communications, collaboration between countries and their citizen's, the awe inspiring "one world" where everyone communicates peacefully and solves all of the problems we as humans and the planet face. It sounds great, too bad that is not what happened. Society was not ready for the explosion of the "Internet of Everything" discussed in the previous chapters.

So what did we end up with? It is commonly referred to as a global network of interconnected devices capable of communicating at the speed of light. The social, economic and cyber warfare impact of the Internet will follow us for generations. The Internet can and is being used for some good things, but what most good "netizens"

T. Singletary (✉)
Techncial Director, Cyber Security Services, Harris – Information & Cyber Solutions,
474 Phoenix Drive, Rome, NY 13441, USA
e-mail: Tim.Singletary@Harris.com

© Springer International Publishing Switzerland 2015   107
M. Blowers (ed.), *Evolution of Cyber Technologies and Operations to 2035*,
Advances in Information Security 63, DOI 10.1007/978-3-319-23585-1_8

don't understand is the darker side of the internet. Most people think of Microsoft™, Apple™, or Google™ when you say the Internet. In reality, those companies are only a fraction of the Internet's traffic. There are some metrics for how much of the Internet Google indexes, which is as low as 4 % and as high as 40 %. You would think with all of the computational power of the Internet that this would be an easy number to calculate. The problem is there are literally millions of web sites, and specifically non-registered web servers that Google knows nothing about. If it does not know about them, it cannot index them. If it cannot index them, then unless you know the transmission control protocol/internet protocol (TCP/IP) specific address, you will never get to them.

Another issue is that the "Internet" was built upon TCP/IP. There are many different pieces to TCP/IP and other protocols (User Datagram Protocol [UDP]) that are allowed over the internet transmission lines. What most consumers see are just the systems responding to a Hyper Text Transfer Protocol (HTTP) request.

Caveat Emptor, any site Uniform Resource Locator (URL) after this section should be visited only in a secure computing environment.

DeepWeb

The Deep Web, also sometimes referred to as "Deepnet" is specifically defined as public facing systems that are not indexed by Google, Bing and Yahoo. The Deep Web has commonly been associated with an iceberg, where parts are visible but underneath the water lays a large and more ominous threat (Fig. 1).

The Deep Web is exactly that, where the type of content found within is most likely not suitable for the average person. The Deep Web is filled with sites that will allow you to test your morals on many different levels. From bootlegged music and videos, pornographic material, to scams of every shape and size. There are specific search engines used for searching the Deep Web.

Housed within the Deep Web, you are going to find the majority of the "script kiddie" scams, Advanced Persistent Threats (APT), Malware and individuals with malicious intent. This is the place you go late at night while bored and thinking no one is watching you, and suddenly you end up with endless porn popups careening across your screen faster than you can close them. The next thing you know you have somehow downloaded a "dropper", and everything on your computer is exfiltrated into the vast darkness of the Deep Web. On top of that, every person that was in your contacts list is now getting emails from you, inviting them to visit the same nefarious website that started this.

The DeepWeb is filled with unlinked content (web pages not linked to other web pages), private web pages that require authentication to access, controlled access content (using technical means to control what is indexed for example Robots.txt file), scripted content that is only accessible through JavaScript, non-HTTP(S) content like Gopher and File Transfer Protocol (FTP) servers filled with just about

Fig. 1 http://www.taringa.net/posts/humor/18533513/Te-gusta-el-iceberg-de-la-deep-web-pasate-papu.
html

anything that one could imagine. You can find intellectual property and trade secrets stolen from corporations, government secrets (supposedly), and personal information on individuals that have had their identity stolen. In short, if you can imagine it, you can probably find it. The problem with the Deep Web is that it is festering with individuals seeking to be anonymous and cyber-criminals.

The individuals that have content on this part of the Deep Web know that the people that visit their sites are usually the ones that stumbled across them accidentally, or they are the type that are gullible enough to fall for an obvious scam.

FACT: There are no Nigerian Royalty that you are distantly related to that has 5 million EUROS that they want to share with you, if you will only send them

$500.00US and your bank account information. (This is an old example, but still active and relevant today.)

The Deep Web is also where the majority of the criminal entities on the Internet lurk. Criminal organizations like the "Russian Business Network" (RBN) routinely use the Deep Web for selling private information stolen off of computer systems around the world, such as medical records, banking and credit card information most commonly used in identity theft. This is a multi-billion dollar industry that is ever-growing each and every week. This portion of the Internet is that dark alley on the bad side of town you do not want to get caught in.

This is also the portion of the Internet that is constantly being monitored by not only nefarious types but by government and law enforcement agencies. It is easily monitored as most of the traffic going across it is through unencrypted Hyper Text Transfer Protocol (HTTP) or Hyper Text Transfer Protocol Secure (HTTPS). Don't be fooled by the "S" secure portion of that protocol, it is far from secure in the Deep Web. A basic "man-in-the –middle" attack, where a malicious individual is able to get into the data stream between your browser client and the secure server, is quite easy if you have been targeted or if the attacker has control over one of the endpoints.

DarkNet

The DarkNet, this is the deepest area of the Deep Web, and the hardest to get to. The DarkNet is a level of the Internet that only the computer savvy should be venturing into. This is where the great white 0day lives and thrives. You can find anything and everything known to man here, both legal and illegal. Illegal drugs, weapons, even hitmen advertise in this part of the web. All of it can be conveniently delivered to your front door via UPS and Fed-Ex.

The major difference between the DarkNet and the Deep Web, other than the caliber of criminal, is how you get there. The DarkNet does not always rely on TCP/IP for the transport. Other protocols are involved and it seems that every time the mainstream public (or law enforcement) catches wind of a new method being used, a newer and different method starts being used to reach this portion of the Internet. Below are some of the different methods of connecting to the DarkNet.

DarkNet-IRC

Internet Relay Chat, also known as IRC, has been around for years. It is a distant cousin of the old Bulletin Board Networks (BBN's) of the modem and dial-up age. IRC is mostly text based "chat rooms" and forums that are created by users, monitored by a moderator, and can even have controlled access. If you are not invited into a controlled room, you simply do not get in. Many of these rooms are not publicized. However, there are many that are publicized and open for anyone to join. These chat rooms can cover every range of subject areas, from the benign conspiracy theory, to organized crime groups coordinating an attack.

IRC works on a client-server model. You must install client software and point it to a server in order to connect to the IRC network. The server then "relays" messages to other clients in the room or "channel". It is estimated that there are roughly 1500 servers globally supporting the IRC networks. Some of these servers are public and anyone can connect. Many of them are private and you must pay a subscription based fee to join the servers. This subscription based model helps restrict the servers to those that are looking for privacy on IRC. Some of the largest IRC networks are Freenode, IRCNet, Quakenet, EFnet, Undernet, and Rizon. There are very few IRC servers that can utilize SSL/TLS to communicate; if you are not on one of those few, your IRC communications are susceptible to interception.

IRC utilizes TCP/IP protocol for its primary communications. Several of the more modern clients now support Client to Client Protocol (CTCP), Direct Client to Client (DCC) and TCP/IP version 6. To increase security and anonymity a few clients support DNS based Authentication of Named Entities (DANE), Online Certificate Status Protocol (OCSP), Certificate Revocation List (CRL), Simple Authentication and Security Layer (SASL), and Off the Record (OTR). IRC servers utilize TCP/IP ports 6660-6669, IRC clients use 6668. If you are using Direct Client to Client the software will dynamically open ports above port 1024 and below port 5000.

Next is a list of the different clients and the protocols they support (Fig. 2).

DarkNet-TOR

The TOR (The Onion Router) network is your first deep-dive into the DarkNet. It is aptly named after an onion which has many layers to it. Once one layer is peeled away, you must peel away another layer and another to get to the heart of the onion. TOR uses a custom browser that can be downloaded from https://www.torproject.org/. Once downloaded and installed, it will connect to a secure server and start routing your browser request through several "TOR" servers to mask your identity. The TOR network was developed to keep websites from being able to track a person's identity via their web browser signature and TCP/IP address. So how does TOR work? Let's take a look.

1. Install the TOR browser (link above)
2. Once the TOR browser is installed, select the TOR browser icon to start the browser.
3. When the browser starts, it automatically connects to a TOR server and downloads a list of servers open for connection.

Client ▲	CTCP ♦	DCC ♦	IPv6 ♦	SSL ♦	TLS ♦	DANE ♦	OCSP ♦	CRL ♦	SASL ♦	OTR ♦
AdilRC	Yes	Yes	Yes	Yes	?	?	?	?	script	No
AmIRC	Yes	Yes	No	No	No	?	No	No	?	No
Bersirc	?	Partial	No	No	?	?	?	?	?	No
BitchX	Yes	Yes	Yes	Yes	Yes	?	?	?	?	No
ChatZilla	Yes	Yes	Yes	Yes	Yes	?	Yes	Yes	script	No
Colloquy	Yes	Yes	Yes	Yes	?	?	?	?	Yes	No
Convos	?	?	?	?	?	?	?	?	?	?
DMDirc	Yes	Yes	Yes	Yes	?	?	?	?	?	No
ERC	Partial	Yes	Yes	Yes	Yes	?	?	?	Yes[Note 1]	No
f-irc	Yes	Yes	Yes	?	?	?	?	?	?	No
HexChat	Yes	Yes	Yes	Yes	Yes	No	No	No	Yes	Yes[Note 2]
HydraIRC	Yes	Yes	?	No	No	?	No	No	?	No
IceChat	Yes	Yes	Yes	Yes	?	?	?	?	Yes	No
ii (IRC IT)	?	No	Yes[Note 1]	Yes[Note 1]	Yes[Note 1]	?	?	?	?	No
ircII	Yes	Yes	Yes	No	?	?	?	?	?	No
IRCjr	Yes	No	No	No	No	?	No	No	No	No
Ircle	Yes	Yes	?	Yes	?	?	?	?	?	No
Irssi	Yes	Yes	Yes	Yes	Yes	Yes	No	?	script	Yes[85][86][Note 2]
jIRCii	Yes	Yes	Yes	Yes	?	?	?	?	?	No
KiwiIRC	Yes	No	Yes	Yes	No	?	No	No	No	No
Konversation	Yes	Yes	Yes	Yes	Yes	?	?	?	Yes	No
KVIrc	Yes	Yes	Yes	Yes	Yes	?	No	No	Yes	No
LeetIRC[34]	No	Partial	No	No	No	?	No	No	?	No
LimeChat	?	Yes	Yes	Yes	?	?	?	?	Yes	No
Lingo	Yes	Yes	Yes	Yes	Yes	?	Yes	Yes	Yes	No
Linkinus	Yes	Yes	No	Yes	?	?	?	?	No	No
Mibbit	?	Partial[Note 3][Note 4]	No	Yes	?	?	?	?	Yes	No
mIRC	Yes	Yes	Yes	Yes	?	?	?	?	script	No
Neebly	Yes	Yes	No	No	?	?	?	?	?	No
Nettalk	Yes	Yes	No	No	?	?	?	?	?	No
Opera	Yes[97]	Yes	Yes	Yes	Yes	?	?	?	?	No
PIRCH	Yes	Yes	No	No	?	?	?	?	?	No
PJIRC	?	Yes	No	No	?	?	?	?	?	No
Quassel	Yes	No	Yes	Yes	Yes	?	No	No	Yes	No
qwebirc	Yes	No	No	Yes	No	?	No	No	No	No
rcirc	Partial	No	No	Yes	Yes	?	?	?	?	No
Scrollback	Partial	No	Yes	Yes	?	?	?	?	No	No
Smuxi	Yes	No	Yes	Yes	?	?	?	?	No	No
Snak	Yes	Yes	Yes	Yes	?	?	?	?	?	No
Textual	Yes	Yes	Yes	Yes	Yes	?	Yes[Note 5]	Yes[Note 5]	Yes	Yes[88]
Visual IRC	Yes	Yes	No	No	?	?	?	?	?	No

Fig. 2 http://en.wikipedia.org/wiki/Comparison_of_Internet_Relay_Chat_clients#cite_note-patch-100

4. The TOR browser then selects a "path" to send the Hyper Text Markup Language (HTML) request utilizing several of the TOR servers.
5. Every time you start a new session with another website, the TOR browser selects a different path to that server. This ensures that no one server can be used to track you.

That's the basics of how the TOR network connects. Again this system was originally designed to protect a user's identity on the internet and prevent tracking. The TOR network can be used to visit any website either on the visible Internet, Deep Web, or DarkNet. Like with all technology, it can be abused, and the TOR networks are no different. It quickly became the standard for underground or DarkNet websites. This prevents the day to day internet users from seeing specific websites designed to be only seen by a TOR server. The web sites usually end in a ".onion" name as opposed to a .com URL.

When you first establish a connection to the TOR network, the first page that opens by default in the browser is the TOR "Startpage" which is a basic search engine similar to Google. Although it is a search engine, it is not all encompassing of the TOR network or the DarkNet, it is simply a starting point. In order to get deeper into the DarkNet you have to use a different search engine or know where the site address resides. One of the most popular DarkNet search engines is https://ahmi.fi. Here, you can start your deep-dive into the sites that most people do not see and quite frankly may not want to see.

Other search engines on the TOR network:

Search engine	Address
TorBlackmarket	http://7v2i3bwsaj7cjs34.onion/
Zanzibar's underground marketplace	http://okx5b2r76olbriil.onion/
Black Market Reloaded	http://5onwnspjvuk7cwvk.onion/index.php
The Black Market	http://ie66qw46jejj4zn2.onion/
IsraService	http://fpgigmfnlscyok5h.onion/
GermanWeed	http://yyz57kb55zslet4c.onion/
TorDrugResource	http://y47ylcppnh3afqk4.onion/
Sheep Marketplace	http://sheep5u64fi457aw.onion/

The DarkNet is overflowing with every type of website one can imagine, from political activist's, to illegal drug sales, to Hackers and Malware for hire. It is not a place for the novice to hang out. And although the TOR browser does somewhat hide your identity, it is not perfect either. TOR browsers are based off of Firefox™ and have been known to contain vulnerabilities just like any other browser. The browser also by default turns off quite a bit of the "normal" attack vectors used by malware and APT. The issue though is that most people like having the "Flash" video from an underground website and will start turning things back on for convenience, even though the browser will prompt you several times and "suggest" you do not turn on those features. Once this happens and your browser is compromised, you might as well be using Internet Explorer to surf the shark infested waters of the DarkNet. Good luck.

So how do we surf the DarkNet and still maintain some sort of security and limit what the attack vectors are? Well, here are a few suggestions. First off never, ever, go to the DarkNet from a corporate or government computer or network. Don't take your corporate or government laptop home and connect to the DarkNet from your home high-speed cable connection. Build a computer that at any given point can be completely wiped, or better yet have the hard drive replaced if you suspect it has been compromised. In other words, do not download anything, copy it to a thumb drive and plug it into your work computer.

Once you have that clean install of your favorite operating system, the next step is to install the free VMWare player (download from VMWare.com). Once you have VMWare player installed, you can either download one of several bootable International Standards Organization (ISO) images (i.e. Anonym.OS, Tails), or create a new Virtual Machine (VM) and install your favorite operating system. Anonym.OS and Tails already have the TOR browser installed so there's no need to install it in those solutions. If your favorite operating systems is Windows™ based, after you create the VM it is suggested that you download a "sandbox" application like Sandboxie™ (http://www.sandboxie.com) and install it. Sandboxie™ will allow you to run your TOR browser in a "sandboxed" virtual environment and not allow anything in that browser session to write to your hard drive. It may seem redundant to run Sandboxie in your VM, but if Windows™ is your host operating system, it is better to be safe than sorry. For those extremely paranoid Windows™ users, another free application that can be useful is Timefreeze™ (http://www. majorgeeks.com/files/details/toolwiz_time_freeze.html). Timefreeze™ installs on your host, not your VM. Once it is installed, start the "timefreeze" application, open your VM, open your sandboxed TOR browser, and then connect to the DarkNet. The Timefreeze application on your host actually shims between your hardware and the host OS and does not allow anything to be written to your host. If some application or process attempts that action, you can just "undo" it by rebooting the host and it goes back to the exact state it was in before you froze it.

One of the more common places on the DarkNet that you may want to check out is a site called Pastebin (http://pastebin.com). Although you can navigate there using a "normal" browser, it is not recommended as it may contain leaked classified government data. If you hold a security clearance with the government and come across this data you are supposed to report it. Depending on the information reported you may end up getting your computer confiscated and wiped. Pastebin is a web site dedicated to all things (data) exfiltrated on the internet, Deep Web, and DarkNet.

The raw output below was actually taken off of pastebin.onion, listing instructions and places to go on the DarkNet to get you started. Remember; enter at your own risk.

Deep web pastebin GO GO!!

How To:

Download Tor + Browser (leaves no trace)

https://www.torproject.org/projects/torbrowser.html.en

Find links! Start out:

http://en.wikipedia.org/wiki/.onion#Onion_Sites

The Silk Road where u can buy drugs =o

http://ianxz6zefk72ulzz.onion/index.php

The Hidden Wiki! Can potentially find everything from here!

http://kpvz7ki2v5agwt35.onion/wiki/index.php/Main_Page

Contains Tor Library

http://am4wuhz3zifexz5u.onion/

Open Vendor Database (discusses non onion drug websites too!)

http://g7pz322wcy6jnn4r.onion/opensource/ovdb/ac/index.php

The General Store (more drugs)

http://xqz3u5drneuzhaeo.onion/users/generalstore/

A bunch of rather popular boards (like Intel Exchange and

http://4eiruntyxxbgfv7o.onion/snapbbs/sitedex.php

Most popular chan on tor (Arguably) comparable to 4chan

http://b4yrk2nkydqfpzqm.onion/mobile/

Directory/list of links

http://dppmfxaacucguzpc.onion/

Another chan

http://c7jh7jzl3taek4eh.onion/

pastebin

DarkNet-Peer-to-Peer (P2P)

The P2P networking concept is not new; it is however, the next step hiding in the DarkNet. Sometimes called Person-to Person, P2P network utilizes a distributed networking architecture where instead of connecting to a server to hide your identity, you connect directly to another peer computer to access the resources on it. The TOR browser actually has plugins that will allow P2P connections right in the browser. Other P2P software applications include Nodezilla™, Vuze™, Morpheus™, Luckywire™ to name a few.

The primary use of the P2P networking these days is for file sharing, which in and of itself is a very dangerous practice on the DarkNet. Regardless of whether it's an application, music, or that latest ripped DVD you have wanted to get your hands on, there is a pretty good chance that it has malware attached to it. Other than fame, political, or social motivations why else would anyone purchase an actual copy of DRM software/music/video, go through the trouble of ripping it to remove the Digital Rights Management (DRM) and give it away for free? Most likely it is because it has malware in it that will allow your P2P "friend" to remotely connect to your machine and steal any other software, thereby continuing the cycle. Worse yet, they could just take all of your personal information and put it out on Pastebin, or sell it to one of the other nefarious groups on the internet. A growing and disturbing trend is using your Personal Computer (PC) as part as a "Pay by the Hour" BotNet in order to launch a Distributed Denial of Service (DDOS) attack on legitimate sites on the internet.

From a security perspective, P2P DarkNet is no more secure than any other method of accessing the DarkNet. If you have to check out this method, remember Sandboxie, and run your client in a sandbox instead of straight from your host.

DarkNet-Invisible Internet Project (I2P)

Invisible Internet Project (I2P) adds another layer to normal internet based traffic. Similar to the TOR network, I2P uses computers and servers running as an I2P node. Once you have installed the I2P client software, it automatically adds your system to the known node list for others to relay through, but you can control how many systems your computer is allowed to relay for. I2P is advertised as pseudonymously and as a secure connection to the internet and DarkNet. The open source specifications were first developed in 2003 and did not really have a robust following until recently when internet privacy became a publicized issue. Like many of the other methods of connecting to the Internet and the darker sides of it (Deep Web, DarkNet), it was originally conceived to address personal privacy concerns. Like every good technology, it has garnered interest from the underground Internet world as well.

I2P works by setting up tunnels from one client to another. Once these tunnels are setup, they can be used by other I2P applications installed on the local system to utilize these tunnels. The tunnels are encrypted and actually enhance the privacy and anonymity of the connections. With that said, this is also the slowest of the connection methods to the DarkNet. Other typical issues revolve around who is actually connecting to your machine for a tunnel. Can they break out of the tunnel and affect your host? What type of data is being tunneled through your system? If the data being sent through your I2P node is considered illegal, you could face issues with law enforcement if your node was the last one traced.

As well as being the slowest, I2P is also the most complex to setup and we have already seen many vendors offering "pay for access" I2P nodes to allow access to specific DarkNet sites. I2P allows for I2P chat sessions, I2P file sharing (including BitTorrent types), and I2P DarkNet web browsing. Users cannot connect to any resources outside of the I2P network, and each application utilizing the I2P tunnel has to be specifically written to work on an I2P network. In other words, you cannot install I2P client software and then open Firefox™ and start browsing DarkNet sites unless they are I2P compliant.

I2P currently has a free email service domain (mail.I2P) run by an individual with the alias of "Postman". Susimail is the most popular I2P web based mail client being used today. Mail being sent via Susimail uses the user@mail.i2p routing domain. Another popular mail system utilizing I2P is I2P-Bote, which utilizes a fully decentralized and distributed mail system. It adds several layers of security by encrypting the emails, and not exposing the email headers. This is very similar to setting up an IPSec tunnel currently used by corporations and government entities today. I2P-Messenger is the final piece of the I2P puzzle allowing real-time chat sessions between users of the I2P networks.

Eepsite (Encrypted-encrypted Peer) are the web sites that are hosted anonymously on the I2P DarkNet. They utilize a proxy based network, including using the peers and client nodes to share routing of packets destined for the I2P network.

Future of the DarkNet

The future of the DarkNet is full of awe inspiring technological feats and dangers at the same time. We only have to look back over the last 20 years of technology advances and analyze their uses, both legitimate and the Darker uses.

One of the biggest issues we face as a society is not some new sophisticated attack or piece of technology, it's the technology that is presented to end users, the maturity of that technology, and how can the bad guys use it against "normal" net-abiding citizens.

We have been continuously plagued with technology that from a security perspective was not ready to be released to the general public. This is not just a Microsoft vs Apple issue; it is much broader than that. From very early on, we have been using TCP/IP protocol to send packets over serial and telephone lines. TCP/IP was designed just for that. However, once someone realized that every home in the world could have a home based computer and telephone line connected to it, they should have taken a step back and thought twice.

Using serial cables to connect two computers together only comes with a finite number of threats involved, mostly physical. Add a telephone line where the end points can be miles and even continents apart, and you have just upped the game. Put a computer in every home connected to this phone system, add faster computers, Digital Subscriber Line (DSL) and cable connections, wireless and well, you see where this is heading.

Today's computers and networks are built on the same principles of TCP/IP and internet routing. TCP/IP was never designed to be secure. It is a clear text protocol that anyone between the two points could tap into and see traffic going and coming between the nodes.

The other pieces of the protocol stack that ride on top of TCP/IP, such as FTP, Simple Mail Transfer Protocol (SMTP), Telnet, NetBIOs, and Server Message Block (SMB) to name a few, are all clear text based as well. Yet even today all of our technology is based on the same flawed protocol and way of thinking. Every piece of technology, both hardware and software that relies on the "standard" TCP/IP stack, is subject to being subverted by anyone that wishes to do so.

Vendors back in the early days of the Internet knew of these risks, but the chances of anyone exploiting them were remote. So what did they do? They made the decision to push it out to see if the general public would accept it and worry about issues later. Another great example is wireless technologies. The original wireless 802.11 protocol had no security implemented whatsoever when it was first released, even though it was a broadcast technology. They put it out to the general public to see how receptive it would be. Corporations figured out it saved them money in infrastructure costs, then the general public got wind of it and vendors started making "home" wireless devices, again clear text and insecure. Finally after a few rounds of protocol releases, mostly for speed and distance, someone sounded the alarm and made it known that those wireless transmissions were broadcast in the clear and anyone could see them. The vendors, who were now seeing their dreams of wireless internet in every home disappearing, scrambled and implemented Wired Equivalent Privacy (WEP). The day they released WEP, they knew it was flawed and that it would be soon defeated, which it was. At the time though it was better than nothing and it showed their consumer base that they really did care about security. Fast forward to today's Wi-Fi Protected Access (WPA, WPA2), they are more secure than WEP but they were eventually broken. And let's not forget about Wi-Fi Protected Setup (WPS). The one button configuration script that sync's your devices to your new access points. This new security implementation was for the home user that did not understand the technology enough to configure it securely. The vendors implemented this feature to get people off of default configurations and force them to use some form of encryption. It did not work because the users left the default configuration in place and the hackers figured out a way to have the access point broadcast their access PIN in the clear.

As a society we accepted the flawed solutions because they were cool, and we have always been in a race to be the early adopter. This has fueled social contests such as "my refrigerator talks to Facebook and yours doesn't", and "my watch has more computing power than the first lunar module and yours is just a Timex". In the rush to have the latest and greatest, we have forgotten the most basic principles of privacy, if you don't want others to know, don't tell them. Opening up our entire lives to technology that has so many flaws in it and then expecting bad guys to not take advantage of that is, well, crazy.

Since the dawn of time there has always been someone out there trying to figure out how to make a dollar (Yen, Ruble, Yuan) without having to actually earn it. Hackers originally were not necessarily bad guys. Hackers were technologists that liked finding holes in technology more than anything else. From there, nefarious types got into the game and figured out they could make a living out of stealing your credit card information, personal health records, and all of the stuff we readily put out there on the internet for the taking. We don't even think twice about the "Internet of Everything" until someone steals our identity and ruins our credit and then our lives.

Even worse are the Gen-Y/Millennials that were raised with an Internet connection since birth. Parents that would stick their children in front of a computer or tablet to entertain them did not realize that these young citizens and contributors to society have their entire lives posted on the Internet. Social media technologies such as MySpace, Facebook, Twitter, SnapChat and the likes have created a treasure trove of information that if mined correctly, can allow one to be tracked on the Deep Web and DarkNet easily. Once information is placed on the Internet it is always on the Internet. Want to try it? Go to Archive.org, type in your favorite web site and see how far back it goes with copies of that web site.

To make matters worse, companies that wanted to be on the cutting edge of technology and put those Internet drops in place, with no Firewalls at first, now wonder how their corporate secrets keep getting out. Well, let's start with the fact that the bad guys were in your networks BEFORE you had that first firewall installed and placed themselves strategically so that no matter what, they always have access. Or let's consider that smaller company that you just bought out and integrated into your corporate infrastructure without proper segregation. We like the ease of use and simplicity of technology over the security of technology. It has been said a million times, "security does not mean easier", which is true, but a more fitting representation is that security is the process of working at being secure.

The bad guys, nefarious types, our personal enemies all know this and it just takes a little digging on the Internet to find out everything they need to know about you. Do you want to take a look at all of the people that have installed security cameras or baby monitors in their homes and businesses? Take a visit over to www. Shodanhq.com for a search engine that will list them. It also will link you to their login pages and inform you if they are using the default user names and passwords. If you want to see your neighbor's wireless network and what (if any) security protocols they are using, go to www.wigle.net (please spell that correctly before hitting the return key). There you can sign up for free and then search the entire world by street address for wireless networks. Once you navigate to your street, look at all of the open wireless devices and those devices that are using default configurations. Look at the Printers that have wireless cards, cameras, lightbulbs, and security systems. You name it and it is there. If yours is there, please change your Service Set Identifier (SSID) and password.

We as a society are using technology that was never ready for the wide open worldwide Internet. We were not ready to accept responsibility for securing it ourselves, because that's the vendors job right? Then we raised our children on the Internet allowing them to post everything about themselves for the world to see. Why are we shocked that the bad guys would take advantage of how easy we have made it?

The issues we see today on the Internet, Deep Web, and DarkNet are not going to get any better unless we take a stand for secure technologies, and take responsibility for our own net actions. The bad guys will always have the upper hand because they do not share the same principles as normal law abiding citizens. Every time a new piece of security software or hardware comes out, the bad guys have ten ways to defeat it before it hits the market. It is easy money in their pockets.

DarkNet Intelligence

The Future is here, Open Source Intelligence (OSINT). Over the last 3–5 years, OSINT technologies have been one of the fastest growing areas of the Internet. Before OSINT was coined as a term we had "Grey Hats". These were typically security professionals that worked by day to try and help secure corporate and private information and trolled the Deep Web and DarkNet at night to find out what was the next big attack they were going to have to defend against. These were the unsung heroes of the security world that most managers and Chief Executive Officer's (CEO's) thought were crazy, and I can't tell you how many times I have heard "that would never happen to us", "but we are not connected to the Internet" or the famous "if it's a threat, how come we have not been hacked already?".

It seems now that DarkNet intelligence is as simple as installing an "App", as OSINT is finally cool and everyone wants it, or wants to be involved in it. For every level of OSINT there is a use, and this is where things start getting sticky. Remember those children that we raised with their lives on the Internet and those devices we connected and did not secure? Well the bad guys have been mining that data for years. Now the good guys are mining it as well. Corporations are now using that public information you freely posted to profile possible weak links in their employee chain. Human resources departments now are running that application on information you posted against their OSINT DB so they can see what you have been up to over the last 20 or so years, as it's all out there. Those crazy pictures of you on Facebook™ drinking from the funnel in college, the multiple dating sites you belong to, the speeding ticket you received because you were late picking up the kids, it all reflects on your personality and behaviors. If you are applying for a position that requires a security clearance or access to sensitive corporate information, it could become an issue.

Human resource departments are not the only groups using OSINT. Many Fortune 500 companies now have their own "Corporate Intelligence Departments". These are not solely focused on digging up information on employees; they can be used to keep tabs on what the competition is doing. If your company can beat them to market and have a better widget than the competition at a better price point, you stand to take market share. These departments are also sometimes charged with looking for corporate or employee leaked information on the Deep Web and DarkNet. This could be an indicator of a compromise somewhere in their organization, either human or machine. The Government is using OSINT along with traditional Intelligence to track events happening around the world.

Everyone is getting into the OSINT world. IBM's offering is their QRadar cloud based analytical engine and their X-Force Exchange. Intel's (McAfee) Threat Intelligence Exchange, Alien Vault (commercial and free version), Symantec, SANS are among the others that are providing near real-time threat intelligence. The majority of these are not free or cheap, although a few of them have demonstration or free trial versions. Another great resource for threat information is Threatcrowd.org which allows you to follow malware campaigns and see their associated network domains.

One of the first open source platforms developed for general use was by Paterva Inc., "Maltego". Maltego started out as a free open source intelligence platform that eventually went to a pay version. Because of its open source roots, there is still a free version available for download. The free version is limited to how many transforms you can run at once and every 3 days you have to log back into their server to verify your identity, but it is well worth it. Because of the large open source community following, there are plenty of transforms to download and support from many forums.

Maltego uses what is known as "transforms" which are nothing more than scripts which perform functions like searching for a particular entity. It has groupings of these transforms based upon what type of intelligence you are trying to perform. For example, if you are trying to find out information from a person's email address, it will concurrently run a batch of transforms looking for any combination of the name, email domain, alias', and then link those together in a viewable diagram. You can then select any of those objects and continue running other transforms. If you found someone's Facebook alias, it will now look for other social media accounts, scour those for phone numbers associated with those accounts and then keep digging. Not all of the information may pertain to your target, and after analyzing the data output, you can remove particular entries and mark them as irrelevant. The more info you start gathering the more accurate the results start getting. Maltego also has what they call "engines" which are scripts that run transforms on a timer. For instance, you can setup a Twitter engine and transform it to look for a particular Twitter ID. It will kick off the transform and get an initial dump of data and then run the engine based on your setup, once a day or once an hour, and then look for changes or updates to that twitter alias information or new posts by them.

Maltego is an extremely powerful intelligence tool, and relatively easy to learn how to use. The transforms can be downloaded from Paterva, or you can download custom transforms from several forums and sites where people are still contributing to the software. Maltego also supports other open source intelligence platforms that may not be quite as mature. A good example would be Canary, which at one time was a competing OSINT tool but now there are transforms to integrate Canary transforms into the Maltego interface. Discussed before, the Shodan web site that allows you to query the "Internet" for webcams and network devices with default configurations. The community has developed transforms that will run a query on the Shodan website and pull in the results. Maltego also allows you to export your transforms, which comes in handy when moving to a different machine or just backing up your settings. Maltego also has a team view that will allow several analysts work and have their results merged on one machine. This can be very helpful when splitting up tasks for a team and getting fast results.

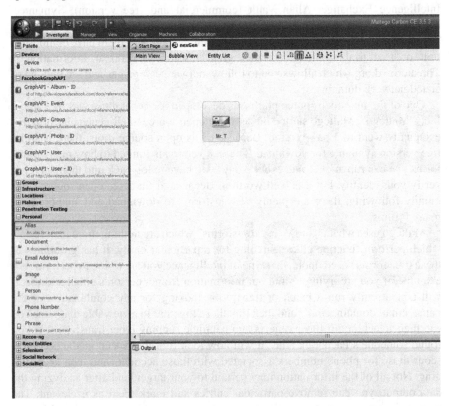

Another source of intelligence information is One World Labs' OWL Vision, and the OWL Vision Professional Tools product line. Although OWL Vision is not free or open source, it does warrant looking into. OWL specializes specifically in Deep Web and DarkNet content. They have developed an algorithm that spiders the DarkNet and Deep Web every day looking for new and/or changed intelligence information. You can utilize the OWL Analyst and let them do the searching and analysis for you or you can perform the tasks yourself using their web interface to the toolset. What makes their tool a little different from the competition is they thrive in the deepest and darkest corners of the DarkNet including Web, IRC, I2P, P2P sites and servers. If you use their tools and do not see any immediate information in their database (DB), just wait a few hours and re-run the query and you are almost guaranteed to have results. Once you execute a query, the OWL algorithm will add that query to the top of the index list for the next spider run. Currently OWL has over 800,000 DarkNet and Deep web sites archived in its secure DB for easy and quick retrieval.

Bottom line is there are many different tools and resources both commercial and open source that will allow one to do as much DarkNet and Deep Web intelligence gathering that they wish to do. The key is to find a methodology that works for you and master it, but also keep yourself open to new tools and techniques that are opening up almost daily.

DarkNet 2035

DarkNet 2035 will look much different than it does today. All you have to do is look at history and quite frankly your favorite technology movie or TV series. Back in the days of Star Trek, the thought of having small pocket communicators was unheard of, now we call them cell phones and Personal Data Assistants (PDAs). Technology is growing faster than most people can keep up with it. That includes security companies and security professionals. Look at Google Glass™, the new Apple watch, and Microsoft's Holo-lens devices that we only once dreamed of 10 years ago which are now making their way to the consumer market. Every time we jump on this new and exciting technology we lose a little bit more of our privacy, and personal information. These devices utilize insecure code and protocols, and hackers and bad guys can take advantage of this much faster than security professionals can find ways to secure them.

For those of us that remember the "Minority Report" Sci-Fi film released in 2002, where actor Tom Cruise played "Pre-Crime Captain John Anderton". The "Pre-Crime" division was responsible for working with "Pre-Cogs" who could see crimes that had not taken place yet, and the Pre-Crime division was responsible for stopping those crimes from happening and arresting the would be offenders. In April 2015 it was announced that the Miami-Dade Police Department, using the IBM Predictive Analytics cloud based system and DarkNet intelligence is now predicting patterns on who, what, where and when crimes are most likely to occur. No one is being arrested on the premise of a crime that has not happened yet, although it is a very slippery slope.

Drones are now not only being used on the battlefield for reconnaissance and offensive actions, but in US cities as well. Although they assist with traffic control, natural disasters and rioting, did we step back though and ask ourselves, can these devices be used to spy on citizens? Can they be taken over by nefarious types and used maliciously? The fact is that every one of those scenarios has already been proven a viable attack vector. Hackers are implanting Near Field Communications (NFC) chips in their hands that run a script to exploit Android ™ phones that are within range. Will we all be required to wear these NFC chips to verify our identity? People can't leave them at home if they are implanted, right?

By the year 2035 there will be so much digitized information on each and every person on the planet that it will take several cloud based zettabytes (1 trillion gigabytes) to hold it all. Who will secure this data? Who will use it and why? Unless you go off the grid with no technology access whatsoever, not even a digital watch, your data and personal information footprint will exponentially grow.

The government will no doubt eventually be responsible for maintaining the security of this data. Corporations have already proven that when security gets in the way of profits they will not make it their priority to protect your data. What the government can't do though is protect your data. Hackers and individuals with malicious intent have always had the upper hand when it comes to security and by 2035 it will not change. As law abiding citizens we cannot "hack back", that's illegal. The government cannot retain the security talent required to protect our data. By the time a security professional reaches a high level of expertise, some corporation will make them an offer they cannot refuse.

The hackers have always had the upper hand. The deeper we dig into their world to uncover and disrupt their malware campaigns and botnets, the deeper they dive. By the time we find out where they are, they are long gone.

The Future Global Neural Network (GNN)

In 2025, the US Government in response to all of the security breaches, political tensions, cyber warfare, and terrorism have now developed the GNN (Gin-Net). The "Internet" as we knew it has turned into a global media network overrun with gamers, spam, malware, and APT. Now it is only used for gaming, entertainment, and advertisements.

The GNN is a cloud based Artificial Intelligence (AI) secure cloud enclave. As part of the 2025 economic stimulus package, the GNN utilizes direct satellite communications which the government has hired hundreds of thousands employees to build this new infrastructure. Every small town and big city now has satellite uplinks. Access points are placed throughout the towns and cities everywhere. The new GNN protocol utilizes mesh networking technology that has been developed and used by the military. Each person is a walking node, each local, state, and federal owned vehicle is outfitted with transceivers, receivers, and amplifiers to re-broadcast signals. As one citizen passes another, their signal is routed to the next node, which eventually makes it to an uplink point. The GNN holds all of your personal information, linking you to state, local, and federal records. It has reduced processing time and government waste by linking your personal data along with your implanted and wearable bio-devices. Every citizen has an implanted bio-chip with all of their personal data on it, driver license, country of origin information, medical records, arrest records, credit information, etc. The GNN AI engine is able to tell who and where you are, and determine from your bio-devices when you are sick even before you do. It cuts down on the government sponsored health care fraud. You no longer have to go into the DMV or any other government office to renew records; they just pull the data from your devices. Law enforcement is utilizing the data, riots can be dealt with faster, no more missing persons, and criminals have little places to hide.

By the year 2030, the corporate world has been overtaken by security breaches because of mismanagement and lack of proper security controls. The US government decided to allow corporation's access to the GNN to protect citizen's private information. Now corporations are notified by the government when an employee is sick. Purchase transactions between citizens now go through the GNN, which only passes a government purchase authorization to the vendor with the shipping address to the customer, while no customer data is passed to the vendors. By the year 2035, the US is a global leader in the GNN and assists other countries governments to setup their secure cloud enclave to connect to the GNN. The government is responsible for this data, working with corporations so they know who is working and who is not. Data is now flowing all around us on many different types of technology. Individuals now work from home to reduce greenhouse emissions. The AI engine of the GNN learns your travel patterns and tolerance level for speed and security. Before leaving your residence, your devices tell the GNN when you are leaving. Updated routing information is instantly transmitted giving you the safest and fastest route to take. Instead of the PC's and smart phones we all have, holo-glasses devices will allow us to see everything from work related information to entertainment. We interact with voice commands and body gestures. A swipe of our hand across our faces logs us into our corporate systems via the GNN and gives us immediate access regardless of where we are on the planet. Our implants are constantly monitoring our bio-functions and immediately tell us when we need medical attention, and notify our company and the government, so work can be shifted to another employee to reduce downtime.

Hackers have been on the move, the virtual world has merged with the physical world, and they were there first. They back-doored the government GNN and now created the DarkNeuralNet (DNN [Din-Net]). This is where the criminals and activist live and work. They are able to manipulate government records, for a fee of course. Here you can buy information using government credits, a smart chip that allows you with a single voice command to switch identity, and jam surveillance drones overhead. Most importantly, in order to pull this off they have to network with other hackers. The Bio-net and DNN is now born, being a mesh network system comprised of millions of nodes that is constantly moving and changing. Each hacker is a node within this network, and when a threat is detected; they switch identities and pass routed transmissions via innocent citizens walking within range of them. The GNN was a good effort, but there will always be a Dark Side.

Star-Trek and Minority Report were once considered science fiction.

References

1. Anonym-os/ (n.d.) Retrieved 20 Apr 2015, from sourceforge.net: http://sourceforge.net/projects/anonym-os/
2. Cerf-Kahn-bio.html (n.d.) Retrieved 15 Apr 2015, from georgewbush-whitehouse.archives.gov: http://georgewbush-whitehouse.archives.gov/government/cerf-kahn-bio.html
3. Comparison_of_Internet_Relay_Chat_clients#cite_note-patch-100 (n.d.) Retrieved 18 Apr 2015, from wikipedia.org: http://en.wikipedia.org/wiki/Comparison_of_Internet_Relay_Chat_clients#cite_note-patch-100
4. eepsite (n.d.) Retrieved 24 Apr 2015, from eepsite.com: http://eepsite.com/
5. http://inventionmachine.com/the-InvINFOGRAPHIC-Exploring-the-Deep-Web-with-Semantic-Search (n.d.) Retrieved 16 Apr 2015, from http://inventionmachine.com: http://inventionmachine.com/the-Invention-Machine-Blog/bid/90626/INFOGRAPHIC-Exploring-the-Deep-Web-with-Semantic-Search
6. Internet History (n.d.) Retrieved 16 Apr 2015, from Computerhistory.org: http://www.computerhistory.org/internet_history/
7. P2P (n.d.) Retrieved 23 Apr 2015, from wikipedia.org: http://en.wikipedia.org/wiki/P2P
8. Philip Emeagwali (n.d.) Retrieved 15 Apr 2015, from Emeagwali.COM : Philip Emeagwali
9. Sandboxie (n.d.) Retrieved 21 Apr 2015, from sandboxie.com: http://www.sandboxie.com/
10. Toolwiz-time-freeze (n.d.) Retrieved 21 Apr 2015, from toolwiz.com: http://www.toolwiz.com/en/products/toolwiz-time-freeze/
11. TOR (n.d.) Retrieved 20 Apr 2015, from torproject.org/: https://www.torproject.org/
12. Who-Invented-the-Internet.html (n.d.) Retrieved 15 Apr 2015, from govtech.com: http://www.govtech.com/e-government/Who-Invented-the-Internet.html
13. Wi-Fi_Protected_Setup (2015). Retrieved from Wikipedia: http://en.wikipedia.org/wiki/Wi-Fi_Protected_Setup

The Bitcoin: The Currency of the Future, Fuel of Terror

Anais Carmona

Technological advances have created a new economic order, where international transactions can be made at the click of a button. Although most cryptocurrencies were created as a product of innovation in line with technological advances and with good intentions in mind, the use of such technologies by malicious users is not a nuanced concept. The Bitcoin, operating in the cyber realm, has created a currency that can surpass institutions and eliminate transparency, providing a perfect agency for anonymous transactions. As governments grow concerned about taxation and their lack of control over the currency, the Bitcoin also poses serious means of funding illicit activities and terrorist organizations. To what extent can the Bitcoin develop and morph into a serious currency utilized to finance terrorism?

The following chapter will aim to take an in-depth look at how the Bitcoin can manifest a credible security threat by directly changing systems of financial support. The first part of this chapter will describe how the Bitcoin operates, including what features make it appealing to illicit networks and what areas continue to be vulnerable. The second part of this chapter will look at how the Bitcoin is shaping terrorist financing, what government response has been and to what degree it has been effective, and a projection of the role of Bitcoins in the coming future.

A. Carmona (✉)
Georgetown University School of Foreign Service, Class of 2014, Washington, DC, USA
e-mail: anaiscarmona92@gmail.com

© Springer International Publishing Switzerland 2015

M. Blowers (ed.), *Evolution of Cyber Technologies and Operations to 2035*,
Advances in Information Security 63, DOI 10.1007/978-3-319-23585-1_9

Background

The Bitcoin is a "decentralized electronic currency" that was created in 2009 by someone under the alias Satoshi Nakamoto.[1] The currency and its transaction methods eliminate the middleman by getting rid of traditional institutions like banks and create a borderless world where transactions can occur instantaneously. There are low or no transaction fees, and anonymity is prioritized.[2] Bitcoins are available on several marketplaces, called Bitcoin exchanges, which allow people to buy and sell Bitcoins using different currencies.[3]

Bitcoins are unlike any other form of currency because they attain value through mining. Bitcoin "mining" consists of solving arithmetic questions by using software and collecting compensation in the form of Bitcoins for correct outputs.[4] Mining is measured in "hashes per second." [5] For instance, when talking about paper money, a government decides when to print it and how to distribute it; however, the entire Bitcoin currency is based on computational power. Bitcoin exchange also requires running SHA256 double round hash verification process that validate transactions and provide the requisite security for the public ledger of the Bitcoin network.[6] This is what attracts people to mine: not only is it a smart and proactive manner of issuing currency, but it also creates mining pools, which are groups of miners that work together to solve a block or a share of the puzzle, and share the rewards that result. Most Bitcoin miners operate within mining pools, because not only is it more effective, but it is also substantially quicker to accumulate the currency.

Bitcoins do not operate as a tangible good, but rather are completely digitalized and operate in cyber space. They are stored in what is called a "digital wallet" which can be found in either the cloud or a computer desktop.[7] Users, owners, and sellers have virtual bank accounts that allow transactions to occur, but do not function as a bank account that can integrate a country's currency.

Advantages & Continued Vulnerabilities

Up to this point, Bitcoins sound like a "currency of the future" or game with no current substantial value. However, there are relevant characteristics of Bitcoins that attract certain individuals, industries, and markets to the currency. The advantages to using Bitcoins include the anonymous nature of transactions, the operational

---

[1] CNNMoney [2].

[2] CNNMoney [2].

[3] Bitcoin [1].

[4] Bitcoin [1].

[5] CNNMoney [2].

[6] CNNMoney [2].

[7] CNNMoney [2].

environment clouded by the deep web, and the ease and speed at which transactions can occur.

Purchases utilizing Bitcoins are mostly made anonymously. The transactions can be found in public logs, but sellers and buyers are kept completely in the dark. Although each buyer and seller is assigned a "Wallet ID" these IDs can be easily changed per transaction.[8] Users are also not limited to one wallet. In recent years, several programs have been created to design stealth wallet addresses to existing wallets, therefore making transactions even less transparent. These changes to Wallet IDs, coupled with the encryption methods of anonymity provided by portals, such as the Tor network, create a highly untraceable platform for transactions that cannot be identified.

Bitcoins mainly operate in the Deep Web, a portion of the Web that is generally not indexed and in which attribution is difficult, where they are primarily utilized in markets that sell anything from guns to the services of mercenaries. Because Bitcoins mainly operate on the Silk Road, and that system falls outside the narrow parameters established by existing financial and corporate frameworks, it is part of the deep web and not indexed by search engines or additional meta data collection codes, it thus eludes control.[9] Additionally, because the digital transactions eliminate an intermediary player, anyone with a cell phone or computer has access to low-cost banking from anywhere in the world. This will play a substantial role in developing countries and remote areas of the world, where terrorist activity tends to flourish.

Bitcoins also represent a globalized form of trade, where the currency has begun to be accepted, sold, and traded internationally and can be purchased using any other currency. The lack of regulation is particularly appealing because it cuts the middleman out of the picture, thus, jumping another regulatory hurdle that is typically easily traced. In a society where events like the stock market crash of 2008 have led to a large population's mistrust the central government or the financial institutions that operate within its borders, the Bitcoin offers an attractive alternative. Bitcoins are not tied to a country or body; the currency does not abide by laws or politics—it abides by nothing more than the laws of economics. Trading, buying and selling of Bitcoins is trade made simple, where transactions happen solely on the web from any part of the world with access. The ease at which these transactions can happen has incredible reach and scope, particularly if it can operate in remote or conflict areas without record, tracking, or regulation.

There area also some consumer disadvantages associated with the nature of emerging virtual currencies like the Bitcoin. Bitcoins investments are not insured by the Federal Deposit Insurance Corporation (FDIC) and are currently not found in any official legislation in any country. The problem with not being insured is that although the anonymity and security encoding serve as a protective measure and the use of networks like Tor to conceal a user's identity, the ecosystem in which Bitcoins operate is still vulnerable. Cyberspace and the cyber realm continue to be vulnerable to hacking attacks and crime, making Bitcoins susceptible by their very definition. Although one of the attractive features of Bitcoins are the security of identity they offer, there have been reported cases of hacked wallets, which have created losses for

---

[8] CNNMoney [2].
[9] CNNMoney [2].

individuals without any authority to report to. For instance, in February of this year, Mt. Gox, a top Bitcoin exchange filed for bankruptcy, claiming that hundreds of millions of Bitcoins had been stolen.[10] Viruses also have the capacity to destroy Bitcoins from within the virtual wallets. If a computer hacker can gain access to desktop or cloud information, they can also access wallets and steal the currency from unprotected users. There have been additional cases of companies that utilize Bitcoins as their operating currency fleeing with company shares and client Bitcoins, which causes white-collar corporate crime to go unpunished, untraced, and undocumented.

Bitcoins in a Dangerous Theater: The Illicit Market and Terrorism

Because of the aforementioned benefits and limited disadvantages that Bitcoins bring into financing and trade, it goes without question that this currency is becoming an option for actors that gain a tactical advantage from circumventing legal barriers in order to keep funds intact and untraced. Bitcoins, by their very nature, have been found operating in a very dangerous theater: illicit markets. The Internet Organized Crime Threat Assessment (IOCTA) has examined the use of Bitcoins on various dark web sites that sell anything from drugs to people. There have been multiple reports that include the role of digital currency use on child sexual exploitation and organ trade. More and more, the Bitcoin is appearing in police investigations in cases dealing with international ransom and extortion.

Without the global financial system's supervision and close monitoring, groups or organizations that prioritize anonymity, speed, and global sources of income are particularly attracted to Bitcoins. The avoidance of major money conduits and even tangible cash assets that can be frozen is an advantage that may result in the use of this system for financing and fundraising, particularly for terrorist organizations. Although already existing beneficiaries, such as benefactors of the drug and weapons trade and other organized crime rings can be widely found, terrorist organizations at one point or another also become involved in other illicit activities. Given the evolution of terrorist organizations to include business-like approaches to financing structures, Bitcoins are more likely to revolutionize terrorist financing than shape their already existing role in illicit activities. Drug and weapons trading requires a product transaction, where a tangible good needs to be delivered. However, terrorism financing capital is just required to come in as a donation, where no transaction or service is required in return. Although a service in return for donations can manifest itself in terrorist acts, financial supporters do not expect an immediate good the way that drug cartels and other criminal activities do. In this manner, the likelihood of the drug market going completely cyber and utilizing Bitcoins as a currency is highly unlikely. For terrorist networks, however, Bitcoins

---

[10] US Defense Dept. Analyzing Bitcoin as Potential Terrorism Threat [9].

represent an important financial option because it has the potential to integrate into existing funding framework almost seamlessly.

Bitcoins are far more likely to revolutionize the way terrorist organizations operate. Since terrorist organizations have begun to move away from traditional ways of combat and organization, it is not unusual to see the same trend evolving in their funding and financing. While terrorists today continue to rely primarily on sponsors, be it states or individuals, the movement of international illicit markets and organizations away from tangible cash assets, or even slightly away from currencies to diversify the avenues of incoming capital, Bitcoins provide complete anonymity, access, and makes them inherently difficult to trace and be frozen or collected. Seeing as nation-states' first counter-terrorism strategy revolves around eliminating funding through tracing and freezing assets, the Bitcoin poses a credible threat to the manner in which states and institutions address and counter terrorist activities. Should more terrorist networks choose to incorporate the Bitcoin into their financial framework, national and international counter-terrorism policies will have to change and adapt drastically, which is much easier said than done.

The concept that Bitcoins could be used to fund terrorist organizations is not as revolutionary as it sounds. The idea has been longstanding and many of the propositions of regulating the Bitcoin have stemmed from this fear and its increasing feasibility to pressure governments and the international community into regulation. The Islamic State of Iraq and Syria (ISIS), has already publicly proposed utilizing Bitcoins to finance global jihadist operations worldwide. In an article entitled, "Bitcoin and the Charity of Violent Physical Struggle," the author, Taqi'ul-Deen al-Munthir, who has identified as a part of ISIS, wrote:

> This system [Bitcoins] has the potential to revive the lost sunnah of donating to the mujahedeen, it is simple, easy, and we can ask Allah to hasten its usage for us.[11]

In the article, he makes the argument that in order for ISIS to fund its terror operations, it must operate outside the traditional western financial system.[12] The pseudonymous transaction capability of the Bitcoin offers ISIS a form of currency and capital that fits well within the needs of jihadist organizers, pleading for sources of money from a caliphate they claim to be sympathetic and supportive to the cause. In that vein, the Bitcoin's borderless nature increases jihadist dependency on the "*sunnah*" or the religious community who identify with the struggle to donate from all corners of the world to grow and to feel as if they directly contributed to the group's operations. That type of identification poses a viable and serious security threat because it is inherently counter productive to American and international counterterrorism efforts, which aim to fragment that very sentiment. On a more operational level, because Bitcoins and the operating network make it incredibly difficult for anti-terrorist financial authorities to halt transactions from taking place or from freezing assets, we will begin to see groups considering and utilizing Bitcoins to financially support their operations. The key idea here is that Bitcoins

---

[11] Higgins [3].
[12] Nimmo [5].

can facilitate some of the fundraising needs, but it is highly unlikely that a group would completely abandon tangible and volatile currency. Rather, the Bitcoin would compliment the financing of such networks in conjunction to the tangible financial sponsorship and other donations.

The question of feasibility must also be addressed. Some critics believe that the Bitcoin is too volatile and others make the argument that terrorist networks will not be able to use adopt Bitcoins into their financing due to the lack of mining capabilities. While terrorist networks do lack mining capabilities, they do not lack the will to diversify their source of income, which could lead to Bitcoin outsourcing. Terrorist networks would have no direct need to mine: terrorist networks could outsource Bitcoin mining. Bitcoins would begin as fundraising mechanism and be based on donations from organization sympathizers, rather than transform into the main source of funding. Although some may argue that terrorists networks may trade tangible cash assets for Bitcoins, at the early stages of currency diversification it does not seem logical nor effective to do this because the Bitcoin cannot compete with the immediate use of tangible assets—like currency. Additionally, given the volatility and continued risks associated with the operational environment of Bitcoins, there is no real argument that can be made that terrorist organizations would ever choose to rely completely on virtual currency, rather what this chapter aims to argue is that Bitcoins offer a way to diversify their incoming capital, which could serve as a substantial lifeline should other assets be frozen or intercepted by counter-terrorism efforts.

Failed Response

There is a concerted effort by governments and banks around the world to destroy the Bitcoin and the cyber currency movement. There is no question that banking authorities in the United States, Europe and Australia view the growing cryptocurrency ecosystem as an emerging threat. The New York Department of Financial Services, for instance, has suggested regulating the conduct of business involving virtual currencies, with a particular focus on the Bitcoin.[13] Regulations included licensing and background checks, as well as reports required for users. In July of 2014, the Dutch criminal justice system was granted the right to confiscate digital currency holdings, while lawyers in Poland recently demanded more consumer protection surrounding the use of Bitcoins in trade.[14] The United States military and the Combating Terrorism Technical Support Office, which is a division of the Department of Defense that identifies and develops counterterrorism abilities and investigates irregular warfare and evolving threats, have already put the Bitcoin on the radar as a possible terrorist threat.[15] While the Department of Defense is

---

[13] Sand [7].
[14] Nimmo [5].
[15] Neal [4].

concerned with the blurring of national lines that has facilitated the transfer of virtual currencies, the anonymity built into the architecture and design of the Bitcoin is the top point of concern as it aids the formation of illicit operations that place a nation's security at risk.

The Bitcoin, given its boundlessness has also sparked an international awareness and created cooperative reactions in both policy and practice that aim to deter the currency from existing without regulation. Operation Onymous is an international law enforcement operation that brought together the Federal Bureau of Investigation (FBI) and the European Union Intelligence Agency Europol to target online marketplaces that were operating through the Tor Network.[16] On November 5th and 6th, 2014, websites in the Deep Web and portions of the Silk Road, Cloud 9, and Hydra were shut down.[17] These sites were identified as prime realms of cybercrime, where money laundering and contraband was traded. Operation Onymous resulted in the arrest of 17 individuals, and $1 M in Bitcoins seized, along with 180,000€ in cash, gold, silver and drugs.[18] While the operation was deemed an overwhelming success, the reality is that the results—in comparison to the scope and size of the illegal market in the deep web—were not impacting. Other drug markets, such as Agora, Evolution and Andromeda were not impacted by government action.

After Operation Onymous, Bitcoin trading volumes more than doubled as markets were stimulated by a surging price. The Bitcoins market frothed directly after Operation Onymous as price soared to a high of $458.[19] Trading volumes rose by 2.3 times to nearly 6 m BTC traded over the week after the international operation. Counter intuitively, after the crackdown, Bitcoin prices went up by about $3.[20] This was not anything out of the ordinary, seeing as the same response was seen after the 2013 closing of the Silk Road that gave birth to the Silk Road 2.0. The Bitcoin and its illegal operating ecosystem seem to be affected minimally to government action regulatory efforts. What is more alarming is that the Bitcoin and the Silk Road have reacted counter intuitively to the worldwide efforts, which makes creating an effective counterterrorism strategy that incorporates Bitcoins nearly impossible to formulate, should networks decide to diversify their financing frameworks. The next section of the chapter will take a look at a futuristic prediction of where the Bitcoin is going in relation to terrorist network financing and overall role in the market.

---

[16] Thoughts and Concerns about Operation Onymous [8].

[17] Thoughts and Concerns about Operation Onymous [8].

[18] Thoughts and Concerns about Operation Onymous [8].

[19] Wong [10].

[20] Wong [10].

The Prophecy of the Bitcoin

Although extremely innovative and globalized, the Bitcoin continues to be extremely volatile, which is an important disadvantage that will force the currency to compete with other forms of cryptocurrencies and even traditional forms of funding.[21] The Bitcoin's supply is limited, but the demand is variable, where the variability has made its price very uncertain and created a bubble-bust cycle in the Bitcoin market. Some economists argue that the safest prediction is that Bitcoin will "eventually be displaced by alternative cryptocurrencies with superior features."[22] However, so long as the Silk Road and markets like it continue to exist, the Bitcoin, which is the preferred currency utilized in the Deep Web, will continue to be relevant. Although somewhere down the line more competitive and appealing virtual currencies may arise, the Bitcoin is relevant in current security dilemmas concerning terrorist financing.[23]

If we were to assume the status quo, where government and law enforcement agencies worldwide continue to supervise the legal financial markets heavily, terrorist networks and other illicit actors will be forced to diversify their financial framework in order to survive. This need for diversification, coupled with the aforementioned advantages of anonymity, will push terrorist networks to the Bitcoin, probably in a greater degree than we see today. By no means will it be a complete movement away from tangible currency, but the Bitcoin's ability to find an effective and seamless niche into terrorist financing will make it an asset and a weapon that the state currently does not have a way of tracking, intercepting, or eradicating.

If the Bitcoin response to government and international crackdowns is an increase in price with minimal operational damage to illicit markets coupled with the lack of existing laws and failure to regulate it, the state is left at a stalemate where it has no resources or effective strategy to eradicate terrorist financing. This is perhaps the most crucial part of the argument: should terrorist organizations be able to obtain monetary assistance from sympathizers worldwide and keep that available and ready for use should their primary source of funding be frozen, Bitcoins have the ability to provide a much needed lifeline to terrorist organizations. Bitcoins are weapons that have the capability to completely outdate state and institutional counterterrorism policies, making one of the strongest tools against terrorism completely invalid. Terrorist networks, in comparison to state and institutional policies and strategy, will adapt in a much quicker fashion, proving state and international failure in the cyber theater of conflict. Currently, diversification of financial frameworks is the next strategic move for terrorist networks, like ISIS, because it steps into a realm that no government or organization has the capability to interfere in. The nature of the Bitcoin and digital currencies will continue to

---

[21] Wong [10].

[22] Prisco [6].

[23] Prisco [6].

provide incentives that outweigh the risks and volatility. If the Bitcoin develops and manifests itself into a secure and effective opportunity, there is no question that terrorist organizations will begin to integrate it into its financing plans.

Closing Remarks

It is evident that the Bitcoin can morph into a credible threat that has the potential to shape terrorist financing by increasing the opaqueness, transactional speed, and overall efficiency of terrorist organizations. The Bitcoin inherently revolutionizes terrorist network financial support systems, making the traditional and most effective counterterrorism policies we employ today completely outdated. The features that are integral to the Bitcoin manifest a viable option for terrorist networks to adopt into its financing structure, making it even harder to target them. As has been discussed in this chapter, if government response in the form of crackdowns has yielded little to no results, the international community will be facing incredible challenges in limiting terrorist financing in the future. Innovation for the sake of improving trade in the globalized era that we live in is absolutely necessary; however, it is too often that we find ourselves creating tools that get turned into the very weapons that we are not prepared to counter in the continued struggle against terrorist networks around the world.

Works Cited

1. Bitcoin (n.d.) How does Bitcoin work?. Bitcoin Project. Web. 10 Nov 2014
2. CNNMoney (n.d.) What Is Bitcoin?. Cable News Network. Web. 15 Nov 2014.
3. Higgins S (2014) ISIS-Linked blog: bitcoin can fund terrorist movements worldwide. Coin Desk. Coin Desk. Web. 20 Nov 2014
4. Neal RW (2014) Bitcoin A terrorist threat? Counterterrorism program names virtual currencies as area of interest. International Business Times. International Business Times. Web. 28 Nov. 2014.
5. Nimmo K (2014) Bitcoin dismissed as a currency for terrorists and drug dealers. Infowars. InfoWars. Web. 1 Dec 2014
6. Prisco G (2014) Cato Institute – Bitcoin will be displaced by cryptocurrencies with superior features – CryptoCoinsNews. CryptoCoinsNews. Cato Institute. Web. 20 Nov 2014.
7. Sand A (n.d.) New York State Department of Financial Services Proposed New York Codes, rules and regulations: n. pag. Virtual currencies. New York Department of Financial Services, 2014. Web. 28 Nov 2014.
8. Thoughts and concerns about operation onymous (n.d.) Thoughts and concerns about operation onymous. Tor Network. Web. 20 Nov 2014.
9. US Defense Dept. Analyzing Bitcoin as Potential Terrorism Threat (2014) RT USA. RT USA. Web. 1 Dec 2014.
10. Wong JI (2014) Markets weekly: trading volumes spike amid price surge. CoinDesk RSS. Coin Desk. Web. 20 Nov 2014.

The Rise of Social Media and Its Role in Future Protests and Revolutions

Paul Klench Rozumski

The rise in popularity of social media in protests and revolution in the present age presents a host of possibilities in the coming decades. Just a decade ago peer-to-peer services such as Napster enabled millions to globally exchange digital music content. Now, there are scores of such services that provide the ability to not simply share data. The multitude of information passed across the world's broadband infrastructure, has given rise to Big Data. How to leverage Big Data dominates the business world today, but governments and non-state actors are also interested.

This chapter explores the role of social media in the present to gain a better understand of how the medium is likely to impact future conflict. While major combat operations involving multiple nations are always a possibility, the trend indicates more low-intensity, but frequent, conflict within the urban environment. To that point, there is an examination of two recent protests in Hong Kong and Ukraine. Both examples are interesting because not only did both event leverage social media for political purposes, but the outcomes were different. Why the outcomes were different, and if governments took notice, frame the following discussion. Ultimately, it is the author's position that basic human psychology and habit patterns observed today will greatly inform our understanding of how social media will be used in the future.

The Rise of Social Media

How people and governments communicate is moving rapidly along a course away from conventional forms of mass-media. In the early Twentieth Century, most people received their information on world affairs from newspapers, telegram,

P.K. Rozumski (✉)
United States Air Force, 32d Intelligence Squadron at Fort Meade, Fort Meade, MA, USA
e-mail: paul.rozumski@us.af.mil

© Springer International Publishing Switzerland 2015   137
M. Blowers (ed.), *Evolution of Cyber Technologies and Operations to 2035*,
Advances in Information Security 63, DOI 10.1007/978-3-319-23585-1_10

photographs, Morse and radio. By the last quarter of the century, cable and broad-cast television projected political debates and violence of war into the living room. At the end of the Cold War, the twenty-four hour news cycle provided a minute by minute accounting of the first Gulf War and the Tiananmen Square demonstrations in Beijing. While conventional forms of mass-media persist in the present era, they are becoming a legacy and secondary means to on-line social media accounts that can digitally document, archive, and share activity to millions in near-real time.

On-line statistic portals report the number of social media users in excess of two billion.[1] This staggering sum continues to climb and projections indicate that by 2020 the Big Data market will reach $76 billion annually with over half the global population logging on as a digital consumer.[2] Coinciding with this upward trajec-tory is the sharp increase in the ownership and availability of cellular phone, Smartphone, and internet access. Internet and social media use varies by region and country, but at least a third (Bolivia) to ninety percent (Lebanon) of emerging and developing nations participate.[3] The most avid users across all nations fall into a common demographic of being under thirty in age and primarily use text messaging services. While a vast majority prefers social networks to communicate with friends and family and share digital entertainment, a small but significant rise in religious and political debate is worth noting.[4] A tipping point is evident that in the next decade, the vast portion of the global population will prefer to receive and share religious and political information via social media.

The United States State Department and Department of Defense note these trends and are actively seeking a greater role within social media. In particular, the military struggles to discern situational understanding within a population's envi-ronment and how to provide effective strategic communication. In exercises fore-casting future force constructs, the conclusions routinely point toward accepting that limited situational understanding is probable, despite the multitude of social media products and services and the Big Data cottage industry feeding the Defense Department. Nonetheless the efforts persist in trying to understand social media's effect on the population and how to harness the medium to full advantage.

Social Media's Effect on a Population

The ability to interact with people in the same city or across vast distances is about clustering the population by political, religious, economic, and social viewpoints. Just as neighborhoods defined by racial and social demographics subdivided the cities of today, millions of users now and increasingly in the future will form a loose confederation bound by like-minded interests within virtual communities. While

---

[1] The Statistics Portal [25].
[2] Liebman [9].
[3] PewGlobal.Org [16].
[4] PewGlobal.Org [16].

the clusters will grow and contract daily by the thousands, the core will contain millions of regular users. These clusters will overlap others in predictable and sometimes unpredictable ways.

The appeal of social media and the observed clustering effect is based on three key reasons. First, on the most fundamental heuristic level is that humans function more efficiently in small clusters of 150 people or less.[5] The human capacity to manage and maintain larger relationships is too unmanageable.[6] This is true even the ability to associate, friend, or follow with thousands of other users in virtual spaces. To manage or cope with this shortcoming, social media enables users to bin information into manageable topical categories, feeds and conversations. Of no surprise is that users tend to gravitate toward other users that share the same views and interests.

What is not always obvious is that each these clusters are led by a small collective of actors that have the ability to command and control the content, provide intent and purpose, and establish a rules-based governance structure of the information shared. While providing products and services, the ultimate goal of the collective is to influence thought and action. This is akin to modern mass-media where the 24/7 new cycle seeks to draw and retain loyal viewership, shape public opinion, and at times, compel the population to action.[7]

The social cluster exists if two conditions are met: (1) Subscribers are free from active participation or terms of membership (2) Subscribers know a close friend or relative participating within the cluster. See Fig. 1.

The second reason is based on biases and effects. In 2006, Charles Tabor and Milton Lodge conducted a study and published their findings after considering several biases and effects. While not focusing on social media, their results do explain why the cluster effect occurs, why people find social media so compelling, and also why information gleaned from social sources is often dubious. Their study demonstrated that humans have a large number of biases and associated effects when sharing and evaluating data. Overwhelmingly, there is a tendency toward confirmation bias, where people will gravitate toward information that supports a previous supposition, despite evidence to the contrary.[8] Moreover, this bias is compounded with the attitude strength effect. The effect works by overloading an argument with a flood of one-sided information. The net result is users are influenced on an unconscious level based on a multitude of biases and motives.

Third, social media is compelling because it requires less effort to interact with people virtually. Instead of activating emotional and cognitive processes within the brain to promote interaction with others, machine to machine communication relaxes those processes. The result is an absence of non-verbal cues, tone, eye contact, and other factors humans have learned to analyze and assess when determining trust and

---

[5] McRaney [12], 146.
[6] McRaney [12], 147.
[7] Cary [3].
[8] Yudkowsky [30].

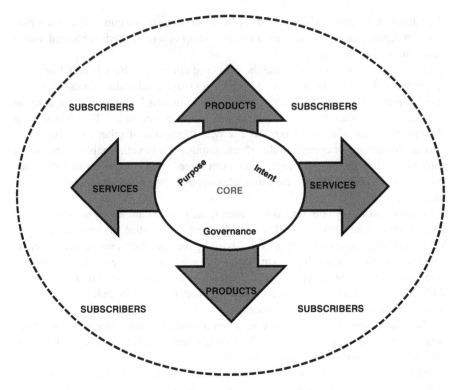

Fig. 1 Social media construct (created by author)

acceptance.[9] The net result is a greater uninhibited willingness to participate within a group and more likely to trust the available content. Trust in the available content is enhanced when a user knows a participating close friend or relative.

The three reasons just explained are generally understood by government and non-state actors. For example, The Islamic State (ISIS) uses popular trending hashtags to post their propaganda.[10] The movement employs automatic computer "bots" to locate the popular trends then subverts the forum with large volumes of posts and redirects to other online locations. This brute force tactic is effective because diverting a fraction of the millions of daily traffic provides a presence and topic of conversation that equates to legitimacy. Table 1 is a sample of the popular United States hashtags from Twitter in 2014. They range from professional sports, popular culture and social causes.

The United States Government also seeks to shape global public option and is at the forefront of promoting equal access and use of the internet. The Internet Freedom initiative, led by the State Department, is aimed at preventing international

---

[9] Margalit [11].
[10] Sharkov [19].

Table 1 2014 popular twitter hashtags

#BringBackOurGirls	#ICantBreathe	#YesAllWomen
#HandsUpDontShoot	#IAmLiberianNotAVirus	#CosbyMeme
#CarryThatWeight	#HeForShe	#WorldCup
#WhyIStayed/#WhyILeft	#UmbrellaRevolution	#IceBucketChallenge

Created by author

states from blocking access to the internet.[11] The notion of promoting freedom of information abroad is aimed at increasing internal dialogue and discourse among the targeted population. It is also based on the notion that citizens with access to Western information from Wikipedia, YouTube, and other sources will be more likely to promote peaceful democratic reform.[12] What is assumed is that the there is a high perceived value the on the information to offer and the willingness abroad to receive such information. However, as the social media model in Fig. 1 indicates, social groups require a core collective that can provide intent and purpose based within the targeted population cluster. Thus, buy-in at the local level is necessary to advance an agenda.

In a piece for *The New Yorker*, Malcolm Gladwell wrote about the social media phenomena and its perceived ability to incite revolution.[13] The author examined civil rights activities in the 1960s and compared them with the Moldovan and Iran protests in 2009. He noted that the impact of social media to incite and conduct a revolution is misunderstood and overstated. The civil rights phenomena required thousands of participants willing to spread the cause by word of mouth and to significant invest their physical well-being to the cause. In contrast, the student protest in Tehran was reported on Twitter, but mostly by western observers writing in English, not Farsi. Ultimately, social media enhanced awareness of the situation to outsiders, but did little to actually perpetuate and resolve the situation.

To Gladwell, social media is not activism. Activism requires recruits with a close friend within the organization that have the same values and goals and are also willing to physically take action. While online texts inform people of a situation, there is little emotion or physical stake in the weak ties that subscribers share.[14] Commonly, social media asks for a "retweet", a "like" or even a small monetary donation to show support for a cause because requiring anything more would break the social media construct. Thus, social media skews public opinion and understanding of a situation by asking for minimal support and that support is no true measure of the true intent and purpose of the public.

The next several pages explore two recent protests where social media played a significant role in the way the protests unfolded and concluded. It is to the reader to

---

[11] U.S. State Department [26].

[12] Shirky [20].

[13] Gladwell [7].

[14] Gladwell [7].

determine social media's ultimate effect on social protests, but consider the effect of social media to foment peace or violent, organize the demonstration, and the ability of government to coordinate a response. The first study considers the non-violent Occupy movement's Hong Kong protests and the second examines the violent Euromaiden protests in Kiev that toppled a government.

Hong Kong Protests

The governance of Hong Kong operates within a one country, two systems construct. There is a generally accepted understanding that Hong Kong enjoys a certain degree of autonomy from the Mainland. However, civil unrest does exist and protests occur with annual frequency. In October 2014, three disparate groups, the Hong Kong Federation of Students, Scholarism, and Occupy Central with Love and Peace, converged on the business and financial center of Hong Kong.[15] Their non-violent civil disobedience was aimed at universal suffrage in determining Hong Kong's top political leadership. This demonstration also marked a continuation of annual protests in the city.

While the official count varies, it is possible nearly 500,000 participated in the 79-day movement.[16] In previous demonstrations, social media played a large role in organizing and informing protestors, the Mainland, and the world. 2014 continued this trend. As before, the Chinese Central Government took significant measures to censor the flow of information. Twitter, Facebook, Instagram, Youtube, and Weibo (the Chinese version of Twitter), were banned and associated servers and proxies aggressively firewalled.[17] Meanwhile, Chinese mainstream media news outlets, such as Xinhua and the People's Daily chose a narrative that downplayed the activity, deflected coverage to other events, or simply decided to avoid publishing photographs or details.[18]

As in the case of the Occupy Wall Street movement in America, the protests eventually waned and Hong Kong returned to normalcy. Aside from raising awareness, it appears the passive demonstrations did little to achieve their political aim. Additionally, while global interest was present and peaked at the initial height of activity, very little in the form of financial, humanitarian, or political action flowed forth in support. The reasons are varied, but here are a couple for consideration.

First, Occupy Central is a movement with a millennial majority from Hong Kong. Their founder, Professor Benny Tai Yiu-ting, and student leaders have no significant political leverage, generous financial support, or a clear plan of action other than massing protestors in a non-centralized manner and

---

[15] **Wong** [27].
[16] Cheung [4].
[17] Parker [15].
[18] BBC News [14].

using social media to spread awareness.[19] As a result, within a week, much of the effort lacked steam.[20] With no clear and sustained means for political reform, the Central Government contained the situation by effectively waged a strategic communication campaign that focused on the economic future of Hong Kong and blamed international subversive elements responsible for the unrest.

Second, while the protests massed, the online political discourse and agenda experienced significant fog and friction. Social media often fueled paranoia, spread misinformation and created a false sense of international support. For example, the opening days, rumors abound implied the Chinese People's Liberation Army's local garrison would fire upon the masses and images of Tiananmen Square increased paranoia. Instead, Hong Kong police employed tear gas with no international reports of mass-violence toward the population.[21] In addition to police, the government organized and fielded their own anti-occupy force, both physically and virtually. The aim was to barrage the internet with misinformation and misdirection. It worked. As the protests grew in greater number it became extremely difficult to command and control the mass. As a result, students began to cluster into smaller groups and form camps. Their social media activity also reflected this behavior. As the groups began to get smaller and cluster, the government was able to contain the demonstrators.

In the realm of support abroad, many students anecdotally reported that seeing a post from a foreigner encouraged them to rally and continue. Conversely, foreign supporters felt a connection because they could interact online. However, both sides were simply swayed by confirmation bias. The evidence shows that despite the virtual pledge of support, no significant political rallies, demarches, or financial support flowed into Hong Kong or occurred internationally. In fact, the students did little to win the sentiments of the general public in their own city because of their disruption to the streets and public services.[22]

Ultimately, the 2014 civil protests in Hong Kong reveal that social media has its limitations and did little to foment violence or achieve desired political aims. While global awareness did increase, it failed to translate to support beyond positive sentiments of encouragement. Moreover, due to efforts by the Central Government and opposition groups, the students experienced confusion and paranoia and these conditions were exacerbated by taking action in a virtual environment. The annual civil disturbances will continue, but it is unlikely massing for a cause via social media and participating non-violently will lead to political reform in Hong Kong.

---

[19] So [21].

[20] Wong [29].

[21] Tay [24].

[22] Ryall [18].

Euromaiden Protests

For months leading to the Russian invasion of Crimea, then Ukrainian Prime Minister Viktor Yanukovich faced two choices: adopt policies to normalize relations with the European Union (EU) or maintain the status quo with Russia. Facing a financial crisis and mounting pressure from Russian President Vladimir Putin, Yanukovich close the latter option and signed a $15 billion bailout deal. That decision sent shockwaves from Kiev across Europe. In the aftermath of that decision, peaceful pro-EU demonstrations turned violent and Kiev burned in what is now called the Ukrainian Revolution of 2014. [23]

The protestors, calling themselves Euromaiden, succeeded in applying the necessary pressure to remove Yanukovich from power by February and enabled the creation of an interim pro-EU government. However, as the interim government was forming, Russia branded the revolution as a coup de tat and seized control of the Crimean Peninsula. Russia still maintains its occupation and pro-Russian sentiments within the Ukraine threaten to further de-stabilize region.

Most of the Euromaiden activity took place in Kiev and in the capital cities of EU nations. Initially, social media spread awareness of the pro-Russian stance Yanukovich adopted and the implications of the bailout agreement. Reports vary, but as the movement culminated, nearly 1 million people stormed Kiev's Independence Square. Once it became evident that the Pro-Russian government would not normalize relations and seek a bailout option with the EU, the violence peaked. In the aggregate, scores of activists were killed and much of the critical infrastructure in vicinity burned or became inaccessible.

Similar to the Occupy movement in Hong King, Euromaiden leveraged forms of social media. Their approach indicates a sophisticated understanding of each of the strengths and weaknesses of the various formats. During the protests, the Russian VKontakte (VK) and Odnoklassniki networks accounted for the largest share of social media use in the Ukraine with over 30 million subscribers.[24] Twitter was also popular, with at least half a million accounts in the country. During the protests, several Twitter hashtags, such as #euromaiden, #євромайдан, and# евромайдан showcased the violence and spread the cause to the broader global audience. At the height of the protests, 130,000 tweets were posted daily and peaked to a quarter of a million on February 20 when dozens of protesters lost their lives.[25] To coordinate efforts within the Square, a Euromaiden Facebook page provided an interactive map, complete with information on where toilets, showers, and supplies were located.[26]

With social media playing such an integral part in recruiting, informing, and even galvanizing the protest effort, there are several points worth considering. First, and as initially highlighted, there was a clear distinction between how Facebook, Twitter,

---

[23] Baczynska [1].

[24] Lokot [10].

[25] Lokot [10].

[26] Talaga [23].

and other forms of social media were used. In particular, most of the information posted in The Euromaiden Facebook page was written in Ukrainian in order to coordinate efforts and to provide news updates and dispel rumors.[27] On Twitter, it appears nearly 70 % of the tweets originated within the country with the purpose of informing the larger global community and to attract new followers. In fact, the data indicates that a spike in Twitter user registration always occurred after each major demonstration. In essence, as the word spread, more users got online to learn more information. In turn, the new users posted their support for the cause. However, their posts did not equate to physical proximity to Kiev.[28]

Second, the older portion of the population, not the Millennials, represented the largest majority of protestors. The average age of Euromaiden members were over 30 and nearly 25 % over the age of 55. This distinction is important because those between ages 30 and 55 identified themselves as the first free and independent generation born without Soviet control of the country. While the Millennials protested for broad conceptual norms, such as human rights and ending corruption, the independent generation called for more tangible aims and took it upon themselves to ensure that the Ukraine remained free from an existential Russian threat. Given the age and the anti-Russian themes that emerged, it is very likely age and historical context played a crucial factor in spurring violence.[29]

Third, social media played a major role in the recruitment of Euromaiden. As mentioned, Twitter spread the message to a broad audience, but what is interesting is that recruitment still needed conventional mass media to initiate the recruitment process. Most of the analysis on the recruitment of Euromaiden indicates that most the new protestors learned about the situation by first watching television or listening to the radio. Interest turned to action after receiving texts and emails from friends and also reading Facebook posts.

Moreover, there was a concerted effort to filter and target information to social media users via a well-coordinated news team of volunteers.[30] The news team tailored their messages. For example, youths turned to Twitter for quick news updates and the older generation used Facebook and blogs for engaging in discourse and to post detailed information on demonstration activities. Finally, Youtube allowed users to record and post near real time videos. Ultimately, the variety of mediums operated in synergy and created and disseminated information much faster than traditional mass media formats.

Fourth, the Revolution demonstrates that the private telecommunications industry and government will either cooperate or work against each other to advance an agenda. During the height of the protests, Ukrainian-based internet service provider Volya-Cable increased internet bandwidth in Kiev. The company advocated for and provided several open and freely available wifi hotspots.[31] These actions enabled a

---

[27] Matzger Barbera [13].

[28] Matzger Barbera [13].

[29] Matzger Barbera [13].

[30] Frediani [6].

[31] GlobalVoicesOnline.Org [8].

massive ad hoc and uncensored internet infrastructure to emerge across Kiev's temporary tent cities.

The Russian government took notice and underwent a different approach in the aftermath of the Revolution. Their approach is now to censor and control the content and flow of social media on the internet. In recent months, a close ally of President Putin, Alisher Usmanov, owner of Russian mail provided mail Ru, acquired VK. VK is Russia's version of Facebook and by controlling the largest email and social media networks in Russia and the Ukraine, Putin is in a position to regulate much of social media's content in the region and to gain access to personal data of political dissidents. [32]

Future Implications

By examining the rise and effect of social media and the use of social media in two recent political demonstrations, there are several useful implications for the future. While these implications are gleaned from the current use and state of technology, they are enduring. First, let us consider how social media clusters a population. Earlier, was shown that basic human heuristics appreciate and prefer to form small manageable groups. Both demonstrations also supported this seemingly psychological truth. If clustering is in fact commonplace, then the most effective way to influence a population's thoughts and actions is via the center of the cluster.

As mentioned, cluster's function and stay functioning based on the perception of trust in the information shared and that there is an actor or set of actors that establish and maintain a rules and governance structure. Governments and non-state actors that wish to influence a cluster have several options. One approach is denial, disruption, or degradation of service. This will serve to effectively cascade the cluster into fragments. Done across a large area during a social uprising the participants experience anxiety, look for alternate means to gather information, or will simply disband.

Another approach is to supplant or re-route users to alternate means of information. This is accomplished via brute force tactics in which internet traffic is automatically misdirected or done more subversively by locating the popular discussion threads or websites and posting large volumes of posts and advertisements to other online locations. The net effect in this approach is that the cluster will break apart as users join new clusters.

A second implication is the perception that awareness spread by social media foments peaceful or violent social uprising. The two examples and Gladwell's writings indicate that in fact true activism that translates to physical action requires a connection to others within the cause that have the same values and goals. More than often, tweets, posts, likes and other such indications of support from afar failed to translate in foreign intervention. Instead demonstrators, spurred on by confirmation

---

[32] Bicchierai [2].

bias, continued their campaign. This misperception of hope and support will continue well into the future. The Hong Kong uprisings show that unless the online participants have a personal stake, social uprisings will likely stay localized and lose momentum.

However, Euromaiden shows how a peaceful demonstration can turn violent when there is a history of political discourse and specific grievances against the government. Fueled by history of Communist rule and a belief that the Russian government continued to influence Ukrainian politics, the older population took a leadership role and used social media to launch a well-coordinated strategic communication campaign that enabled the uprising to last several months and eventually force political change.

As social media useage increases, industry, government, and non-state actors will clash. This third implication is presented based on the recent moves by the Russian government to control their region's email and popular social media accounts. Should that government decide to conduct a mass denial of service or internet disruption operation, it will likely encounter significantly less blowback than a Western government. For example, in the United States, Google and Apple's decision to encrypt data and hardware is making it more difficult for the Federal government to obtain access to private data and as a result, judicial proceedings persist.[33]

Last, there is the perception that one can gain situational understanding based on social medial. As the two examples indicate, this is not entirely correct. With respect to social uprisings, situational understanding is best measured in city blocks. As mentioned, populations cluster together and those clusters are joined together in a mix of facts, assumptions and rumor. In addition, each form of social media has its own uses. Some accounts are designed to convey information to post maps and agendas while others are for the spread of propaganda. To gain situational understanding, one most find isolate the core members of the uprising, determine what accounts and online venues they are using (many of which no available to the general public), and engage with those members directly. The further one goes outside the core group, the more likely there is less fact and more assumption and rumor.

Conclusion

The exploding use of social media is staggering. The ability for populations and governments to stay connected is unprecedented. Over the next several years the norms and rules of behavior to govern its use and oversight by government will continue to mature.

Ultimately, social media is simply a hyper-expedient means of communication that is on the same evolutionary path as the signal flare and the telegram. The

---

[33] Devlin [5].

presence of a multitude of social media options are changing the dynamic of how people communicate with each other and how governments and non-state actors interact with a population. More than ever, it is becoming increasingly difficult to operate without detection and impunity and populations and governments will clash over privacy and access.

References

1. Baczynska G (2014). Timeline: political crisis in Ukraine and Russia's occupation of Crimea. Retrieved 13 Mar 2015, from Reuters: http://www.reuters.com/article/2014/03/08/us-ukraine-crisis-timeline-idUSBREA270PO20140308
2. Bicchierai L (2014). Russian email giant takes over VKontakte, 'Russia's Facebook'. Retrieved 15 Mar 2015, from Mashable: http://mashable.com/2014/09/16/mail-ru-takes-over-vkontakte
3. Cary M (2010) 5 ways new media are changing politics. Retrieved 24 Jan 2015, from U.S. News and World Report: http://usnews.com/opinion/articles/2010/02/04/5-ways-new-media-are-changing-politics
4. Cheung T (2015). Central government researcher warns radicalsed Hong Kongers. Retrieved 5 Mar 2015, from South China Morning Post: http://www.scmp.com/news/hong-kong/article/1715773/central-government-researcher-warns-radicalised-hongkongers?page=all
5. Devlin Barrett DY (2014). Apple and others encrypt phones, fueling government standoff. Retrieved 27 Mar 2015, from The Wall Street Journal: http://www.wsj.com/articles/apple-and-others-encrypt-phones-fueling-government-standoff-1416367801
6. Frediani C (2014) How Ukraine's EuroMaidan revolution played out online. Retrieved 15 Mar 2015, from Techpresident.com: http://techpresident.com/news/wegov/24790/how-EuroMaidan-play-out-online
7. Gladwell M (2010). Small change, why the revolution will not be tweeted. Retrieved 24 Jan 2015, from The New Yorker: http://www.newyorker.com/magazine/2010/10/04/small-change-3
8. GlobalVoicesOnline.Org. Ukraine's #Euromaidan Protests. http://globalvoicesonline.org/specialcoverage/2013-special-coverage/ukraines-euromaiden-protests/. Accessed 14 Mar 2015
9. Liebman L (2014) Big data market projected to reach $76 billion by 2020. Retrieved 24 Jan 2015, from Bloomburg.Com: http://bloomberg-datacap.cms.newscred.com/article/big-data-market-projected-to-reach-76-billion-by-2020/8a294bc75ace8344d1ef969f1e4416f3
10. Lokot T (2014). Russian social networks dominate in Ukraine despite information war. Retrieved 15 Mar 2015, from GlobalVoices: http://globalvoicesonline.org/2014/09/01/ukraine-russia-social-networks-information-war/
11. Margalit L (2014). The physchology behind social media interactions. Retrieved 26 Jan 2014, from Psychology Today: https://www.psychologytoday.com/blog/behind-online-behavior/201408/the-psychology-behind-social-media-interactions
12. McRaney D (2012) You are not so smart: why you have too many friends on facebook, why your memory is mostly fiction, and 46 other ways you're deluding yourself. Gotham, New York
13. Metzger PB (2013). How Ukrainian protestors are using Twitter and Facebook. Retrieved 15 Mar 2014, from The Washington Post: http://www.washingtonpost.com/blogs/monkey-cage/wp/2013/12/04/strategic-use-of-facebook-and-twitter-in-ukrainian-protests
14. BBC News (2014) China 'censors Hong Kong protest posts on social media'. Retrieved 5 Mar 2015, from BBC News: http://www.bbc.com/news/world-asia-china-29411270
15. Parker E (2014). Social media and the Hong Kong protests. Retrieved 15 Mar 2015, from The New Yorker: http://www.newyorker.com/tech/elements/social-media-hong-kong-protests

16. PewGlobal.org (2014) Emerging Nations Embrace Internet Mobile Technology. Retrieved 24 Jan2015,fromPewResearchCenter:http://www.pewglobal.org/2014/02/13/emerging-nations-embrace-internet-mobile-technology
17. Ukraine's #Euromaidan Protests (2013) Retrieved 14 Mar 14 2015, from GlobalVoices: http://globalvoicesonline.org/specialcoverage/2013-special-coverage/ukraines-euromaiden-protests
18. Ryall J (2014) The goverment tries to win the Hong Kong battle with mind games. http://mashable.com/2014/10/05/hong-kong-mind-games. Retrieved 28 Mar 2015, from Mashable: http://mashable.com/2014/10/05/hong-kong-mind-games
19. Sharkov D (2015). ISIS 'Piggyback' on Manchester United, Comedy Central and Taylor Swift Hashtags.Retrieved26Jan2015,fromNewsweek:http://www.newsweek.com/isis-piggyback-manchester-united-comedy-central-and-taylor-swift-hashtags-301271
20. Shirky C (2011) The political power of social media. Retrieved Jan 2015, from Foreign Affairs: http://www.foreignaffairs.com/articles/67038/clay-shirky/the-political-power-of-social-media
21. So P. HKU satisfied over occupy donations from Benny Tai Yiu-ting. http://www.scmp.com/news/hong-kong/article/1671601/hku-satisfied-over-occupy-donations-benny-tai-yiu-ting?page=all. Accessed 6 Mar, 2015
22. South China Morning Post (2014) HKU 'satisfied' over Occupy donations from Benny Tai Yiu-ting. (31 Dec 2014). Retrieved 8 Mar 2015, from South China Morning Post: http://www.scmp.com/news/hong-kong/article/1671601/hku-satisfied-over-occupy-donations-benny-tai-yiu-ting?page=all
23. Talaga T (2014). How social media is fuelling Ukraine's protests. Retrieved 13 Mar 2015, from TheStar.Com: http://www.thestar.com/news/world/2014/02/05/ukraines_revolutionary_movement_euromaidan_stays_organized_with_social_media.html
24. Tay H. Hong Kong student umbrella revolution movement takes to social media to separate fact from fiction in pro-democracy protests. http://www.abc.net.au/news/2014-09-30/feature-social-media-use-in-hong-kong-protests/5780224. Accessed 8 Mar 2015
25. The Statistics Portal (2014) Number of worldwide social media users. Retrieved 24 Jan 2015, from Statistica.Com: http://www.statista.com/statistics/278414/number-of-worldwide-social-network-users/
26. U.S. State Department (2015) Office of international communications and information policy. Internet Freedom. Retrieved 24 Jan 2015, from Internet Freedom: http://www.state.gov/e/eb/cip/netfreedom/index.htm
27. Wong K (2014). Occupy central: a Hong Kong protest evolved from planned sit-in to leaderless umbrella movement. Retrieved 3 Mar 2015, from Forbes Magazine: http://www.forbes.com/sites/kandywong/2014/10/08/occupy-central-a-hong-kong-protest-evolved-from-planned-sit-in-to-leaderless-umbrella-movement
28. Wong K (2014). Occupy central: a Hong Kong protest evolved from planned sit-in to leaderless umbrella movement. Retrieved 8 Mar 2015, from Forbes Magazine: http://www.forbes.com/sites/kandywong/2014/10/08/occupy-central-a-hong-kong-protest-evolved-from-planned-sit-in-to-leaderless-umbrella-movement/
29. Wong K. Occupy central. A Hong pong protest evolved from planned sit-in to leaderless Umbrella movement. http://www.forbes.com/sites/kandywong/2014/10/08/occupy-central-a-hong-kong-protest-evolved-from-planned-sit-in-to-leaderless-umbrella-movement/. Accessed 6 Mar 2015
30. Yudkowsky E (2008) Cognitive Biases Potentially Affecting Judgment of Global Risks. Oxford University Press, New York

Is Skynet the Answer? Rules for Autonomous Cyber Response Capabilities

Jarrod H. Stuard and James McGhee

Introduction

You awake to the soft sounds of your favorite music growing louder as you listen. The lights slowly begin to brighten. You can already smell the coffee wafting into your bedroom through the climate control system. As you stretch and stand up, rubbing the sleep from your eyes, your T.V. turns to your favorite news channel. You can hear the shower start as you lay out your clothes for the day. After breakfast, you get into your car. You speak the command, "work" and your car begins the drive while you read the latest news feed being projected onto your glasses. When the car stops at a red light, you glance out the window. Overhead you see an Unmanned Aerial Vehicle (UAV) silently glide past, checking on traffic ahead. Your smart phone beeps, alerting you to your tasks that await you at work. You review the tasks and discover one of your clients has been hacked – again. You see the computer system at work has decided during the night to trace the source of the hack and attempted to disable the offending bot. You hope it made the right decision and found the right culprit. If not, it may be a long day. This scenario may sound far-fetched, part of some imagined future, but the year is 2013 and the time is now.[1]

---

[1] Capt Stuard is Chief, Cyber Operations Law at the 67 Network Warfare Wing, Joint Base San Antonio, Lackland AFB. Mr. McGhee is an attorney with the 24th Air Force, Joint Base San Antonio, Lackland AFB. The views expressed in this Article are those of the authors in their personal capacities and do not necessarily represent those of the US Air Force or any other US governmental entity.

J.H. Stuard (✉) • J. McGhee
Cyber Operations Law at the 67th Network Warfare Wing,
Lackland AFB, San Antonio, TX, USA
e-mail: jarrod.stuard@gmail.com

© Springer International Publishing Switzerland 2015
M. Blowers (ed.), *Evolution of Cyber Technologies and Operations to 2035*,
Advances in Information Security 63, DOI 10.1007/978-3-319-23585-1_11

Automation is quickly moving into every facet of our lives. Smart homes are not new, but have become progressively more sophisticated, even ordering groceries without human input, based on the contents of the refrigerator. Google has recently introduced a self-driving, autonomous vehicle, capable of driving without any human input. Autonomous military weapons, especially UAVs, have been around for a while too, but also are becoming much more sophisticated and independent in their operation. Financial markets are handling volumes of trades at speeds which necessitate a degree of autonomy for the computer systems which govern them, and the list goes on to touch almost every facet of modern life. Likewise, new cyber capabilities, both offensive and defensive, are responding to increasingly complex and voluminous cyber threats to government networks. Yet rules regarding those responses are either lacking or antiquated and unable to adequately include emerging technologies. Indeed, every day, it seems our capability to unleash an autonomous creation into the wild on our behalf outpaces the degree to which we have pondered and resolved the myriad legal questions that arise in this new environment. For instance, who is responsible if something goes wrong? Can responsibility even be determined? What rules should apply? What law governs? Should autonomous cyber responses be allowed at all? This chapter outlines some of the key questions in this regard and seeks to explore these questions in light of the developing law for other autonomous systems. It will discuss the aspects that make cyber unique and propose rules that address such distinctions.

Cyber Background

The cyber threat is not new, but it is serious and growing. According to the Government Accountability Office, just 9 years ago, in 2006, the number of actual breaches reported by federal agencies was 5,503 and grew to 42,887 in 2011.[2] Today, DoD receives over six million malicious probes every day.[3] While most of these probes are automatically blocked by DoD systems or represent a minor threat, which can be remedied with a simple anti-virus program, the few root level threats that do penetrate the defensive systems represent serious problems. Mandiant, a cyber security consulting firm, revealed in a widely-publicized report that just one group in China (referred to as APT1) had maintained malicious access to critical systems of government and industry entities around the world for as long as 1,764 days. In that time, the perpetrators stole many terabytes of protected information.[4] Indeed, the threat environment is pervasive and varied in nature.

---

[2] Testimony of Gregory C. Wilshusen before the Subcommittee on Oversight, Investigations, and Management, Committee on Homeland Security, House of Representative, April 24, 2012.

[3] Lawson [1].

[4] Mandiant [2].

By now, most people are familiar with reports of the Stuxnet intrusion on Iranian nuclear infrastructure, but just a brief glance at the news reveals a more pervasive cyber threat. In early 2012, the Middle East was embroiled in a heated standoff, culminating in escalating cyber exchanges between multiple nations and the targeting of national centers of economic power. If you missed it, that is because it happened in cyberspace. The circle of hacks started when a Saudi Arabian hacker posted the credit card numbers of over 60,000 Israelis online. Israeli hackers fought back by posting private Facebook information about Saudis online. Then both sides escalated the growing "conflict." In the ensuing weeks, the websites of national airlines, stock exchanges, and defense forces went down across Israel, Palestine, Saudi Arabia, and the United Arab Emirates. More recently, multiple news outlets reported that Iran is suspected of attacking and destroying 30,000 computers belonging to the Saudi oil company Aramco, nearly two-thirds of that vital oil-provider's computer infrastructure.[5] While the lasting effects of these hacks were minimal, they revealed how vulnerable national assets and services could be to nefarious online activity. This was a warning that the nation of Georgia learned a bit too late.

It was 2008; Russia and Georgia were on the verge of conflict over the split-away region of South Ossetia. When Georgian troops entered the region to counter Russian incursions into the area, Russia decided to invade Georgia proper. Just before and during the invasion, Georgian websites, one by one, started to drop out of service. The President's website changed to images of Adolf Hitler. Defense and financial web services went down, and even the national news agency's website ceased to operate. In essence, the nation's online communication capabilities collapsed. The response from Georgia was slow and largely unsuccessful; the government rerouted internet service through servers in Germany, but to no avail. As this was happening, Russian forces moved into Georgia in a coordinated cyber/kinetic assault that was truly the first of its kind.[6] It demonstrated what cyber forces could bring to the fight as a first wave attack and the dangers of not being able to respond.

In addition to dangers to physical infrastructure, the danger to information is perhaps even greater. Cyber espionage is becoming all too common, and the information theft of mountains of classified materials or the equivalent of the entire blueprints of America's newest weapons is disturbingly not surprising anymore. In July of 2011, the Pentagon admitted to the loss of over 24,000 sensitive files from a single intrusion in a cleared defense contractor's network.[7] Mandiant's APT1 report details the activities of only one hacker group, yet that one group managed the theft of many terabytes of sensitive data from ten different industries over several years, with impunity.[8] These are real thefts with real consequences. Open source reporting also widely implicates the Chinese in stealing aircraft designs for the West's next

---

[5] Perlroth [3].

[6] Carroll [4].

[7] Peralta [5].

[8] Mandiant [2].

greatest airplanes, to include the F-22 and F-35. Coincidently, new stealth fighters, such as the Chengdu J-20, designed in China are appearing sporting marked similarities to America's newest stealth jets.[9] Through cyber tools, China is effectively leap-frogging generations of research and development to secure a prime spot on the world stage of technologically advanced militaries. If continued unabated, China could soon be a near-peer military force to the United States. The threat is real; the question then becomes how to counter the threat.

Law of Autonomous Systems

The laws applicable to fully autonomous systems are still in various stages of infancy, leaving lawyers to the task of applying traditional legal constructs to new technologies. In some cases, this is relatively easy; in others, it can be very difficult. Still, in others, the traditional rules are unworkable and inadequate.

The Google car, as it is affectionately known, is a self-driven, autonomous vehicle that does not require any human oversight. The vehicle relies on video cameras, radar sensors, lasers, and a database of information collected from manually driven cars.[10] On March 1, 2012, the Nevada legislature authorized self-driven cars for the state's roads. The Nevada DMV handed Google the very first U.S. license for a driverless vehicle. The law allows the vehicles to be tested on Nevada's roads. For now, two people must be present in the vehicle, one in the driver's seat and the other in the passenger seat. Google's system permits a human driver to take control by stepping on the brake or turning the wheel, but the Nevada law acknowledges that the operator will not need to pay attention while the car is operating itself.[11]

What if you own a "Google" car and it is involved in an accident while you are merely a passenger. Are you responsible? Is Google? Is someone somewhere in the manufacturing chain to blame? These questions are no doubt complex. However, even with the new technology, the old laws, such as the common law of torts and, more specifically, products liability, can apply. To be certain, many vehicles currently operate accident avoidance systems and if they fail, products liability would apply. The Google car is akin to an advanced form of cruise control, a common automobile function which has a long history of legal action tied to it. In *Watson v. Ford Motor Co.*, a plaintiff, the driver of the car in question, sued Ford after the cruise control function in the car malfunctioned and the car crashed, killing one and rendering the driver a quadriplegic. The theory of the case was that electromagnetic interference interfered with the car's computer systems and therefore the deceleration function. Ford ended up suffering a judgment of $18 million (even though the case was overturned later on unrelated, procedural grounds).[12] The point is that the car crash sce-

---

[9] Piore [6].

[10] http://gov.aol.com/2012/05/08/nevada-issues-first-license-for-self-driven-car/.

[11] http://www.leg.state.nv.us/Session/76th2011/bills/AB/AB511-Enpdf.

[12] *Watson v Ford Motor Co.*, 389 S.C. 434, 13 Sept 10.

nario is one that the civil courts are well practiced at, and the addition of a little more autonomy is not a legal game-ender. Courts can evaluate in the open the shortcomings of commercial autonomous systems and provide legal remedies for those wronged by them in the initial phases. These are all regulatory and legal advantages often not enjoyed in the world of military defense and offense. Yet, the automation trend has not passed over the world of weaponry either.

Drones have been around for a long time. The earliest drones were simple balloons and dirigibles that had rudimentary surveillance devices attached to them. We have progressed remarkably since then. As one of many examples, the Navy is currently working on a new Drone, referred to as the X-47B. It is an unmanned combat air system. It currently does not carry weapons, but has a full-sized weapons bay. Eventually the system will demonstrate autonomous carrier launches and recoveries, as well as autonomous in-flight refueling with a probe and drogue.[13] Currently, military drones have a "man in the loop." This simply means they are not completely autonomous but controlled by a human to some extent, yet even today, when that connection is lost, automated systems take over to guide the drone to safe territory, among other functions.

Presently the U.S. military uses drones in countries like Iraq, Pakistan, Yemen, Syria and even some African nations to target terrorists. Drone strikes are not few, but their numbers are still small enough for humans to make case-by-case decisions to assure legal compliance with the traditional laws commanders are used to being bound by on the battlefield. These laws generally include the Laws of Armed Conflict and theater-specific Rules of Engagement. In fact, recent media reports indicate the Obama administration is striving to develop a "Rulebook" for the use of drones. Perhaps as a starting point for such rules, the Department of Defense recently issued a new directive, entitled Autonomy for Weapons Systems.[14] This directive mandates that weapons systems with autonomous or semi-autonomous capabilities, such as drones, comply with certain limitations to include maintaining communication with a military operator, minimizing the ability for enemy tampering, to include the capability of a kill-switch to disable or disengage the drone if certain criteria are not met.[15] The rules included in this directive demonstrate hesitancy to fully release autonomous weapons systems from human control. Yet, a typical drone does not deal in the volume of threats or speed of attack as a system entrusted with our cyber defense. Indeed, one can argue the rule set needs to be fundamentally different for cyber systems, and, in fact, this directive exempts cyber systems from its limitations. The net result of these examples is a world where laws have attempted to tackle the novelty of autonomous systems, but nowhere have those efforts sufficiently tackled the unique dynamics of the cyber age.

---

[13] http://www.as.northropgrumman.com/products/nucasx47b/assets/UCAS-D_DataSheet_final.pdf.

[14] http://www.dtic.mil/whs/directives/corres/pdf/300009p.pdf.

[15] Id.

Unique Issues in Cyber: Is Autonomy the Answer?

The challenge for an operator charged with defending valuable networks, information, and infrastructure is how to evaluate, process, and respond to hundreds of threats to millions of targets in a relevant timeframe? The importance of this challenge cannot be overstated when only one mistake can lead to the loss of a vital national infrastructure system or years' worth of research and technological advantage over an adversary. The traditional process of carefully analyzing a piece of malware, building a signature and implementing that signature is simply not efficient or effective in the current environment. Halting or limiting a response to determine the proper agency (e.g. FBI, CIA, DoD) to counter a bad actor is not a useful rule set either. Autonomous systems that can detect, evaluate, and reach out in response to bad actors in real time, without the sluggish input of the human brain or time-consuming processes of inter-government coordination, may provide the answer. Indeed, this technology is being developed as these words are written.

It is widely reported that the Fujistu Corporation, in conjunction with the Japanese government, has developed software to automatically navigate through the myriad springboard computers used in a typical hacking attack to find the original culprit. The software's next action is up to the creativity of the designer. It can stop or disrupt the attack, gather information of the original culprit or perhaps direct malware of its own onto the offending computer.[16] The need for such systems is clear, but the implications are daunting. The technology is here, but the policy has yet to catch up.

Policymakers approach cyber policy with caution for good reason. Professor Stephen Dycus from Vermont Law School suggests that Congress must better define limits and authorities for cyber warfare, but he emphasizes that one of the central tenants should be to "Expressly forbid automated offensive responses to actual or threatened cyber attacks on the United States under any circumstances."[17] Surely, that is too broad a statement. He recognizes that there is a fundamental difference between cyberspace and the traditional war-fighting domains of land, sea, air and space. Unlike traditional domains characterized by geography and time-spans more discernible to a policymaker's mind, cyberspace transcends physical boundaries onto logical and virtual dimensions. The result is a trifecta of problems stemming from concerns of speed, geography, and attribution. These concerns present both the need for and the reasons against autonomous cyber defense systems. The challenge is not overly generalizing autonomous response options, perhaps excluding valuable defenses in the process. This trap seems to ensnare far too many scholars.

The flow of information and software code occur at such a speed that a piece of malware can spread from an entry point in a network to lateral connections throughout it before a responder can even turn on his/her computer, much less analyze the code and formulate a response. James Lewis writes in *Thresholds for Cyber Warfare*,

---

[16] Daily Yomiuru Online [7].
[17] Dycus [8].

"While the preparation for a cyber-attack may be lengthy, the speed of the actual attack is measured in seconds irrespective of the distance from the target. The cost of an attack is low, and surprise and stealth are normal attributes."[18] In the time a drone missile can strike one target, a piece of malware can infect millions of users. The speed element here is a distressing factor for the defender in terms of protecting friendly networks. Equally troubling is making sure our response is appropriately tempered. An automated response that creates an adverse effect against an attacker's network may generate an escalation of action on both sides before any human is involved in the process. Jay Kesan and Carol Hayes of the Illinois College of Law write, "While automated counterstrikes arguably increase the deterrent effect, the potential damage from automation likely exceeds the benefit from removing the human element. While automating detection may be acceptable, we suggest that humans should execute counterstrikes instead of relying on an automated process, provided that a human also verifies the existence of a threat."[19] This view may underestimate the threat to our networks and oversimplify our response options, automated or otherwise, thus eliminating valuable response options through unnecessary generalizations. The volume and mobility of cyber threats to our networks necessitate some form of rapid response, and dismissing all of those responses as equally too risky does not do justice to the technical nuances available to us. Instead of a blanket dismissal, policy makers should instead attempt to maximize the response ability of automated cyber capabilities within the rule sets that mitigate these legitimate concerns. We describe such a rule set below.

The speed and ease of access available to bad actors in the cyber realm also opens up the entire world as a front line. Attacks can come from anywhere on the globe. Rule sets for cyber defenders that are only specific to certain categories of nations, or distinguish between domestic vs. international restraints, or differ between various Areas of Responsibility are inherently too constraining to provide for a uniform defense of networks. At the same time, such geographic rule sets allow bad actors a map of permissible routes into our networks. If it is harder and takes more time and coordination to respond to a threat from U.S. soil, then bad actors sitting in China need only originate the attack from the U.S., wait for our bureaucratic coordination to kick in, and enjoy the spoils in the meantime. Indeed, when Georgia suffered its cyber onslaught from Russia, the actual servers from where the attacks originated sat in Brooklyn, USA.

When it comes to international law and the use of force in cyber, the complexity of the geographic element is apparent in the continuing confusion nations are experiencing. A clear example is the bounty of law review topics, international conferences and, collaborations of legal experts, unable to produce clear and distinct cyber international law. Article 2(4) of the United Nations Charter demands that nations "refrain in their international relations from the threat or use of force against the territorial integrity or political independence of any state." One can only use force in self-defense if subject to an Armed Attack (or authorized to do so by the Security

---

[18] Lewis [9].
[19] Kesan [10].

Council). Where that line lies in cyber for both force and armed attack is the subject of much debate. While a Stuxnet-style shut down and destruction of critical national systems seems clearly in the realm of an unauthorized use of force, deleting data from a single, unimportant computer does not. Reality usually lies somewhere in the middle, and presents more questions than answers. Michael Schmitt writes, "In particular, automatic "hack-back" systems that might involve a response amounting to a use of force are neither necessarily lawful nor unlawful. Their use must be judged in light of many factors, such as the reliability of the determination of origin, the damage caused by the attack, and the range of available response options." This ambiguity in itself creates caution before using automated systems, yet it does not recognize that there is a base level of actions that are surely below the realm of an Article 2(4) use of force that we should be exploring. Our rules below explore such a potential.

Closely related to geographical fluidity or perhaps because of it, attribution poses another obstacle. Obfuscation techniques, source address spoofing and anonymizers increase the difficulty of attribution. In a traditional kinetic war, the foe is usually obvious, as satellites and electronic signatures unmask the country that launched the missile or fired the shot. Even when the foe is not definitively known, we may still respond to a kinetic attack, in limited circumstances. For instance, if a submarine was able to get close enough to our coast and launch a missile on the homeland, we would likely respond and sink it even without knowing which country was responsible. The critical factor is identifying the source of the attack, not necessarily the actor behind it. Similarly, with cyber war, the foe is not so obvious. Cyber-weapons may bounce from botnet to botnet across multiple international borders, leaving questions about whether terrorists, organized crime, or unfriendly countries launched the assault. It is not terribly difficult for a nation or even a rogue element to conduct a cyber-attack while pretending to be someone or something else (a false flag operation). To complicate matters, adversary nations may very well have complex relationships between state agencies, criminal elements, and civilian patriot hackers that do not resemble or respect the lines drawn by U.S laws. If we must evaluate the dynamics and identity of each attacker before a response, we inevitably handicap ourselves in trying to respond quickly. Recognizing damage to our networks and information is equally as bad from a state actor or criminal element, the cyber defenders would be right to advocate for some limited, automated response authority that precedes a more focused analysis into attribution, akin to the kinetic submarine example above. The proposed rules below outline a starting point for such authority.

Moreover, the attribution problem may not be as big a hurdle as initially thought. As our technology and experience increases, so too does our ability to identify culprits. To be sure, Leon Panetta has stated that, "Over the last 2 years, DoD has made significant investments in forensics to address this problem of attribution and we're seeing the returns on that investment. Potential aggressors should be aware that the United States has the capacity to locate them and to hold them accountable for their actions that may try to harm America."[20] To be clear, Secretary Panetta was discussing cyber-attacks, which would necessitate a proper response under the UN Charter

---

[20] Remarks by Secretary Panetta on Cybersecurity to the Business Executives for National Security, New York City, October 11, 2012.

and Law of War, but the point also applies to lesser forms of cyber intrusions. Attribution is almost always needed when dealing with a response to an attack, for discrimination purposes. Nonetheless, his point lends support for the emergence of autonomous response capabilities.

Proposed Rules

With the above discussion in mind, this paper proposes three broad rules to temper concerns about autonomous cyber capabilities while permitting our technicians to explore opportunities in this area.

Below Force Effects

Autonomous cyber capabilities should be limited to effects not likely to implicate international law "use of force" concerns, such as Article 2(4) of the UN Charter or the LOAC.[21] At first glance, this rule may seem either too expansive in that it will eliminate a large portion of desired cyber responses or in addition, naïve in that it is foolish to believe such ambiguous legal parameters can be captured in a series of if/then statements. Yet, when we strip cyber attacks and responses of their novelty and provocative language, reality mitigates these concerns to a degree.

As explained above, the definition of a use of force in cyber is hardly a decided issue. Yet, cyber intrusions and "attacks" happen on a day to day basis, and few, if any, would argue we are under an armed attack worthy of an Article 51 analysis and diplomatic actions at the United Nations. These intrusions and relatively minor cyber effects represent the vast majority of what troubles our networks, and creating similar effects on outside networks would similarly not raise "use of force" concerns. More specifically, we need autonomous cyber capabilities that could automatically trace back the origins of an intrusion and, to the degree possible, terminate such actions by the intruder. Specific associated rules could include: (1) blocking connections to our networks; (2) gathering information from an intruding machine and machines associated or laterally connected to the intrusion; (3) lacking the ability to influence the root level software or hardware of target machines so as not to threaten the overall operation of hardware or entire systems; (4) being reversible in nature in that they do not require complete reformatting of a system or replacement of hardware.

---

[21] We also recognize there are domestic legal considerations in this regard, even for cyber activity that falls below Article 2(4) thresholds. Prohibitions in the Computer Fraud and Abuse Act (CFAA) may complicate this proposal, but given that the CFAA is currently under rewrite by Congress, it already allows broad exemptions for intelligence and law enforcement activity, and other laws (i.e.: the Wiretap Act) permit extensive exceptions for network defense purposes, we think similar network defense provisions to the CFAA could easily allow such autonomous defense activity.

Expansive Initial Reach/Restrictive Follow-up

The attribution question plagues the cyber defender, especially when one contemplates automated defense. It is all too easy for an intruder to utilize domestic networks or decoy state networks to create effects on government systems. A worry is that the government would automatically collect information on or target US persons or uninvolved nation states. Nonetheless, given the restrictions in the first set of rules, we believe the risks are acceptable when coupled with restrictions on the utilization of data after it is collected. First, there should be a timeline rule, which permits the gathering and retention of information, even US person information. This initial time would allow a proper analysis and disposition determination. To be sure, current intelligence oversight rules allow for up to ninety (90) days temporary retention to make such an analysis. As we recognize with signals collection, there is a distinct benefit to putting the legal burden on the tail end of the action instead of the front end. If our automated response works correctly, we can mitigate the intrusion and gather important information with no more risk than we accept with our intelligence organizations that incidentally gather and properly dispose of US person data on a routine basis. Second, when we create minor, reversible effects on uninvolved state networks, there should be a notification requirement at a later date to the affected nation. This requirement could obviously be subjected to a variety of policy restrictions for specific nations or sensitive scenarios.

Accountability

While the need for autonomy dictates a certain degree or freedom at the start of the action, it nevertheless should mandate strict oversight during the development and also after employment of the capability. Autonomous capabilities would not be fire and forget weapons. We certainly would not want to simply release a rogue capability into the "wild." To avoid that possibility, we propose building in accountability. First, as the DOD now requires for certain autonomous and semi-autonomous weapons systems, autonomous cyber capabilities should undergo thorough testing and be subjected to a legal analysis during the acquisition phase of the capability. Second, during a response, an autonomous capability should always be able to report actions and information back to military operators. Once such a capability is lost, there should be a kill switch mechanism so the capability ceases any adverse effects or self-deletes. Third, autonomous capabilities should be confined to immediate responses but should hand-off to human operators within a reasonable amount of time; not sustain operations. If human approval for the continuation of an operation is not obtained within a certain time period, the capability should self-delete.

Conclusion

Autonomous cyber capabilities, bounded by the proper rules, would allow us to stop intrusions on our systems and project out beyond our networks to stop the intrusion at the point of origin. If we harden our systems with a robust, layered defense and then include an autonomous response capability - allowing us to respond at the speed of the attack - we can begin to achieve the protection we need. If we make our own systems dangerous for intruders perhaps they will think twice before launching an intrusion in the first place. Indeed, Kesan and Hayes have stated, "automated counterstrikes arguably increase the deterrent effect."[22]

It is abundantly clear that the application of rules, policy and law in the cyber arena is seriously lacking. The old rules are proving unworkable and no new rules are being proposed or even considered. Our enemies are taking advantage of this void. The intrusions upon our systems are not only increasing, but will continue to increase. The boldness of the "attackers" is also increasing. Unless and until we do something to better protect our systems, we can expect exorbitant losses to continue. These losses not only equate to billions of dollars every year, but also to strategic and classified information losses. It is becoming increasingly easy for nations to counter our technological advantage because they already have the plans they stole. Congressional legislation or an Executive Order regarding cyber is only a start and unless we get serious about it, will only prove to be a Band-Aid on an arterial wound.

We need real solutions and capabilities. We need the ability to not only protect, but also to respond and to do so as quickly as possible with the fewest constraints possible. We have already witnessed what cyber capabilities can do. They can damage pipelines. They can destroy and disrupt SCADA systems. Even if one believes that our systems are robust and redundant, they are not bullet proof. It has been observed by many professionals in this area that, given enough time and effort, all of our systems can be attacked. We think it better to be prepared and not need it, than to need it and not be prepared. A robust, autonomous response capability would give us a solution and allow us to react at the speed of need.

References

1. Lawson S. Just how big is the cyber threat to the Department of Defense; Forbes.com http://www.forbes.com/sites/firewall/2010/06/04/just-how-big-is-the-cyber-threat-to-dod/. Last accessed 13 Mar 2013
2. Mandiant (2013). APT1 report: exposing one of China's cyber espionage units. http://intelreport.mandiant.com/. Last accessed 13 Mar 2013
3. Perlroth N. Hackers lay claim to Saudi Aramco Cyberattack; NY Times, 23 Aug 12, http://bits.blogs.nytimes.com/2012/08/23/hackers-lay-claim-to-saudi-aramco-cyberattack/. Last accessed 13 Mar 2013

---

[22] Kesan [10].

4. Carroll W. Cyber war 2.0 – Russia v. Georgia; Defense Tech, 13 Aug 08, http://defensetech. org/2008/08/13/cyber-war-2-0-russia-v-georgia/. Last accessed 13 Mar 2013
5. Peralta E. Pentagon Says 24,000 Files Were Stolen in Data Breach; NPR, 14 July 11. http:// www.npr.org/blogs/thetwo-way/2011/07/14/137858361/pentagon-says-24-000-files-were-stolen-in-data-breach. Last accessed 14 Mar 2013
6. Piore A. Digital Spies: The Alarming Rise of Electronic Espionage; Popular Mechanics, 24 Jan 12. http://www.popularmechanics.com/technology/how-to/computer-security/digital-spies-the-alarming-rise-of-electronic-espionage-2. Last accessed 14 March 2013
7. Gov't working on defensive cyberweapon; Daily Yomiuru Online, http://www.yomiuri.co.jp/dy/national/T120102002799.htm. Last accessed 14 Mar 2013
8. Dycus S (2010) Congress' role in cyber warfare, 4 J. Nat'l Security L Pol'y 155(169)
9. Lewis JA (2011) Does China's new J-20 Stealth Fighter have American technology? Center for Strategic and International Studies. Accessible at: https://csis.org/publication/does-chinas-new-j-20-stealthfighter-have-american-technology
10. Kesan JP, Hayes CM (2011) Mitigative Counterstrike: Self-Defense and Deterrence in Cyberspace, Harvard J Law Technology 415:452

Ethical Considerations in the Cyber Domain

Justin M. Hubman, Zachary B. Doyle, Robert L. Payne III,
Thomas F. Woodburn, Branden G. McDaniel, and Joseph V. Giordano

Introduction

Cybersecurity is a dynamic and ever-changing field. In today's information intensive environment, cyber-related incidents such as online fraud, cybercrime, cyber terrorism, and cyber espionage are on the rise. Our national security, personal safety, and economic health are at risk because of our dependence on cyber technologies. Threats from the cyber domain can include hacking, white collar crime, fraud, identity theft or stealing proprietary information. The perpetrators exist on a continuum (basic hackers, organized cybercrime groups, terrorists and even well-funded nation state actors). Recently, we have seen a proliferation of Internet-connected devices such as automobiles, set-top boxes, home appliances, and energy consuming devices on a smart-grid. This proliferation is projected to continue as we move towards the Internet of Everything. This will only serve to increase the number of entry point that the adversaries can exploit.

Ethics as applied to cybersecurity has become an increasingly prominent concern with regard to the field. The cyber society is not one specific area or one specific group of people; there are no real common goals or common rituals. In the real world, ethical standards are the moral guidelines taught to specific groups and individuals. It is the responsibility of the individual to recognize situations involving ethical standards and act accordingly. Ethical standards have not been established to the degree necessary to ensure proper behavior in the cyber domain. In order to establish these much needed ethical standards, the cyber society will first need to reach a consensus regarding the primary ethical concerns, eventually establishing corresponding ethical standards. The cyber society is not in a specific area

J.M. Hubman • Z.B. Doyle • R.L. Payne III • T.F. Woodburn
B.G. McDaniel • J.V. Giordano (✉)
Economic Crime, Justice Studies and Cybersecurity, Utica College,
1600 Burrstone Road, Utica, NY 13502, USA
e-mail: jgiordano@utica.edu

© Springer International Publishing Switzerland 2015
M. Blowers (ed.), *Evolution of Cyber Technologies and Operations to 2035*,
Advances in Information Security 63, DOI 10.1007/978-3-319-23585-1_12

nor is it a specific person. This "society" is global, further complicating the issue. What needs to be done to set these standards?

Ethical conduct in the cyber world is as undefined as the cyber world is. Ethics, in general, is not easily defined in the actual physical world in which we live. Defining proper ethical behavior in the cyber domain will be a difficult challenge. Making sure all societies and governments agree on cyber ethics will be an arduous, if not impossible, undertaking. Under current circumstances, democratic nations could be willing to reach bilateral agreements. Yet, in the face of it all, other nations might not be so willing to take on the ethical definitions of the U.S., Europe and its allies. Within the next 20–25 years, the present ethical concerns in the cyber domain will become increasingly prominent.

Ethical Considerations in the Cyber Domain

The cyber society is a combination of legislative actions, state and non-state actors, the military and public-private partnerships. It is difficult to establish a set of standards when the cyber world is used for essentially everything, both good and bad, and the parties which constitute the cyber society often come from geographically separate and ideologically diverse worldviews.

As the cyber society changes and advances, the ethical and philosophical concerns become increasingly complex. To further complicate matters, the cyber society has yet to be declared a "society." According to Webster's Dictionary, a society is defined as "people in general thought of as living together in organized communities with shared laws, traditions, and values." While many would argue the cyber arena is a place where there are shared laws, especially within the United States, people in cyberspace generally do not live together, have similar traditions, or share the same values. Ethical conduct in the cyber world is still quite undefined; much like the cyber world is undefined.

A major concern and source of debate is the right to privacy and the right of the government to collect data on individuals. Recently, the National Security Agency (NSA) faced criticism regarding their data collecting programs. Edward Snowden, a contractor for the NSA, leaked highly classified information containing the details of this program in 2013. This program was given the codename PRISM. Snowden leaked the information pertaining to PRISM to *The Washington Post* and *The Guardian*.

PRISM was a highly classified government-sponsored data collection program which used other service providers to aid in the collect the data. This program "piggybacked" off well-known commercial companies. People understand that these companies are collecting data about them, and they tend to accept this. However, when the government collects data on the same people, there is public outcry. The NSA and other government funded departments have the job of protecting national security and the safety of the United States. The only job these companies have is making billions of dollars of profits.

The U.S. government, including the NSA and the Intelligence Community, performs data collection with the overall mission of protecting the nation from numerous and varied threats. However, what tends to escape notice in times of public outcry is that numerous commercial, financial, and advertising online businesses collect as much as, if not more, information than these government agencies. Why the double standard?

With the continual explosive growth of cyberspace, the threat of conflict in that domain becomes a serious concern. It is the sole responsibility of modern cyber-intensive organizations to take extra precautions in protecting the information they collect. This will soon be the norm, making necessary that the data collecting process will be subject to government regulation.

Public – Private Partnerships

Critical infrastructure protection has been vastly efficient since the Cold War. Critical infrastructures include systems and organizations such as power plants, power grids, oil and gas pipelines, telecommunication, and other facilitates that are critical to the nation's government. Public and private partnerships are an essential part of our homeland security. According to Givens and Busch, "approximately 85 % of the nation's critical infrastructure is under private sector control, alliances between government and businesses are essential for homeland security" (year). Throughout the Department of Homeland Security, there are different levels to coordinate to establish awareness between the public and private sectors. The Office of Infrastructure Protection (OIP), for example, assists in vulnerability analysis, national and local coordination with businesses and government agencies, and risk mitigation. On the cybersecurity side, information technology firms are very essential to achieve national cybersecurity objectives. Recent incidents regarding hacking have become more prevalent and common in the private sector. Analyzing the source of the threats and methods of attack will allow for better knowledge of cyber threats to these private and public sector organizations.

Cyberterrorism is a huge threat to the public-private critical infrastructure. Cyberterrorism refers to the manipulative use of computer systems to bring about a political change or to cause chaos and fear. Cyberterrorism has major influences on government as well as military computer systems. These threats are posed in many ways, but are mostly logical threats. Each threat is analyzed, and this process is forever evolving with new discoveries in technology. Although there are no physical attacks in cyberterrorism, public and private partnerships are important when identifying the measures that have the potential to reduce or eliminate the threats that are posed.

Another important aspect of public-private partnerships is preventing cyberespionage. Cyberespionage is the use of computer networks to gain illicit access to sensitive information, typically held by a government or other organization. Cyberespionage frequently deals with computer networks being hacked through the

Department of Defense (DOD). The attacks focus on and manipulate the weaknesses in the DOD computer networks. The public-private partnerships can serve to help minimize the impact of the intrusions. The Federal Bureau of Investigation (FBI) plays an important part in working with the public-private partnerships. FBI officials will collect reports from various industries to try and minimize the theft of trade secrets. While cyberespionage is a very serious crime, there are several others crimes that can be committed in the cyber domain as well.

Cybercrime refers to the crime that is conducted over the Internet or a network. Cybercrime is a term that most people have heard and possibly can relate to in today's society. With hackers becoming more abundant as technology improves, public-private partnerships are increasing in importance. These partnerships must take on more responsibility in order to prevent cybercrime and other breaches. As of 2015, cybercrime data breaches have become more prevalent more than ever.

Surveillance has an important role in the studying of data breaches. Originally, surveillance in police work was conducted on foot, in cars, and frequently by undercover agents. This surveillance still occurs today. However, there is a whole new area of surveillance as well, which now occurs in the cyber domain. Surveillance is extremely important in counterterrorism efforts in today's world. Potential targets can be located and mapped in order to assist with the physical security of those locations. More importantly, however, surveillance is used for scanning ports and assessing vulnerabilities in computer networks. The private sector plays a major role in this by building a network intrusion detection system that can point out when a port is being scanned. This brings much opportunity for public and private partnerships to mitigate cyberespionage. According to Givens and Busch:

> Much of the work involved in halting cyberespionage is quite similar to that involved in stopping cyberterrorism. To better understand how public-private partnerships can stop cyberespionage, it is helpful to use conventional spying, also known as human intelligence (HUMINT), as a framework for analysis (Busch and Givens 2014) [3].

It is also very critical to understand that in order to mitigate threats that IT infrastructure requires public-private cooperation.

Although there are many advances in the way we try and reduce cyberterrorism, cyberespionage, and cybercrime, there are still gaps to fill and important questions that remained unanswered. Givens and Busch consider the questions regarding the still-growing framework of local, state, and federal cybersecurity laws, which leaves open gaps for prosecuting crimes and advancing civil suits. They provide that "government and business interest do not align perfectly, leading to potential conflicts. Sharing resources and information can be difficult. And the public and private sectors must deepen their cooperation with one another to avoid complacency." These challenges will be very difficult to overcome without finding ways to resolve them in a systematic, efficient way.

According to the 2014 Verizon Wireless Data Breach Investigations Report [1], 92 % of the 100,000 incidents analyzed from the last 10 years were all described by nine basic patterns. These patterns include point-of-sale (POS) intrusions, web app attacks, insider misuse, physical theft/loss, miscellaneous errors, crimeware, card skimmers, denial of service (DOS) attacks, and cyber espionage. In the past few years, the United States has been exposed to the most cyber attacks in history, and many people now question the efficiency of the private sector's information security. Companies such as JPMorgan Chase, Home Depot, and Target were all exposed and infiltrated that year. A survey conducted by the Ponemon Institute showed that the average cost of cybercrime for U.S. retail stores more than doubled from 2013 to 2014, jumping to an annual average of $8.6 million per company in 2014. The average annual cost per company of a successful cyber-attack increased to $20.8 million in financial services, $14.5 million in technology sector, and $12.7 million in the communications industry (Accroding to the Ponemon Institute [1]).

According to Riley Walters in Brief 4289 on National Security and Defense, based off the practices and ideas of Steven P. Bucci, Paul Rosenzweig, and David Inserra, there are three main reasons to improve the private sector's ability to defend itself and Congress's action towards this. First, Congress should create a safe legal environment for sharing information, which entails that:

> As leaders of technological growth, private companies are in most ways at the forefront of cybersecurity, whereas like government agencies, companies must share information that concerns cyber threats and attacks among themselves and with appropriate private and public partnership organizations (Walters 2014) [12].

This environment for sharing information becomes extremely important, because it will make the process much more efficient and effective. This will increase the ability and the desire for private sector businesses to work hand in hand with public sector government agencies. Secondly, the United States needs to work with international partners, and Walters explains that attacks can infect hundreds (and more than likely thousands or more) of computer systems and networks. These infections can spread across international borders rapidly, so international cooperation is a vital part of the security of the United States. This cooperation must involve foreign companies as well as governments working with domestic companies and governments. This will greatly strengthen the public-private partnerships that already exist. Lastly, we need to encourage cybersecurity as a whole. Walter concludes, "With the number of breaches growing daily, a cybersecurity insurance market is developing to mitigate the cost of breaches. Congress and the Administration should encourage the proper allocation of liability and the establishment of a cyber-insurance system to mitigate faulty cyber practices and human error."

Trying to predict the future ethical policies for cyber critical infrastructure is a difficult task to perform. However, there are some things that can be predicted to happen within the near future that will be the basis for practices in 25 years. First, as expected, public-private partnerships will expand overall. Data will be increasing exponentially and this will directly affect the number of attacks, including cybercrimes, cyberespionage and, cyberterrorism. The government will need to interact with businesses in order to avoid and counter these attacks as much as possible. When this is not possible, cooperation will be necessary to recover from successful cyber-attacks.

One aspect of preventing unethical behavior is to prevent private sector leaks. Going back to Busch and Givens:

> As more government functions are outsourced to the private sector, there is increased potential for private sector leaks of sensitive or classified government information. This can happen in at least three ways: external electronic data breaches, internal electronic data breaches, and conventional human disclosures (Busch and Givens 2014) [3].

In the future, public-private partnerships will continue to grow, and the two sectors will work more together than ever before. The work will involve dealing with and mitigating cyberterrorism, cyberespionage, and cybercrimes. Both sides need to work together to achieve the common goal of a more secure, safe cyber environment. In fact, both the Department of Defense and the Department of Homeland Security are reaching out to the innovators in Silicon Valley to help them deal with and counter the growing cyber threat and to ensure that America's military and government have the cutting-edge technologies it needs [2, 5]. In addition to the exchange of technical information, one of the main drivers for this will be cyber ethics, as the ethical policies and codes of conduct will be crucial in dictating how these partnerships and information sharing models will work. With a strong cyber ethics philosophy in place, public-private partnerships will serve to increase cooperation and help to reduce cyber attacks in all facets of the industry.

Military Considerations

When considering the military and warfare the first thing that comes to mind is front line combat, hostile areas, air raids, and troop deployment. However, practices and strategic measures change, making drastic differences in war tactics. The four military domains of warfare are land, air, sea, and space. These traditional, physical domains of warfare have now been joined by a fifth domain, cyber. Former director of the National Security Agency and Central Intelligence Agency and U.S. Air Force retired General Michael V. Hayden [8] stated in *The Future of Things 'Cyber'* that he sees cyber as a domain and this is now listed in doctrine. Very recently, the U.S. Department of Defense has released a strategy document that states the Department "should be able to use cyber operations to disrupt an adversary's command and control networks, military-related critical infrastructure and weapons capabilities" [2]. It is impossible for man to change the land mass, the seven oceans or anything of that magnitude created naturally. Due to the fact cyber was created by mankind, it can and will constantly continue to change and evolve.

At the highest level, the military is authorized by law to engage in cyberwar. Cyber operations in the military require the understanding of the following terminology: Computer Network Operations (CNO), Computer Network Defense (CND), Computer Network Attack (CNA), and Computer Network Exploitation (CNE) [10]. These terms may look confusing and start to raise questions. CNA involves an attempt to deny, degrade, or destroy information of the enemy, or even possibly destroy networks or computers within a specific network. CND involves the ability to monitor, analyze, and protect the network to ensure that attacks won't cripple or entirely compromise a network. Lastly, CNE is the monitoring of networks in order to recognize when information is being stolen and used maliciously [10].

Cybersecurity issues are always evolving, and it is necessary to keep looking forward in order to prepare for what may be next. Every system and network is as vulnerable as the next. When trying to protect assets and resources, there has to be the assumption that anyone could penetrate, exploit, disrupt, degrade, or deny services to a system at any time. If vulnerabilities are found in a computer network, there is a strong chance an adversary can access a system and use that access to disrupt the service. Failure to explore common issues can lead to destructive attacks on critical infrastructures and can potentially lead to cyberwar.

On July 19, 2008, a Georgian Internet security firm was hit by a distributed denial of service attack (DDoS). The DDoS attacks happened prior to the Russian invasion of Georgia, and again during the invasion, leaving Georgia's communication system down. In response, Georgia moved important assets to the United States without being granted access by the United States [9]. However, the article explained that most of the Internet in the United States is controlled by third-party private sector organizations, which raises the question: does the United States remain neutral in the situation? A typical DDoS attack is constituted as a cybercrime on Article 4 of the Council of Europe Convention. However, does it become cyber warfare when it coincides with traditional military physical force attacks? These are key questions that must be addressed.

It's clear that these concerns can be researched further. Stuxnet is another example of the ethical ambiguities that can be found within cyberspace. With an attack as powerful as Stuxnet, which attacked and manipulated a nuclear facility in Iran, the potential to destroy or take down power plants, nuclear infrastructures, and other critical infrastructures give cause to prepare for these types of attacks. Altering any of the critical infrastructures could cause failure, leading to catastrophic damage and affecting the economic and national security of a given nation. Future cyber experts need to set guidelines for these issues before adversaries begin to take full control of nuclear facilities and are able to launch and guide nuclear missiles. This leads to the questions about cyber attacks against a nation's critical infrastructure. Is such an attack ethical prior to an armed conflict? Is such an attack ethical during an armed conflict? Is such an attack prior to an armed conflict considered an act of cyber war?

With the constant evolution in this field, new threats, as well as developments may begin to be predictable. Military defense should be at the highest level of cyber strength as possible. The possibility of an enemy obtaining access and control of a guided missile and turning it around to strike a different target on the ground is a high risk. DARPA, a military research organization, intends on developing a drone which limits the possibility of this happening; an "unhackable" drone. The United States currently has drones that are capable of carrying guided missiles that are controlled by an operator in a secure base halfway around the world. Securing the systems related to drone technology including command and control, weapons control, communications and all other aspects of the system, becomes a high priority in the new and emerging world of cyber-based, semi-autonomous, robotic warfare.

Cyber-Ethics Related to State and Non-state Actors

Of course, cyber ethics can be applied in a variety of areas across different disciplines. This can be broken down into several categories, including state and non-state actors. For the purpose of this discussion, a state actor, as defined in United States law, is "a person who is acting on behalf of a governmental body." Obviously, by this definition, a state actor would have to abide by United States laws, and would be subject to various regulations to protect certain rights and freedoms of the citizens. On the other hand is non-state actors, which are essentially anyone or any group who does not qualify as a state actor. There are several types of non-state actors, including corporations, terrorist organizations, and independent entities. Both state and non-state actors will be greatly affected by cyber ethics, but in very different ways.

In general, ethics is the branch of philosophy that is concerned with what is right and wrong, and is greatly influenced by society. So, ethics change as time passes, and as society's attitude as a whole changes. This can be seen throughout history in almost every society, and this will be no different with cyber ethics. However, this change may not be as cohesive and consistent as one may expect. This is especially true for non-state actors. Since there are so many different non-state actors, they will all be affected, or not affected, differently. Of course, legal regulations will affect how corporations operate. But cyber ethics will also affect how companies advertise their products, and what information they collect about their customers or potential customers. In the future, it appears that companies will continue to collect more information about customers, and it seems to be unavoidable. This is because people are willing to put more information online constantly, including personal information about likes, dislikes, habits, and more. This will influence how companies operate on a daily basis, and they will need to be careful not to upset the people who are buying (or considering) their products or services.

Some ethical concerns of business specific to the cyber world will be privacy policies and data security. While corporations will surely abide by legal regulations (for the most part), they may have to take extra steps in the future to keep their business practices in line with ethical concerns of the consumers. This could include preventing data breaches, and sharing or not sharing consumer information with third parties.

One controversial topic in this area is Amazon's proposed use of drones for delivery. In 2014, Amazon requested exemptions from the Federal Aviation Administration that would allow the company to deliver small packages by drones [11]. This raises several ethical concerns in the cyber world. Should drones be allowed to fly for commercial purposes? What are the risks associated with commercial drones? As of now, commercial drones are not being used. However, it is a certainty that this will change in the future. As the technology and capabilities of drones advance, the security must improve as well. This should reduce some of the concerns of both the Federal Aviation Administration and consumers. It will take some time, but in the next 10–15 years, one can expect that drones will be integrated into the commercial airspace.

It's one thing to examine commercial entities and how cyber ethics apply to their world. It's another thing to examine cyber ethics in the context of terrorist organizations. Obviously, terrorist organizations have no regard to the law, and this can be said about conventional ethics as well. "Normal" ethical procedures are ignored by terrorists as noted by Bruce A. Clark [4] in his article *The Ethics of Terrorism*. Clark notes that terrorist organizations such as al Qaeda seem to "have no legitimate grievance over which to attack," and that "there aren't any" ethics when it comes to terrorism [4]. This carries over into the cyber world, where terrorist organizations will continue to ignore ethics, ethical conduct and ethical behavior. According to James Comey, director of the FBI, cyber-attacks are now one of the biggest threats to the United States. The cyber world is "where the bad guys will go," according to Comey, and this will only continue in the future [6]. This is already happening; one example is the ISIS hacking of the United States Central Command Twitter and YouTube accounts in January. In addition, ISIS has shown to be a sophisticated user of social media to spread their message throughout the world. So, when it comes to cyber ethics, terrorist organizations will ignore all commonly accepted cyber policies and standards, and there are no indications that this will change in the future.

Another interesting way to look at cyber ethics is from the view of "hacktivist" organizations. The most well-known hacktivist group is Anonymous, and they have been responsible for several attacks and breaches into various systems and networks. Anonymous identifies itself as a "non-profit organization" on its website and Facebook page. The Facebook page also claims that Anonymous is "Supporting the poor and powerless. Bringing justice to the world." However, the cyber-attacks and breaches they are responsible for violate both laws and ethical cyber practices. So, when it comes to cyber ethics, it seems that Anonymous is only concerned with its own agenda, and will not abide by widely accepted ethical standards; essentially, they have created their own code of ethics. Again, there is no reason to expect this to change, as organizations like this operate without any regards for accepted codes of ethics.

Clearly, some non-state actors, such as corporations, will be affected in a large way by cyber ethics over the next 20 years. On the other hand, non-state actors such as terrorist organizations and hacktivist groups will not really be affected, because ethical practices do not concern them. However, the other side of this discussion is state actors, as previously mentioned. These people and agencies will most certainly be affected by cyber ethics, and they will also be molding the laws concerning the cyber world to fit in line with cyber ethics.

In the United States, government laws, rules, regulations, and policies have always been influenced by the ethics of the American society as a whole. This can be seen on several occasions, including the abolition of slavery, the civil rights movement, and the women's rights movement. So, looking into the next 20 years, it can be expected that the same will happen with local, state, and federal laws applying to the cyber world. As with anything, the cyber world will need to have laws governing what is acceptable or unacceptable, allowed or prohibited, and so on. These laws will surely govern how the Internet is used by citizens, as well as what is acceptable in terms of government data collecting.

This has already become an issue, as illustrated with the National Security Agency (NSA). It is now public knowledge that the NSA was collecting and storing massive amounts of phone records of American citizens. While many American citizens were outraged, some called it an acceptable measure to counter potential terrorism. No matter which side is taken in this discussion, this clearly presents the issue of cyber ethics affecting state actors. What is acceptable, and how far can the government go in regulating and monitoring cyber activity and for what purpose?

If the example of the NSA data collection is taken, several questions may arise. What was being collected, and how much? Why was this information being stored, and for how long? However, when it comes to cyber ethics one question rises above the rest. Simply, why was the government doing this secretly? The answer to this can be directly related to cyber ethics.

Cyberspace: An Evolving and Uncertain Domain

In his book, *Future Crimes*, Marc Goodman [7] discusses what we can expect in the future related to crime and malicious activity in cyberspace. Goodman brings to the forefront the fact that most everything of value is created, stored and processed in the cyber domain. In addition, as stated by Goodman, the movement to the Internet of Everything means that everything is connected and that everything is vulnerable. This is a true double-edged sword. The opportunities and advantages provided by cyberspace are limitless: health and disease research, enhanced communications, increased efficiency in business, streamlined government, "just-in-time" production, customization, etc... With essentially everything being stored electronically in the cyber domain there is an increased need to protect, defend and secure all of this data. DNA databases, financial information, personally identifiable information (PII), protected health information (PHI), product databases, supply chain information, and so much more is stored in cyber databases.

Government, military, intelligence and law enforcement information is stored in the cyber domain. The critical need for protecting this data is paramount and must be taken seriously. Taken together, this information nothing less than the actual digital representation of the modern organization or individual. Criminals or malicious actors hacking into any of the aforementioned systems can essentially take on the identity of whom or what they've hacked into. Hack into any of these systems, gather up the sensitive information and an individual or organization has lost both its intellectual property and its identity. The ethical consideration of the modern day organization is to do all that they can to protect the information that they have been entrusted with. Not providing the most protection possible is a lack of ethics on the part of the modern day organization. The result of such a lack of protection of the digital and cyber infrastructure can be losses amounting to billions of dollars, serious harm against national and economic security, ruination of organizational reputation and even loss of life.

Conclusion

Cyber ethics is a topic that has tremendous implications for the future. Our dependence upon cyberspace is only going to grow as we look ahead to 2035. That being said, there are numerous hurdles that must be overcome as we seek to understand cyber ethics. The world of cyber ethics has many players: technologists, lawmakers (e.g., Congress), organizations (e.g., business, industry, and critical infrastructures), governments (e.g., defense, military, Intelligence Community, law enforcement), and society. Technology developments will continue to march along at an amazing pace. New technologies continue to come to market in what seems to a day-to-day model. It's doubtful that over the next 20–25 years that anything will stop either this pace of development or the consumers' insatiable desire to own and use the latest and greatest technology development. Lawmakers play a key role in defining cyber ethics. The problem on the legislative front is that things move slowly and for good reason as complex issues and problems need to be examined, analyzed and debated. However, for the fast moving world of cyber, this slow moving model might not be conducive to addressing the need for cyber laws that address ethical concerns (e.g., information sharing, surveillance, metadata, use of drones, etc…). Despite the herculean efforts of some members of Congress, development of cyber laws has not been a successful endeavor. Organizations are in the mode of buying, integrating and using all of the latest technologies that they can get their hands on, sometimes without understanding the legal, social and ethical impacts that these technologies have on their organizations and society in general. The past few years have seen numerous controversies arise that have brought to the forefront the tradeoff between national security and personal privacy. All of a sudden many government agencies have become targets as violators of personal privacy. The details of national surveillance programs have been leaked by the likes of Edward Snowden and others. The national agencies that have been vilified have a legitimate mission to protect the American public. However, these agencies need to do things properly and with a strong ethical underpinning. Finally, society in general needs to gain a much better understanding of what it means to live in the cyber age. People need to realize that their surfing habits, social media accounts, financial records, cell phone records and other forms of personal information are constantly being tracked and traced by a multitude of players (for the most part by non-governmental institutions).

To address the complex and somewhat confusing topic of cyber ethics, it is critically important that lawmakers, organizations, government, the American public and technology companies engage in thoughtful, meaningful debates. As we look to the future, we see more people across the globe joining the online population. Systems are being developed that enable people and organizations to store more information than ever thought possible. The emergence, growth and evolution of social media systems require new thinking when it comes to cyber ethics. The "Internet of Things" is yet another emerging trend in which a wide variety of physical objects will be connected to the Internet, making data collection and surveillance a serious issue. The government, the military, defense organizations, the Intelligence Community, and law enforcement organizations are the protectors of society. They need access to data to carry out their very important missions, while also determining a way to ethically collect, sanitize, analyze and store information that is sensitive and private. A future without an intellectual and moral understanding and implementation of cyber ethics will most certainly be a dystopian future.

References

1. 2014 Verizon Wireless Data Breach Investigations Report (2014). In Verizon Enterprise. Retrieved 26 Apr 2015. http://www.verizonenterprise.com/DBIR/2014/reports/rp_dbir-2014-executive-summary_en_xg.pdf
2. Baldor LC (2015). New Pentagon strategy warns of cyberwar capabilities. http://abcnews.go.com/Technology/wireStory/pentagon-strategy-warns-cyberwar-capabilities-30520063
3. Busch NE, Givens AD (2014) The business of counter terrorism public- private partnerships in Homeland Security, vol 4. Peter Lang, New York, pp. 87–137
4. Clark BA (2008) The ethics of terrorism. In: Spectacle. Retrieved Apr 2015, from http://www.spectacle.org/0408/clark.html
5. Eng J (2015) Homeland security to open satellite cyber office in Silicon Valley. http://www.nbcnews.com/tech/security/homeland-security-open-satellite-cybersecurity-office-silicon-valley-n345706
6. FBI: Cyber-attacks surpassing terrorism as major domestic threat. 14 Nov 2014. In RT. Retrieved Apr 2015, from http://rt.com/usa/fbi-cyber-attack-threat-739/
7. Goodman M (2015) Future crimes. Published in the United States by Doubleday, a sub division of Random House LLC, New York, and in Canada by Random House of Canada Limited, Toronto, Penguin Random House companies
8. Hayden M (2011) The future of things cyber. Strat Stud Q 5(1):3–8
9. Korns SW, Kastenberg JE (2009) Georgia's cyber left hook. Parameters 60–65
10. Lai RC-II, Syed (Shawon) Rahman P (2012) Analytic of China cyberattack. Int J Multimedia Appl (IJMA) 4(3):46–47
11. McNeal GS (2014) Six things you should know about Amazon's drones. Forbes. Retrieved from http://www.forbes.com/sites/gregorymcneal/2014/07/11/six-things-you-need-to-know-about-amazons-drones/
12. Walters R (2014). Cyber attacks on U.S. companies in 2014: issue brief 4289 on National Security and Defense . In: The Heritage Foundation. Retrieved from http://www.heritage.org/research/reports/2014/10/cyber-attacks-on-us-companies-in-2014

Ethical Challenges of 'Disruptive Innovation': State Sponsored Hactivism and 'Soft' War

George Lucas

This chapter discusses the phenomenon of "soft" war. This concept offers an obvious comparison with a concept now well-established in international relations: namely, "soft power" [9], according to which diplomacy, trade agreements and other policy instruments may also be used, alongside or in lieu of threats of military force or other "hard-power" (kinetic or forceful) measures, in order to persuade adversary nations to cooperate more readily with any given state's strategic goals.

"Soft war, by analogy," is a comparatively new term designating actual warfare tactics that rely on measures other than kinetic force or conventional armed conflict to achieve the political goals and national interests or aspirations for which wars (according to Clausewitz [3]) are always fought. Importantly, I argue that "soft war" is fully equivalent to what Chinese military policy strategists earlier deemed "unrestricted" warfare: i.e., "warfare" carried out within domains in which conventional wars are not usually fought, employing measures not previously associated with the conduct of war. Cyber conflict is included within the purview of such measures, as a form of "unrestricted" warfare or "soft war," which is what makes this topic of special interest and concern. Accordingly, I begin with a background review of malevolent activities in cyberspace itself.

G. Lucas (✉)
U.S. Naval Postgraduate School, Reilly Center for Science, Technology & Values, Notre Dame University, Notre Dame, IN 46556, USA
e-mail: george.r.lucas.jr@gmail.com

© Springer International Publishing Switzerland 2015
M. Blowers (ed.), *Evolution of Cyber Technologies and Operations to 2035*,
Advances in Information Security 63, DOI 10.1007/978-3-319-23585-1_13

A Brief History of Cyber Conflict (Or Malevolent Activities in the Cyber Domain)

Not so long ago, cyber "activism" (on the internet, at least) was limited to pranks, practical jokes, and random acts of vandalism carried out by individuals or perhaps small groups or "gangs." Pranksters attached software "viruses" to emails that, when mistakenly opened, quickly spread through an organization's internal network, posting goofy messages and perhaps even erasing valuable data or software store on hard drives. Cyber vandals posted offensive messages or unwanted photos, or otherwise defaced an organization's website for no apparent reason. About the only crimes committed in those early days were trespassing (technically, by "invading" a private company network or an individual's computer itself) and destruction of property. Apart from mean-spiritedness or a perverted sense of humor, however, about the only reasons given for such malicious activities were a collective grousing by disaffected programmers and computer "geeks" about the monopolistic practices, and mediocre software distributed by Microsoft Corporation.

Malicious behavior in the cyber domain, however, quickly evolved into a variety of more serious and sinister activities. On the one hand, it was not long before sophisticated individuals and criminal gangs exploited the very same software vulnerabilities as pranksters, but did so in order to steal bank deposits, credit card numbers, or even one's personal identity. On the other hand, cyber "activism" itself likewise evolved into ever more sophisticated acts of political sabotage: defacing or even temporarily shutting down government or commercial web sites with so-called "DDoS" attacks (distributed denial of service), dispatching software "worms" that traveled from computer to computer, penetrating each machine's firewall and virus protection software in order to gain control over the PC's or laptops themselves, transforming each into a "zombie." These individual machines were then remotely networked with others into a massive "botnet" controlled by political dissidents or criminal organizations, who, in turn, used them to launch DDoS attacks on banks and financial institutions and divert their funds to secret accounts.

"Hacktivism" is a term that came into somewhat indiscriminate use to classify all these distinctive and diverse acts of malevolence and mischief in the cyber domain, ranging from straightforward crime and vandalism, to many forms of political protest carried out on the internet. Technically, the "hacktivist" is one who engages in vandalism and even in criminal activities in pursuit of political goals or objectives, rather than simply for personal satisfaction or financial gain. Well known individuals (like Julian Assange of Wiki Leaks) and loosely-organized groups like Anonymous, LulzSec, and "Cyberwarriors for Freedom," resort to internet malevolence to publicize their concerns, or otherwise further their political aims. These concerns range from personal privacy, liberty, and freedom of expression to opposition to political regimes like Syria or Egypt.

There are many ways of carrying out "hacktivism." I find it useful to focus upon the political goals of the "hacktivist" (as opposed to the financial interests of the conventional criminal). These political goals can be categorized as: transparency, whistle-blowing, and vigilantism. WikiLeaks purports, for example to provide greater _transparency_ regarding the otherwise covert activities of government and large corporate organizations. The actions of _whistle-blowers_ (like U.S. Army Private Bradley (Chelsea) Manning, and NSA Contractor Edward Snowden), somewhat in contrast, aimed specifically to expose what each individual took to be grave acts of wrong-doing or injustice on the part of the U.S. government or military (in these specific cases).

The _internet vigilante_s like "Anonymous," for their part, are a bit harder to pin down, since the loosely organized federation's individual members espouse a wide variety of disparate causes. The organization's behavior in response to each chosen cause, however, clearly involves taking the law (or, in its absence, morality) into the group's hands unilaterally. That is, based upon their shared judgments regarding immoral or illegal behavior by individuals, organizations, or governments to whom the group objects, the group launches attacks against selected targets ranging from the Syrian government of Bashir al Assad (for engaging in massive human rights violations), to organizations and individuals who might be engaged in perfectly legitimate security and defense operations to which members of Anonymous nevertheless object.

This is vigilantism. And, as its name suggests, the members of Anonymous cannot easily be traced or held accountable for their actions. As in all instances of conventional vigilantism, the vigilante's judgment as to what or who constitutes a moral offense is deeply subjective, and often wildly inconsistent or otherwise open to serious question.

Importantly, in all cases involving transparency, whistle-blowing and vigilantism, the _burden of proof_ is on those who deliberately violate fiduciary duties and contractual (legal) agreements into which they may have entered, or who disobey or flout the law itself, in order to expose or protest against activities they deem to be even more egregious than their own actions. This comparative judgment on the part of the protestor or whistle-blower is technically known as "the Principle of Proportionality." It demands of them that the degree of harm brought about through their own actions be _demonstrably less_ than the harm already done by others to which they seek to call attention, or bring to a stop. The problem is that this comparative judgment is notoriously difficult to make. Vigilantes often exaggerate or misrepresent the harm against which they protest, and seriously underestimate the effects of their own activities on public welfare.

Otherwise, the remaining difficulty with such actions is that there is no independent or adversarial review of these decisions. According to what is likewise termed the "Principle of Publicity" or the Principle of Legitimate Authority, the final authority to evaluate the legitimacy of the protestor's or dissident's actions rest not with that individual or dissident organization, but with the wider general public, in whose collective interest the individual purports to act. So, in all these cases, it must be possible in principle to bring the individual dissident's actions and intentions before an impartial "Court of Public Opinion" for independent review. The last criterion is the one most frequently ignored, and most often failed by both vigilantes and would-be whistle-blowers. They are prone to suffer from an abundance of self-righteousness.

The Advent of State-Sponsored Internet Activism

Having established this context for the discussion of cyber hacktivism generally, what now are we to make of its most recent evolution: namely, the rise of state-sponsored or government "Hacktivism?" Nations and governments are entering the cyber fray alongside private groups, either attempting to combat or shut down other hacktivists and stifle dissent within their own borders, or instead, to pursue political objectives against other states that were traditionally resolved through diplomacy, economic sanctions, and finally, a resort to kinetic force. *Many states at present appear to be resorting to massive cyber attacks instead.* Such nations are thought to include pro-government groups or organizations in China (e.g., PLA Shanghai Unit 61384), the Russian Federation, and especially North Korea.

The most recent high-visibility example of such state behavior was the apparent attack by North Korean operatives on Sony Pictures, over the pending release of the movie comedy, "The Interview." Never (it was frequently remarked) had such a bad movie received such first-class publicity. The entire affair seemed itself almost comedic, save for the important principles at stake: interference in the internal affairs of another nation, freedom of expression, violations of personal privacy for foreign state purposes. The kind of extortion and blackmail involved, and its impact on corporate and individual behavior in a sovereign land, might not have seemed so funny in alternative circumstances. The U.S. thus treated this instance of massive, state-sponsored hacktivism as a serious act of international conflict.

In other, earlier instances: the "Russian Business Network," a branch of organized crime in the Russian Federation, is believed to have cooperated with the government in launching a preemptive cyber attack on government organizations and military sites in the Republic of Georgia in 2008, prior to a conventional Russian military incursion into the breakaway Georgian province of Ossetia. The U.S. recently indicted five members of the PLA Shanghai unit by name, for having been responsible for massive thefts of patents and trade secrets from U.S.-based aerospace and defense industries. The indictments were not expected to result in actual arrest and prosecution, but were intended instead to send a message to the Chinese government that its disavowal or denial of state accountability for these crimes under international law was no longer plausible.

One of the most interesting of these earlier developments was the work of "Cyber Fighters of Izz ad-Din al-Qassam," an organization that takes its name from a prominent early twentieth-century Muslim cleric and anti-colonialist. In 2012, on the anniversary of the 9/11 terrorist attacks in the U.S., this group allegedly carried out a massive DDoS attack on U.S. financial institutions. The attack was described in a Twitter post by the group as having been launched in retaliation for the continued presence on YouTube of the American-made film, "The Innocence of Muslims," which portrays Islam and the prophet Mohammed in a very scandalous and unflattering light. The group vowed to continue the attacks until the offending film itself was removed from the Internet.

Two things stood out regarding the resulting, very serious disruptions of American financial institutions. First, despite its claim of independence, the group's attack was not indiscriminate. The institutions targeted were primarily those that had complied with the terms of the ongoing U.S. economic sanctions against Iran. In particular, the group's demand that a film be censored on account of its political or religious content seemed hollow: their leaders had to know that this was a demand that was beyond the power of a democratic government anywhere to grant, even were they willing in principle to comply with this demand.

The second oddity was that the anonymous Twitter site from which this group issued its September 2012 proclamation turned out to be the same account from which messages had flowed a few weeks earlier (allegedly from another vigilante group entirely) in the aftermath of a massive cyber attack on the internal computer network of ARAMCO, the Saudi Arabian oil giant. Those attacks, on 15 August 2012, allegedly carried out by an organization calling itself the "Cutting Sword of Justice," erased data on all affected computer drives, and inserted in their place the image of a burning American flag. U.S. security officials seemed quite certain that the first of these attacks was an act of retaliation by Iranian agents in response to the damage done to their own nuclear and oil infrastructure by Stuxnet and Flame, respectively, both weapons attributed to (but never acknowledged by) the U.S. and Israeli governments.

Suppose all these allegations and counter allegations are true: in particular, suppose that the two attacks in close sequence in 2012 (and others since) were not carried out by distinct and independent organizations, but instead represent the coordinated actions of a state government (Iran), retaliating for similar attacks upon its cyber infrastructure by other states (Israel and the U.S.). Add to these the known and ongoing, state-sponsored, malevolent cyber activities of the People's Liberation Army in China, the "Russian Business Network," and North Korean operatives. The conclusion is that states, as well as individuals and dissident groups, are now directly and deeply involved in hostile activities that increasingly transcend the boundaries of traditional espionage, covert action, and the "dirty tricks" of the past. Rather, this ongoing, high-stakes, but low-intensity conflict carried out by states against one another has evolved into what several colleagues (e.g., Michal Gross [5]) are coming to call "soft war."

Cyber Hacktivism and "Soft War"

By analogy with the concept of "soft power," soft war is a mode of warfare or conflict that is intentionally non-kinetic: i.e., it does not entail the use of conventional weapons, or the destruction that accompanies conventional armed attacks. But it is a disruptive new innovation in international conflict, and *it is still a very grave matter*. Real damage is done, and real harm is inflicted, although rarely (in contrast to the case of Stuxnet) does this involve causing real physical harm to physical objects. Rather, the conflict results in loss of information, loss of access to information processing, and an inability to carry out essential activities (such as banking, mining, medical care, trade, and commerce) that rely largely upon information processing.

Unlike the highly-publicized concept of a "cyber war," however, *the weapons and tactics of "soft war" are not limited to the cyber domain*. They can involve state use of the media, including cyber social media as well as conventional media, for purposes of propaganda, confusion, obfuscation, and disinformation. Soft war could involve the use of non-lethal (or "less-lethal") weapons in conventional attacks. For terrorist "pseudo-state" groups like Hamas, soft war could involve forms of what has elsewhere been called "lawfare," (for example) using civilian volunteers as "human shields" to deter conventional attacks on physical infrastructure or military installations by adversaries, one among a range of non-violent tactics termed "lawfare" [4]: e.g., using the law itself (in this instance, the Law of Armed Conflict) to thwart an adversary. Cyber tactics are only some of a range of options employed in the deliberate waging of so-called "soft" war.

The evolution of cyber conflict itself toward the "soft war" model of hacktivism, specifically, is quite different than the full-scale, effects-based equivalent of cyber "warfare" predicted by many pundits (such as Richard Clarke [2], and Joel [1]) during the last decade. The much-touted "cyber Armageddon," or "cyber Pearl Harbor" was to be a massive disruption and destruction of conventional systems, like air traffic control and electrical grids, resulting in widespread death and destruction on parallel with a massive conventional war. But state-sponsored vigilantism and hacktivism appear to signal something quite distinct from this familiar, but often highly exaggerated and implausible scenario. This state-sponsored conflict is virtual, not physical; non-violent, rather than kinetic; but nevertheless quite destructive and malevolent in other respects, equally capable of causing massive social upheaval, or bringing about a "death by 1,000 cuts" through pilfering of industrial and state secrets, or by interference in trade, commerce, finance, medical care, and transportation.

And, just as with increased reliance on the exercise of "soft power" (diplomacy, sanctions, media relations and the like), the advent of "soft war" has distinct advantages for those nations that engage in it. Essentially, *this kind of warfare substitutes cleverness and ingenuity for brute strength*. It is less costly to wage, less destructive of property, of lives, and of national treasure (as well as international prestige). Yet it is quite capable of achieving the same political goals, when properly utilized, as "hard" kinetic war, as well as capable of undermining or fending off an adversary that relies solely upon "hard" war tactics. It is, in short, the equivalent of bringing Asian martial arts that rely on balance, timing, and tactical sophistication to bear upon an enormous, powerful, but wholly conventional bully. The martial arts expert can hold his or her own, and even prevail, even though smaller, lighter, and perhaps less physically strong than the bully.

This comparison is apt, since "soft" war is directly attributable to two Chinese military strategists, reflecting on the future of military conflict in the aftermath of the lopsided victory of U.S.-led coalition forces in the 1991 Gulf War against the conventional forces of Iraqi President Saddam Hussein. In a landmark essay in 1999 [6] entitled "Unrestricted Warfare," two senior colonels in the People's Liberation Army, Qiao Liang and Wang Xiangsui, argued that the U.S. had become an international bully, physically too strong and too reliant on extensive war-fighting technology to resist by conventional means. Instead, they proposed, new forms of conflict needed to be devised, more indebted to subtleness and cleverness than to brute force, in the spirit of Sun-Tzu, in order to effectively oppose the brute physical power of the American "hegemon."

There is no explicit regime under international law that specifically governs this kind of conflict. Ought there to be? Or is it sufficient to rely on state interests, and the norms emergent from accepted state practice, to serve as a guide for when, and for how, to engage in "soft war?" Ought the same or similar guidelines applicable to kinetic war also guide entry into and conduct during this "soft" mode of warfare as well? Or ought it to remain, as its original formulators speculated, "unrestricted" or "without bounds?"

Earlier, I used terms like proportionality, publicity, and legitimate authority advisedly to describe ways in which vigilante groups like Anonymous, or whistle-blowers like Manning and Snowden, might go wrong. In a similar manner: might we not reasonably require, for example, that states only engage in such conflict when presented with irreconcilable differences sufficiently grave to justify conventional use of force (as, admittedly, happened on both sides of the Iran/U.S.-Israel dispute over Iran's nuclear weapons program)? And, as that example suggests, ought we to demand or reasonably expect that, when faced with the alternative of resorting to "soft" or kinetic warfare to resolve such disputes, that (consistent with a Principle of Last Resort), not only should all viable and reasonable alternatives short of war be attempted, but that the "soft war" alternative should always be chosen in lieu of the conventional resort to the use of kinetic force? Perhaps most importantly, might we demand, or reasonably expect, that nations engaging in such conflict with one another should do their utmost to avoid deliberate targeting of purely civilian, non-combatant individuals and their property, as is legally required in conventional war? Or, as in the example of using volunteer civilians as human shields, should attacks on financial institutions or civil infrastructure that merely involve a denial of access or service be subject to a more tolerant regime in which the combatant-noncombatant distinction is less viable, and perhaps less significant?

"Soft War" and "Soft" Law (Ethics)

The foregoing are chief among the questions waiting to be addressed and clarified in the wake of the advent of "soft war" generally, and specifically in the aftermath of the increased resort by state-sponsored agents to the kinds of tactics once limited to dissident individuals or non-state groups. While the lion's share of such normative work has occurred within the context of existing international law (most notably, the "Tallinn Manual" [10, 11]), I have begun to believe that the legal framework will simply not suffice to provide reliable guidance in this new domain of conflict. There are a number of reasons for this skepticism.

Contributors to the Tallinn Manual, for example, including some of the most eminent legal minds in the world today, brilliantly attempted to interpret and extrapolate existing international law (the regimes pertaining to armed conflict and humanitarian treatment of war's victims, and those pertaining to criminal activity in particular) so as to bring existing legislation to bear upon conflict in the cyber domain. But as I have described above, *"soft war" is not "war,"* strictly speaking, and so not subject to the jurisdiction of international legal regimes pertaining to armed conflict. Neither is it crime (although it sometimes involves the commission of otherwise-criminal actions by state agents).

Finally, as noted above, "soft war" *includes, but is not limited to* the cyber domain. "Media war" is not "war," and it is also not limited to cyber conflict. Use of non-lethal weapons, or tactics of "lawfare" (including human shields) not only occur outside the cyber domain (and so are obviously not addressed within the Tallinn Manual), but (in the latter instance) are also designed precisely to frustrate the bright-line statutes of existing international law, turning the letter of the law against its underlying regulatory purpose.

Even within the cyber domain alone, "soft war" tactics there more akin to espionage than to war or crime, and thus, once again, not explicitly addressed in international law, nor are state parties to existing legal arrangements eager to see such matters addressed there. In fact, this is the chief obstacle to pursuing normative guidance through the medium of law: those who are party to the law, and whose consent would be required to extend or amend it, are deeply opposed in principle to any further intrusion upon their respective interests and activities through treaty or additional legislation. Insofar as international law rests fundamentally upon what states themselves do, or tolerate being done, this opposition to further legislation (the one issue in the cyber domain on which the U.S., Russia, and China seem to agree) seems a formidable obstacle to pursing governance and guidance through legal means.

This is not as unpromising as it might seem, however, when one recognizes the historical fact that the principle bodies of international law pertaining to conflict of any sort largely codify, after the fact, norms of certain kinds of practice that emerge from public reflection by the practitioners themselves upon the better and worse features of that practice, and upon the ends or goals ultimately served by these practices. Law and regulations give the appearance (at least) of being stipulative, and are thought to be imposed externally, often upon unwilling subjects or agents. Best practices, by contrast, *emerge* from the shared practices of the interested parties, and reflect their shared experience and shared objectives.

International law, seen in this light, is more properly understood as grounded in common accord, consensus, and voluntary compliance. Its inherently cosmopolitan character (often overlooked by politically-appointed "Committees of Eminent Persons," eager to impose their terms of behavior on others) instead reflects Immanuel Kant's conception of standards of regulative order that moral agents themselves have both formulated and voluntarily imposed upon themselves, in order to guide and regulate their shared pursuits. Their compliance with principles that they themselves have formulated is thus more feasible and readily attainable.

This is a somewhat prolix manner of expressing a doctrine known in international relations as "emergent norms." This concept is encountered more broadly in moral philosophy as a kind of "trial and error," experiential groping toward order and equilibrium, a process that Aristotle (its chief theorist) described generally as the methodology of the "imperfect" sciences. The great contemporary moral philosopher, Alasdair MacIntyre, is chiefly credited with having resurrected this methodology in the modern era, from whence we can discern it already at work in the cyber domain, as well as in the field of military robotics (e.g., Lucas [7, 8]). Legal scholars, for their part, have dubbed this sort of informal and voluntary regulatory institution (as occurs in the Codes of Conduct of professional organizations, or the deliberations and recommendations of practitioners in the aftermath of a profound moral crisis) as constituting "soft" law.

What is required at the moment is a coherent and discernable body of "soft" law for "soft war." That is, the relevant stakeholders in the community of practice – in this case, frankly, adversaries engaged in the kind of low-intensity conflict that I have described under the heading of "soft" war – to formulate and publicize the principles that they have evolved to govern their practice. In earlier eras, like the Cold War, for example, espionage agents from adversarial nations evolved a sophisticated set of norms to govern their interaction and competition, designed largely to minimize unnecessary destruction, loss of lives in their respective clandestine services, mutual treatment of adversaries in captivity and prisoner exchanges, and other tactics designed to reduce the risk of accidental or unnecessary escalation of conflict (especially conflict that might cross the threshold of kinetic war in the nuclear era). All of these informal normative arrangements intended to facilitate, rather than inhibit, the principle aim or goal of espionage itself: reliable knowledge of the intentions and capabilities of the adversary. In the nature of things, there were no "councils" or "summit meetings," and no published or publicized "codes of conduct." Rather, these norms of prudent governance and guidance came to be "understood" and largely accepted (and complied with) by the members of this interesting community of practice.

What the broad outlines of the content of this "soft law" for "soft war" might be are already outlined above, utilizing somewhat more familiar "just war" terminology, which serves well for this purpose. Adversaries and stakeholders pursuing "soft war" have an interest, for example, in seeing that it does not accidentally "go kinetic," or involve needless and unnecessary "collateral damage" to vital civilian infrastructure, especially of the sort that might lead to widespread physical destruction and loss of life. They share a common interest in proportionate response, and the dictates of military necessity, of the kind exhibited in the conflicts (allegedly) between the cyber warriors of Iran, the U.S., and Israel described above. And adversaries like the U.S., China, and the Russian Federation, still locked into a preliminary mode of "unrestricted" or limitless warfare, need to consult more directly and frankly than has been possible to date on where common interests lie in imposing boundaries and regulative order on their "soft" conflicts, before the incessant damage being done on an ongoing basis to all parties to these conflicts forces an escalation into something far more serious and irreparable.

I have deliberately confined myself to only one very prominent tactic in the arsenal of soft war more generally, in an effort to illustrate how cyber conflict itself is being assimilated less as a new and distinctive form of conflict, as a valuable tactic in a new form of warfare generally. I conclude on a positive note, by observing that this increased resort to "soft war" tactics, including (but not limited to) cyber conflict, holds promise that the very real conflicts and disagreements that have often led nations to make war upon one another may themselves evolve into a mode of authentic opposition and conflict resolution that nonetheless ends up resulting in dramatically reduced bodily harm and loss of life, while doing less damage – and more easily reversible or repairable damage -- to the property of adversaries and innocents than was heretofore conceivable in conventional conflict.

References

1. Brenner J (2011) America the vulnerable: inside the new threat matrix of digital espionage, crime, and warfare. Penguin Press, New York
2. Clarke RA, Kanke RK (2010) Cyber war: the next threat to national security and what to do about it. HarperCollins, New York
3. von Clausewitz K (1830). On War. Edited/translated by Michael Howard and Peter Paret. Princeton University Press, Princeton, 1976
4. Dunlap CJ Jr (2011) Lawfare Today…and Tomorrow. In: "Pete" Pedrozo RA, Wollschlaeger DP (eds) International Law and the Changing Character of War. US Naval War College International Law Studies 87(2011):315–325
5. Gross ML (2014) The ethics of insurgency: a critical guide to just Guerilla warfare. Cambridge University Press, New York
6. Liang Q, Xiangsu W (1999) Unrestricted warfare: warfare without boundaries (超限战,). Eng. Trans. Pan American Publishing Co., Los Angeles, 2002
7. Lucas G (2014) Automated Warfare. Stanford Law and Policy Review 25(June):317–354
8. Lucas G (2015) Military ethics: what everyone needs to know. Oxford University Press, New York
9. Nye J (2004) Soft power: the means to success in world politics. Public Affairs Press, New York
10. Tallin Manual (2013) The Tallinn Manual on the International Law Applicable to Cyber Warfare. Michael Schmitt (eds). Cambridge University Press, New York
11. Tallinn (2012). Michael N. Schmitt, ed. The Tallinn Manual on the International Law Applicable to Cyber Warfare. (Tallinn: NATO Cooperative Cyber Defence Center of Excellence, 2012). Available at: https://www.ccdcoe.org/249.html

High School Student Vision: Disruptive Technologies – A Collection of Works from a 2015–2016 High School Class

Dan Scott, Rose Collins, Ryleigh Peterson, Liz Adams, Kyler Harrington, Eoin Gallagher, Will Fruce, Chris Bedigian, Eve Kyle, Sophia Klemenz, and Dana Tuohey

Introduction: View from a Younger Generation

Dan Scott
Christian Brothers Academy
Syracuse, NY, USA

When presented with the opportunity to participate in the writing of this chapter, my class at Christian Brothers Academy in Syracuse, New York, jumped at the chance. Technology is something that my students have been inundated with from birth. It is something that has become second nature to them, and they can't imagine a world without things like computers and cell phones. So with this unique perspective and upbringing, my students were asked to write about the future of disruptive technologies. More specifically, they were asked to address this question: In the year 2035, what technologies will exist and how will they affect our daily lives?

At first many of the students were tentative about the topic as they found it difficult to imagine what the future would look like. With some help from a few examples the ideas began to flow. In the following short essays you will find topics such as quantum computing, flying cars, solar roads, and artificial intelligence. The last essay brings in the interesting perspective of how this generation views technology, attempting to answer whether or not these technologies are really "disruptive" to them or simply a fact of everyday life.

My hope is that the insight from these students will show the impact that disruptive technologies have had on the thinking of young people today. Their predictions for future innovations are exciting to imagine and I am hoping that some of my

D. Scott (✉) • R. Collins • R. Peterson • L. Adams • K. Harrington • E. Gallagher • W. Fruce
C. Bedigian • E. Kyle • S. Klemenz • D. Tuohey
Christian Brothers Academy, Syracuse, NY, USA
e-mail: dscott@cbasyracuse.org

© Springer International Publishing Switzerland 2015
M. Blowers (ed.), *Evolution of Cyber Technologies and Operations to 2035*,
Advances in Information Security 63, DOI 10.1007/978-3-319-23585-1_14

students will be the one's involved in their creation! On behalf of my students here at CBA, we hope you enjoy the following submissions.

Computer Combat: The Future of Cyber Attacks

Rose Collins
Christian Brothers Academy
Syracuse, NY, USA

There once was a time where international attacks were just done in person. They were brought about through weapons of destruction or diseases that wiped out thousands, but nowadays we are able to attack a lot more impersonally. No need to rally forces and no need to worry about killing people. Through the world of cyber warfare we are able to bring down nations from their cores. We can hack into their most classified secrets, hurt their economies, shut down power grids, and leak information to the public. All it takes is some geniuses, computers, and lines of coding to create a worm that can turn an entire nation into chaos. The future of warfare will never again just be based on weaponry and armed forces, but cyberwarfare to take down the enemy from its center.

Cyberwarfare can do a lot of damage to nations. It cannot alone win wars, but it can cause destruction to infrastructures and the leak of classified plans. In 2007 an Iranian uranium-enrichment center was attacked, but not by any physical weapons. The computer program Stuxnet was able to cause the waste of uranium by turning things on and off and damaging equipment. By doing this it was able to slow the country's nuclear force. This level of interference is not only possible in Iran, but in virtually every country in the world, including the United States [12].

In the United States, many of our basic programs are linked up to the internet or computers, which makes it easier for them to be infiltrated and manipulated. Our subway and train lines, our power grids, and our water treatment plants all work in relation to the cyber world. Researchers have attempted to hack into these places and easily made their way in [15]. It does not take much to get into one of these programs and shut them down anymore. Cases of teenagers being able to hack into railroad systems and systems of navigation have become more common [12].

Our nation has come to the realization that preventative measures for the future of cyber hacking are necessary to keep afloat. Banks have begun to hold drills of what they would do in the case of a cyberattack. Many companies and the government itself have hired hackers to attempt to hack into their systems. The security measures must be tested and retested again, to be sure that there is no chance for an attack to occur. Even with security measures in place, there are some ways that preventative measures cannot help. As the knowledge of our hired hackers increases, so does the knowledge of the hackers working to take us down. The future of hacking will be consistent trying to one up our opposition. Hacking will become more complex as the future continues and the need for advancements and increased knowledge on our part will be even more necessary [15].

It is safe to assume that the United States is already under cyberattack. Many of these programs take a while to detect and will not show themselves for quite a while. These attacks are not like weaponry in the sense of immediate results. They sit and stay for a while, without people even realizing that they are doing anything [2]. Many researchers believe that small grade attacks to our banks are already occurring. The Pentagon opened up to being the target of an attack back in 2008, and other attacks against defense and aerospace organizations are becoming more common. As John Arquilla, professor of defense analysis at the US Naval Postgraduate School, said "Cyberwarfare is a lot like Carl Sandburg's fog, coming in on 'little cat feet" [15].

The future of cyberwarfare holds many uncertainties. Many experts believe that it will not eliminate flat out warfare. There will still be soldiers and there will still be guns. Computers will play a much more vital role, though. In the future, with the integration of wireless communications into so much of our world's infrastructure, it will be much easier to attack other nations. We will be able to blackout cities and shut down water plants [12]. It is realistic to assume that we may very well be impacted by a cyberattack within the next 15 years, but luckily, with preventative measures done by our government and many private companies, we will be able to bounce back.

Cyberwarfare is a new form of war, often seen with anxiety and fear. Many fear the unknown and right now cyber warfare is a very large unknown. Within the next 15 years, we will become more educated, and most likely more acquainted with it. While this poses a lesser threat immediately, its long term effects can alter the fabric of a nation and can last for years. In the future, the leaders of warfare will not be determined on just their military forces. All it takes to fight a battle now is an internet connection and a computer.

Commercial Space Travel

Ryleigh Peterson and Liz Adams
Christian Brothers Academy
Syracuse, NY, USA

To the average human being, the world is a big place. It's crazy to think that beyond Earth, there is such an extensive amount of area in outer space that it is still undetermined what and how much is up there. Ever since the beginning of time, man has wanted to explore and push the boundaries of possible. Americans, Neil Armstrong and Buzz Aldrin, were the first men to step foot on the moon on July 20, 1969. Ever since that historic day in history, only 547 people have been to the moon. Sixty years ago, the idea of space travel seemed nearly impossible. Now, our horizons are being broadened to not just travel to the moon, but other planets as well. In addition to astronauts making the journey, everyday people will have the opportunity as well.

Space is spectacular, for it is filled with the unknown. So far, only astronauts who have mastered and received the highest level of training are the ones who get to make the journey. The idea is to open travel and the opportunity to people who don't do something involving space for a living. The company, Virgin Galactic is trying to make this far-fetched idea a reality, and hopes to make the world's first commercial space line [4]. Virgin Galactic stated, "Once all astronauts are safely onboard, WhiteKnightTwo will take off and climb to an altitude of about 50,000 feet and after performing all necessary vehicle and safety checks, the pilots will release

SpaceShipTwo from WhiteKnightTwo for the start of the next stage of the flight. Within seconds, the rocket motor will be engaged, and SpaceShipTwo will quickly accelerate to approximately three and a half times the speed of sound, producing moderate G-forces and propelling the vehicle and its crew on their way to space. After the rocket motor has fired for around a minute, the pilots will safely shut it down. Having just experienced a thrilling, dynamic rocket ride, the dramatic transition to silence and to true weightlessness will be a profound moment for our astronauts as they coast upwards towards space." ("Your Flight to Space" 2015) For large sum of $250,000 per person, Virgin Galactic is trying to send those who can afford the trip into outer space. For most, the idea of space travel is a hard concept to grasp, especially when adding the idea of sending anyone who has the luxury of paying for their ride, into space.

The Mars One project opened the idea to the public to submit an application to have a one-way ticket to go to Mars. Since the selection process was open, 100,000 people have submitted an application. There are various stages and qualifications of the applicants that the company is looking for, in order to choose the lucky 40 multi-continental group to send into space. The set date to leave for Mars is September 2022, then arriving on Mars in April 2023. The logistics of the trip will include that each person will be able to carry about 5,511 lb of a "useful load" (Juarez, CNNMexico.com, Landau [8]), and after eight missions 44,000 lb of supplies will be on Mars. The reason why this mission can be carried out is because scientists made a major breakthrough. They discovered that the Martian soil on Mars can be evaporated into hydrogen and oxygen. Which means that they are modifying the conditions to make the habitat a livable for the human race.

Whether or not it can it be done, is the question racing through all of our heads. Technology, as of 2015, is not advanced enough to protect people against the exposure of radiation. Reynolds stated, "At this point it's completely infeasible to try to send someone to Mars unless we can get there faster or we develop better shielding for a spacecraft" (Juarez, CNNMexico.com, Landau [8]). NASA is also continuously working on engines to cut the travel time, and the expected date that NASA could successfully do this is in the year of 2030, but that time might be cut shorter because technological discoveries and improvements are rapidly growing every single day. If your mind can grasp around the idea of going into the unknown then you could potentially be the perfect candidate to join the mission to Mars. The most important thing to remember is that once you begin the journey into the unknown, there is no turning back.

Quantum Computing

Kyler Harrington
Christian Brothers Academy
Syracuse, NY, USA

In the year 2035, the quantum computer will be the computer that drives science. It will allow for complex analysis and processing speeds that will expand the bounds on how we reason about complex systems in our Universe. It will allow us to make advancements in data processing of the growing number of data collection capabilities. Some of these include satellites, ground telescopes, super-powered microscopes, probes for the human body, probes for underwater exploration, seismic sensors, thermal sensors, and even computer network monitoring and control sensors, and many more. This new found capability will empower the age of knowledge and science that will be hungry to use this technology for the betterment of humanity, advancement of exploration, and enlightenment.

In today's computing and technological era we use devices and computing power on a daily basis. Although this seems to be taken for granted by my generation, we are not too far removed from the generation who created it. When the computer was first invented many people thought it was too fast and most countries would only need a few. Those predictions were very wrong as most aspects of our lives today have evolved to be influenced by computers in some way. This is why we must ask ourselves what makes a computer "tick". What makes a computer have the ability to store data and run several calculations simultaneously without crashing. Since computers were first invented their basic functions could always be broken down in either a 1 or a 0. This allowed the computer to store data as either "on" represented by a 1 or "off" represented by a 0. This allows the computer to make sense of what it is reading in its own language, however the computer must store this information in its circuitry and it must record it and translate it, this is why some computers are slower than others. This process has slowed many programs and software down in all applications of computers. Many people are frustrated because they are limited to either having a computer that is just the right size but too slow and small in regards to computing power to fit their needs. Others are restrained based on the fact that the faster, more sophisticated "quantum computers" are to massive in size to be portable. Even the fastest binary computers today still don't have the capabilities scientists and industries need to transfer massive amounts of data in a short amount of time. They are limited by processing speeds when having to calculate massively complex simultaneous equations or build detailed models of complex systems.

This is not the case however if we look at computers based on quantum mechanics and advanced computing technologies. In future years, a new species of computer will evolve which will be unbounded by binary representation. This new species is called the Quantum Computing. This computer will encode information as quantum bits. These quantum bits represent atoms, ions, photons or electrons. These components in a quantum computer can contain multiple states simultaneously which allows a computer to operate at speeds exponentially faster than traditional computers today.

With these new applications scientists will be able to run software and shift through more data than ever thought possible. The advantages of quantum are substantial and many scientists are eager to see what the future holds in regards to the quantum computing field. With an emerging generation of technically savvy, cyber hungry people to drive the technological race, we may someday have computers that can exceed processing speeds which are faster than every thought possible and be equipped with the potential to go beyond human thought and reasoning.

Microsoft's HoloLens

Eoin Gallagher and Will Fruce
Christian Brothers Academy
Syracuse, NY, USA

In today's ever changing technology field there is one new invention that is particularly changing the lives of many young adults. The Microsoft HoloLens is a new invention that brings holograms to your world. The HoloLens are glasses that are worn and they are usable by people of all ages. These holograms are also integrated with your physical surroundings. The main reason however as to why these glasses are unique is that they will make completing tasks easier. These glasses make it easier to see how you can build something or fix something as complicated as a motorcycle.

The HoloLens can have many other convenient uses other than fixing things. By the swipe of a finger you can watch television, check the weather, and have the recipe for dinner that night all right in front of you. Not only can you use this at home but this new technology can be brought to the classroom. If teachers and students use these HoloLens glasses, learning will be more personal and right in front of you. Say goodbye to the terrible view in the back of the classroom because now the holograms the teacher is using are right in front of you. Another advantage the Microsoft HoloLens brings to teenagers is in the video game department. With the HoloLens the game is brought right into your living room.

In the future one advantage we may see are the HoloLens may be able to turn into glasses when you are not using the holograms. Another advantage is the holograms can be another teacher in the classroom. As our knowledge of holograms increases we may be able to program more detailed holograms that can help in the classroom. Like all new technologies, there will be some disadvantages. One disadvantage that we may see in the future could be that holographic teachers could replace real teachers in the classroom. This would limit the amount of teachers needed and leave many unemployed, which could hurt our economy. Another disadvantage is that one day we may all have these glasses and lose sight of what is real and not real.

The Microsoft HoloLens is changing the way people do things. These glasses will hit the market in the United Kingdom in December of 2015 at a price of 300 Euros.

Flying Car

Chris Bedigian
Christian Brothers Academy
Syracuse, NY, USA

A few years ago the only place you could see a flying cars was in the Jetsons, Star Wars, and other futuristic sci-fi television. As kids we dreamed of kissing our spouses goodbye, jumping in our cars and flying to work. However many of us understood that this would probably not be a reality in our life time. Juraj Vaculik had other ideas. The CEO of Aeromobil sees a very near future that includes these flying cars.

The Aeromobil will revolutionize transportation as we know it. Getting from place to place will be faster and easier than ever before. People will be able to pack up their things and fly to Florida instead of hours of boring road games and awful traffic. The official Aeromobil 3.0 was produced and had its maiden flight in October of 2014. The flight was successful and documented on camera. It was not the hovering fly away like in the Jetsons, but that by no means takes away how impressive this feat truly is. The Aeromobil is more along the lines of a small private jet mixed with a crop duster. It has foldable wings that fold inwards to run along the length of the vehicle. It is a two person vehicle with a pod like main body with a long slender midsection, leading to a t shape back wing with two wheels and a propeller. When driving it has a listed top speed of 99+ miles per hour, and in flight it reportedly reaches speeds of 124+ miles per hour. Which is not extremely fast but still twice as fast as anyone normally drives.

As amazing as this product seems, there are still quite a few drawbacks I see to this product. First of which is the price. It is estimated to cost the consumers 100 s of thousands of dollars. Which means that these vehicles will by no means be the norm in society. Only the rich will buy it and it may die out before it even gets off the ground. Second is the government regulation. With all the recent terrorism scares, especially in the wake of 9/11 there will be a ridiculous amount of regulations attached to owning and operating an Aeromobil. There will be regulations on where you are allowed to take off, fly and land. I'm sure that there will be restricted no fly areas, and that there will be a tracker inserted in all the vehicles. I believe that there should be an autopilot feature that takes over and lands itself if someone is starting to approach a "Red" area, like the capitol or a major city like NYC. It will be extremely difficult to regulate these and I see there being a large gap between the release and getting past all of the regulations. Lastly people aren't the best drivers. I don't think I would feel safe with some of the people I've seen driving operating a plane. Although I'm sure that they will be required to have a pilot's license, having a driver's license doesn't stop people from driving poorly.

In summation The Aeromobil is a great feat of ingenuity and innovation. It is an exciting yet slightly frightening look into the future of transportation. It could easily lead to a much more convenient way for people to travel and see new places. However there is so much that must go on behind the scenes to ensure the safety of the drivers of these as well as the people around them. If they can somehow find a way to get the proper regulations set in place I believe this could be a phenomenal step forward.

Solar Roads

Eve Kyle and Sophia Klemenz
Christian Brothers Academy
Syracuse, NY, USA

The smell of tar and asphalt are the price we pay for solid roads. But a new innovation suggests using solar power. Conserving energy is not only beneficial to our environment, but solar roads could offer safer, and technologically advanced road systems. Two married engineers from Sandpoint, Idaho, have made a great technological advance with solar power. They call their great achievement, "Solar Roadways."

Solar Roads are made up of hexagonal shaped solar panels that have been designed to replace dark, heat absorbent asphalt. They use the energy to power the small LED lights that power lights on the panels that have road signs, lane markers and turning lanes, which are indicated on the panels. These two engineers have come up with something so delicate and impactful to our society. Imagine the amount of energy we could conserve and use towards other businesses and industries. These solar roadways could lower the cost of electrical energy, resulting in less money spent for energy costs. The panels are also made with recycled materials, making them eco-friendly.

The average cost of a solar roadway is around $10 K for 12′ × 12′ panels (solarroadways.com). This compares to the millions of miles of heat absorbent asphalt. More accurate costs will be available when the new design is completed in few more years. Solar roadways also have a strong economic component that allows them to pay for themselves. They do this by generating electricity, transporting cleaned storm water to municipalities or agricultural centers, and by selling advertising in parking lots with the configurable LEDs (solarroadways.com). Overall, the economic opportunities for solar roadways are far greater than that of asphalt roads. They not only have to be replaced every decade or so, but offer more environmentally friendly alternatives.

As two teens that have grown up with technology, we both agree that solar roads will catch on and soon transform our society as we know it. The only concern we have is how durable they will be and how much it will cost our country. Once more trial runs have been introduced, more people will know the facts and pros and cons of our new tech roads.

Technology: Is It Really Disruptive?

Dana Tuohey
Christian Brothers Academy
Syracuse, NY, USA

Anyone can see that the technological advances in just the past 30 years or so have expedited the advancement of many aspects of our daily lives. How many of us can honestly say we don't use at least one piece of technology that wasn't around before the 1980s? Probably very few of us. Technology is helpful, but where should the line be drawn between helpful and invasive? I personally believe that technology is only invasive if we allow it to be, and that adaptation is key in this period where new technology is coming into play nearly every day.

Many people argue that the youth of today are too distracted by their phones and personal electronics and have lost the ability to communicate in real life. This is only true if you view the world through a straw. The reality is that the youth of today have grown up in a time in which this technology rules our everyday lives, and that it reaches people of all ages. Youth are simply more adept in understanding and utilizing these tools, as it is all we know. As a result, we are more capable of adapting to new advancements. This adaptation can be applied to both personalized technologies as well as technology on a larger scale.

I have always found it interesting how resistant to change the generations before us have become. This encompasses more than just personal or handheld electronics. This attitude can be applied to advancements in new energy sources, technological warfare, and a variety of other things. This mind set has prevailed in the beliefs of many generations of parents ever since the baby boom – and even before. Resistance to change is often a symptom of aging, and I believe this mindset perpetuates the idea of "disruptive technology" to a dangerous degree. This mindset will always be around as long as people have children and get older. The key to dealing with it is understanding this reality. Once you have come to realize that things probably will not change, it is up to the rest of the population to decide what is useful and what is not. Ageism in the field of technology is not the answer, but neither is remaining stagnant.

I understand peoples' hesitation in the advancement of technology when it begins to compromise moral standards that have been around since the beginning of time. I would agree with this and say that sometimes technology treads on some very dangerous moral ground that has yet to be challenged by society. This, however, is where human judgement should come into play. We should be able to freely moderate the technology that has come into being, but without swearing off technology all together. Because when you denounce technology as a whole, that is when you start to move in reverse as a society. I believe that each and every one of us has the capacity to discern what technology is productive for us, or what could potentially be seen as dangerous. Turning against technology as a whole would simply be foolish.

We are all spoiled. That's just the truth. And by saying that we are comfortable with certain technological advances and not others would simply be hypocritical. We can be very quick to judge or denounce technology that does not directly assist us in any way, and this leads to stagnation.

I believe that there are some aspects of technology that are more superfluous than others. Flying cars, for example, are excessive. They have very little practicality and even if they did become a thing, they would be highly expensive and dangerous to use. We would have to expand our rules of the road to moderate air travel, and it could even cause more pollution depending on its energy source. I do believe, however, that if something like this were to find its way into the market, that we have a responsibility as humans to adapt. We could regulate these cars, find a way to make them more fuel efficient, compile a number of "traffic rules" that apply to flying in the sky, and even develop requirements for owning and operating such a vehicle, such as a specialized license or permit.

This logic can be applied to any number of the new inventions discussed in this chapter. From solar roads, to things on a more astronomical scale; the key is regulation and adaptation. If there is one thing that humans are capable of, it is the ability to adapt. We have proven this time and time again through economic, political, and social crises. So how can technology be any different?

I am not against technology. I believe that while many people can potentially exploit it, I am optimistic that humans are capable of moderating the use of new technologies. This, however, will require an open mindedness and knowledge of how and why technology works, and how we can incorporate it into our daily lives without letting it disrupt our lives.

Works Cited

1. AeroMobil: Flying Car. AeroMobil: Flying Car. http://www.aeromobil.com. Accessed 29 Apr 2015
2. Chatfield T (2015) Cyber warfare: fear of system failure. BBC Future, 7 June 2012. Accessed 20 May 2015
3. Cruddas S (2015) Mars one: 'it's important what you do before you die' – CNN.com. CNN, 8 Feb 2015. Accessed 20 May 2015
4. David L (2015) Will commercial space travel blast off in 2014? Space.com. Space.com, 11 Jan 2014. Accessed 20 May 2015
5. HowStuffWorks. How quantum computers work. Howstuffworks "Computer Channel" N.p., n.d. Web. 28 Apr 2015
6. Human Spaceflight – Virgin Galactic. Virgin Galactic. Accessed 20 May 2015
7. John M (2015) Quantum computing is becoming more than just a good idea. New York Times, N.p., 28 Apr 1998. Web. 28 Apr 2015
8. Juarez J, Landau E (2015) More than 100,000 want to go to mars and not return, project says – CNN.com. CNN, 15 Aug 2013. Accessed 20 May 2015
9. Julie and Scott Brusaw, Solar Roads. http://www.solarroadways.com/about.shtml. A New Solution. Accessed 17 April 2015
10. Microsoft HoloLens Preview – CNET. CNET. Accessed 20 May 2015
11. Microsoft HoloLens. https://www.microsoft.com/microsoft-hololens/en-us. Accessed 20 May 2015
12. The Economist (2015) Here's how cyber-warfare started and where it's going. Business Insider, 12 Dec 2014. Accessed 20 May 2015
13. Thibodeau P (2015) IBM's new future: quantum computing. Computerworld – IT News, Features, Blogs, Tech Reviews, Career Advice. N.p., 16 June 2011. Web. 28 Apr 2015
14. USA. AFRL. Cluster State Quantum Computation. By Fanto ML, Alsing P, Lott G. Air Force Research Lab Rome NY Information Directorate, Feb 2014. Web. 20 Apr 2015
15. Weinberger S (2015) Cyber Pearl Harbor: why hasn't a mega attack happened? BBC Future, 19 Aug 2013. Accessed 20 May 2015

Printed in the United States
By Bookmasters